# More About Masonry

Supplements

## The Newly-Made Mason

By H. L. Haywood

and

Completes the Masonic Story

By H. L. Haywood

*Revised Edition*

Macoy Publishing & Masonic Supply Co., Inc.
Richmond, Virginia

COPYRIGHT, 1948, 1980


Macoy Publishing & Masonic Supply Co., Inc.
Richmond, Virginia


PRINTED IN THE UNITED STATES OF AMERICA

# MORE ABOUT MASONRY

## *OTHER BOOKS BY THE SAME AUTHOR*

FREEMASONRY AND ROMAN CATHOLICISM *

FAMOUS MASONS AND MASONIC PRESIDENTS

SUPPLEMENT TO THE CLEGG REVISION OF
MACKEY'S ENCYCLOPEDIA

THE NEWLY-MADE MASON

HOW TO BECOME A MASONIC LODGE OFFICER

GREAT TEACHINGS OF MASONRY

MASONIC ESSAYS

*\* Out of print*

# *Foreword*

"On Saturday afternoon, February 25, 1956, a shadow crossed the sun in Cedar Rapids, Iowa, and the Masonic world was dimmed.

"Harry Leroy Haywood died at the age of 69."

That was the beginning of a tribute to Haywood written by the late Ralph E. Whipple, then Grand Secretary of the Grand Lodge of Iowa.

Many tributes to the Masonic mastery of Haywood followed his death. The Masonic world had lost its most prolific writer. It had truly lost a friend. Even more severe was the loss of a Freemason who understood Freemasonry and knew how to impart it through the written word.

Haywood was never happier than when a young Mason, approaching him with awe, asked a question about the Craft. Like any of the few Masonic educators there are, he was proud to learn he had really reached someone. And during his 48 years in Masonry, he reached many—including the great Joseph Fort Newton.

There is no way Haywood could ever learn of the lives he touched. No other person will ever know. But I was one of those he reached. A little book he wrote for The Masonic Service Association in 1953 actually turned me into something of a Masonic researcher. It also helped me to decide a paper I was writing for my Research Lodge would have to become a book. That turned into *House Undivided.*

This is what Haywood wrote in *Well-Springs of American Freemasonry* that sent me researching (it's under the section on "West Virginia"):

*Foreword*

In 1868 occurred an event which should be observed, at least in spirit, by both Virginia Grand Lodges. The new Grand Lodge, still conscientiously concerned to see that everything as between the two was shipshape, regular, and fraternal, sent two commissioners to Richmond to visit the Mother Grand Lodge. Then it was that the older Grand Lodge welcomed its younger sister with a gesture, the full meaning and beauty of which can be understood by veteran Masons only; all West Virginia lodges were to retain their old charters as far as Virginia was concerned, "and recommended to all lodges in the territorial limits of West Virginia, to surrender their original charters to, and ask new charters from, the Grand Lodge of West Virginia."

How could anyone resist wanting to learn more about this episode? And this is just one of the items Haywood wrote over the years that sent young Masons to libraries or Masonic book companies. And this is such a book; a book loaded with information, yet one that will send the inquiring Masonic mind on a life-long quest for more, and more knowledge.

In *More About Masonry*, Haywood goes to great lengths to explain many of the things every Mason should know about the Craft. He is, as always, meticulous. It might appear at times that he is overdoing a particular subject. But this isn't so, in most cases. He learned, as every Masonic educator learns, and so does every successful businessman, that communication is a peculiar animal. It doesn't matter how a subject is approached, there will always be those who don't get the message. So, he erred on the side of length rather than brevity.

In explaining the "High Grades" for example, he appears to go around his elbow to get to his thumb. But early in his explanation he makes it clear that "no Grand Body in any of the four Rites of the High Grades is superior to a Grand Lodge." In his discussion he is letting the reader join with him in a search for a better term than "Higher Grades"; "Concordant Orders"; "Auxiliary Rites";

## Foreword

"Appendant Rites." He notes, "Side Orders grew like shoots out of the parent trunk." He was convinced the "tendency to proliferate" is a long way from coming to an end. How prophetic he was!

This should be noted about Haywood's comments about the Scottish Rite. For the most part he is correct when he states the Symbolic Lodge degrees are not practiced by the Scottish Rite in the United States. However, Louisiana is an exception. The Grand Lodge does permit three Lodges to use the Scottish Rite ritual for the first three degrees. On October 3, 1972, I witnessed the First degree conferred in the Scottish Rite manner in Albert Pike Lodge No. 376, New Orleans. About half way through I told the late Peter Laguens, Grand Secretary, that I'd not have become a Master Mason if I had gone through that initiation. He told me this Lodge had more Entered Apprentices than any other in Louisiana.

Haywood's account of the formation of the Scottish Rite bodies is well worth the attention of all seeking more light. He notes that "the United States is the homeland of one of the five great Rites of the Craft."

In his account of Royal Arch Masonry Haywood writes: "At the present time of writing, the oldest written record of the words "Royal Arch" is dated December 27, 1743." As far as can be determined, this remains true. It should be noted, though, that John T. Desaguliers who was Grand Master in 1719, made a trip to Edinburgh, Scotland. It is said that during this trip in 1725 he was made a Royal Arch Mason. In 1735 Desaguliers took part in a Masonic ceremony where it is claimed certain Masons were made "Chapiters." There are many who believe the Royal Arch degree was developed concurrently with the Master Mason degree. It is evident that much is yet to be learned about the development of Freemasonry in its many facets.

No man ever wrote a truer statement than did Haywood in this book under "Masonry and the law": "It does not matter if you destroy a man in one minute or in one year, destroy him at one stroke, as in murder, or destroy him piece-meal by destroying his money, or belongings, or his possessions, or his property, or his freedom or whatever else he might have in order to continue to be; to destroy another by any means is to act as a criminal."

Haywood lets us know that Freemasonry and Freemasons don't have to suffer the slanders prevalent during the anti-Masonic craze of the 1830's: "Any libellous, scandalous, defamatory, damaging false statement made about Freemasonry is made about each and every one of those men in particular—it is not the slander of a theory but a harmful slander of known and locally identifiable men; those men can go into court and sue, either separately or collectively." This was written for this book in 1948, yet, even today, I've been criticized for advocating Freemasonry to stop turning the other cheek. Only by protecting the good name of the Craft can much of the anti-Masonic slander still going on be halted.

Under "Masonic Jurisprudence" Haywood tells us: "Jurisprudence separates out those constituents which are concerned with rules, observes them, studies them, and seeks to know and to understand them; but it is not something external to Freemasonry because its subjects belong to what Freemasonry is; therefore, a knowledge of jurisprudence is a knowledge of Freemasonry itself, a way of explaining or describing one of the things which it is; our jurisprudence is not *about* our rules and regulations, it *is* our rules and regulations."

L. B. Blackmore of Ohio said of Haywood: "In writing this book, Brother H. L. Haywood has exemplified the quotation that, 'The talent of success is nothing more than doing what you can—well.' Those who have been privileged to read other works by Brother Haywood have verified the fact that he is unexcelled in this field of Masonic writing." This is true. To read this book, one will be appreciative of the vast talent and knowledge of its author. His love of good books and of Freemasonry shines through on every page.

It was this love of good books that made Harry Leroy Haywood the excellent writer he was. And he spent a lifetime in this lonely, exacting field. It was he who made the ill-fated National Masonic

## Foreword

Research Society, located in Iowa, world renown. He did it through the pages of one of the greatest Masonic magazines ever produced—*The Builder*. As its Editor-in-Chief he was responsible for its content. He encouraged the most knowledgeable Masons of the day to write for its pages. No better testimonial can be given of his work than this by Ralph E. Whipple: "This magazine is considered to be the 'prototype' of Masonic journalism by qualified Masonic students. It was the leader of its day; it was far better than anything that had been published previously, and none since has matched its excellence."

Whipple gives this account of Haywood's Masonic affiliations: he "received his degrees in Acacia Lodge No. 176, Webster City, Iowa, on May 3, May 17 and June 7, 1915. He affiliated with Waterloo Lodge No. 105, Waterloo, Iowa, on December 12, 1916 and later with Publicity Lodge No. 1000, New York City. The latter lodge is quite famous, confining its members to the brethren of the 'fourth estate.' On May 4, 1951, after returning to the midwest, he affiliated with Mizpah Lodge No. 639 of Cedar Rapids, Iowa. He was a member of Tabernacle Chapter No. 52, R.A.M., Waterloo, Iowa, and Zarephath Consistory, A.A.S.R. (S.J.) at Davenport, Iowa."

In *10,000 Famous Freemasons*, William R. Denslow writes: "He was graduated from the Cedarville, Ohio, high school at the age of 13, and attended the Theological Seminary, Dayton, and Lawrence College, Appleton, Wis. Ordained a minister at 18, he gave up preaching in 1919. Although without a college degree, he taught and lectured on religion and anthropology for 13 years in many major colleges of the U.S."

Born on November 1, 1886, H. L. Haywood spent his life-time, practically, with books. It is claimed he began reading at the age of three—reading books designed for fifth grade students! This isn't difficult to believe when the record of his life is studied.

Haywood was buried in the Masonic section of the Cedar Memorial Park, Cedar Rapids, Iowa.

How can this Foreword, really a tribute, to this great man be closed? Only by letting you read something he wrote that isn't

*Foreword*

contained in this book. It's the frontispiece of *The Masonic Essays* of H. L. Haywood:

### Warmth and Welcome

Across the crowd-thronged ways
When night hangs black and friendless there,
A tide of strangers ebbs and sways
Along each cheerless thoroughfare
And never a face lights up to see
One's self to pass, and none to care
How lone and weary one may be.

'Tis then unto one's lodge one turns
For there he finds within its door
The fire of hearty welcome burns;
If one's not known, its flames the more
Send forth a warmth his breast to fill
Until he finds his joy returns
Within that have of good will.

The Mason's secret lies in this—
"A stranger here, ye took me in";
Its Royal Art would stray amiss
Amid the world's harsh hue and din
If warmth and welcome were to die;
Its greatest strength in these consists,
Of these is made its Mystic Tie.

*H. L. Haywood*

This sums up his deep and abiding love for the Craft. It sums up his love for his fellowman. It's a fitting epitaph—for God certainly did take him in, although he was no stranger to Him.

ALLEN E. ROBERTS

Highland Springs, Virginia
1980

## *Preface*

"The proper study of mankind is man."—Pope

"When Masons come to speak about that which is finest in their Fraternity, about that which is nearest to being what religion is elsewhere, which moves on high, reaches level with the most exalted plateaus of thought, they begin to look anxiously about them to make sure that they keep their feet on the ground; they are great believers in masculinity, and hold it to be one of the best things in a man, and it too belongs to masculinity to dread those flights of idealistic fancy which blow the sails away. But there is in the whole universe no better place on which to stand than on the ground, and there is nothing higher or better anywhere than sanity, good sense, and sound wisdom, and there is no better life possible in any earth or in any heaven than the life of work; but while our law is a set of rules and regulations for workmen, and our Landmarks are drawn close to the ground, we are as free as other men to believe that there are great things in man; we bracket together the question—what do you believe about man? with the question—what do you believe about God?—because one is as important to us as the other. We say in our Rituals, "There is a Grand Lodge above." We know what we mean by that saying.

We do not mean that after we have changed our way of *being* and are no longer in this world that we shall find a Grand Lodge, with a Grand Master presiding over it; we do not mean that it is our picture of "heaven"; we believe that there is nothing better in this world than to be a man, and to be in fellowship with other men, *and we do not believe that there will be anything better in any other world.*"

H. L. Haywood

*Quoted from his chapter on Anthropology in "More About Masonry"*

# Contents

## Part One

CHAPTER                                                                PAGE

I. FREEMASONIANA (Origins of Masonry) . . . . .     3
History of Freemasonry from 1350 A.D., to 1717 A.D. First Permanent Lodges, Old Charges, Non-Operatives; The Mysteries, Collegia, Astrology, Kabbalism, Alchemy, Rosicrucianism.

II. THE REGIUS AND COOKE MSS . . . . . . .     11
Resumé of the Historical Contents of The Regius or Halliwell Phillips MSS. Resumé of contents of The Cooke MS. "Old Charges", Corporation Charter, Legal Act.

III. THE POLYCHRONICON . . . . . . . . . .     20
Higdon; Tradition not History; Regius and Cooke MSS. Tradition. Vocabulary of the Craft, Word Examples; Myths and Legends.

IV. THE BOOK OF CONSTITUTIONS (ANDERSON) . . .     31
Resumé of contents; Historical References. Formation of Grand Lodge and its Approval; Ancient Landmarks, Constitutions and Charters; Landmarks Identify Freemasonry; Old Charges.

V. HISTORY OF MASONRY IN THE UNITED STATES . .     39
Early Masons, Record of First Lodges, and Grand Lodges; Provincial Grand Lodges and Grand Masters. Independent Origins of First American Lodges; Account of 48 Grand Lodges. Charters and Separation from English Grand Lodges.

VI. HISTORY OF MASONRY IN OTHER LANDS . . . .     48
Exclusiveness and Divergences. France 1725-30 A.D. Grand Lodge of England, Mother Grand Lodge; Italy 1730's; Papal Bulls—1738, Opposition, Influence of Women and Children.

xiii

## Part Two

| CHAPTER | | PAGE |
|---|---|---|
| VII. | GRAND LODGES | 57 |

Why, When, Where since 1717 A.D. Regular Grand Jurisdiction, Grand Lodge Code; Book of Constitutions; Grand Communications, Grand Officers, Lodges and Grand Lodges.

VIII. THE GRAND MASTERSHIP . . . . . . . . . 64

Duties—Co-ordinate not Subordinate; Ancient Origin Historical. The Grand Master of Masons; Appointments, Authority, Edicts; Grand Master only can "Make Masons at Sight."

IX. LODGE OFFICERS . . . . . . . . . . . 73

Master, His Power and Duties; Wardens, Secretary, Treasurer, Deacons, Stewards, Tiler, Marshal and Chaplain.

X. MASONIC JURISDICTION . . . . . . . . . 82

Definitions of Boundaries of Authority, Definitions of Jurisdiction. First Grand Lodge Jurisdiction, Local and Territorial Jurisdiction, Grand Lodge Jurisdiction.

XI. MASONIC MONIES—MASONIC LODGE FUNDS . . . 89

Original Theory of Wages; Dues are Merely Sharing Necessary Masonic Expenses. Collections, Allocations, Expenditures; Usury vs. Interest.

XII. MASONIC COMITY . . . . . . . . . . . 96

Definition; Comity a Vital Necessity in Freemasonry. 49 Grand Lodges; Provincial Grand Lodge System, Grand Lodge Bodies, Grand Lodge Officers and Local Lodges. Interdependent Rites.

XIII. MASONRY AND ETHICS . . . . . . . . . 103

Recognition, Correspondence, Co-operate Voluntarily: How a "System of Ethics"? Insists on Good Morals but has no System of Morality. Gallileo 1581 A.D. The three Principal Tenets of Freemasonry.

## Part Three

XIV. CIVIL GOVERNMENT—POLITICS . . . . . . 113

Aristotles' Theory; Politics; Masons Do Not Vote as Masons, Prohibited by Landmarks. "Government" in Book of Constitutions. Masonry has no Politics, Members as Individuals have Politics.

## Contents

| CHAPTER | | PAGE |
|---|---|---|
| XV. | MASONRY AND THE LAW | 121 |
| | Freemasonry Subject to the Law; Old Charges. Sovereignty in Principle. "Masons as Makers of America." | |
| XVI. | MASONIC JURISPRUDENCE | 130 |
| | Science of Masonic Laws; Rules Applicable to Masonic Action. | |
| XVII. | MASONIC PARLIAMENTARY LAW | 136 |
| | Conduct of Masonic Business; Stations, Places of Masonic Officers; Performance of Masonic Duties. | |

### Part Four

| XVIII. | MASONRY AND HISTORY | 147 |
|---|---|---|
| | Constitutions, Peoples, Freemasonry's Internal History; William Preston's Illustrations; William Hutchinson's "Spirit of Masonry". Halliwell's Publication of Regius MS. | |
| XIX. | HIGH GRADES I (CHAPTER COUNCIL & COMMANDERY) | 154 |
| | Royal Arch, Cryptic Masonry, Knight Templarism; Oldest Lodge Records. | |
| XX. | HIGH GRADES II (THE SCOTTISH RITE) | 163 |
| | Scottish Rite Originated in France; Councils of Emperors, Albert Pike Sovereign Grand Commander. | |
| XXI. | DIVERGENCES FROM THE LANDMARKS | 169 |
| | Degree Peddlers; The Present System of Uniform Work; Grand Lecturers. Various Suggested Masonic Origins. | |

### Part Five

| XXII. | MASONRY SELF-DISCIPLINED | 179 |
|---|---|---|
| | Reclaiming of Their Freemasonry by Modern Grand Lodge. "A Free Vindication"; The Fraternity as a Political Power. Anti-Masonic Literature; "Use and Abuse of Freemasonry". Leadership or Censorship 1885 A.D. to the Present time. | |
| XXIII. | ANTI-MASONRY | 186 |
| | Its History and Basis, Political and Religious. The Morgan Affair; Roman Catholic Anti-Masonry; The Fascists; World War II. | |

| CHAPTER | | PAGE |
|---|---|---|
| XXIV. | GENERAL TOPICS | 195 |

(Landmarks, Bibles, Secrecy, Sociability) Dr. Albert G. Mackey; The Encyclopedia of Freemasonry. Feasts; 18th Century Lodges.

XXV. QUALIFICATIONS FOR MASONRY . . . . . . 205

Qualifications to do Work, to Receive the Degrees, to be a Lodge Member, to Occupy Office. Voluntarily not for Gain; to live a Masonic life.

XXVI. ANTHROPOLOGY . . . . . . . . . . 212

Freemasonry has Own Anthropology. Thinker's Conclusions and Important Presuppositions; Materialism, The Caste System, Darwin's Philosophy, other Philosophies and Masonry.

*Part One*
MORE ABOUT MASONRY

CHAPTER I

# *Freemasoniana*

(Origins of Masonry)

BETWEEN THE TIMES when the Grand Lodge laid a censorship on Masonic writers and speakers, and the founding of modern Masonic scholarship, a number of theories became active, and in some instances became popular, which have no standing in Masonic knowledge now. Since they are thus more or less dead theories a Mason has no need to take the time to study them; but since he will encounter them here and there in books, especially in old books, or in occasional discussions, it will be useful for him to know enough about them to be able to identify them and to know what is being talked about. The following paragraphs are for that purpose.

From six or seven centuries before the beginning of our Christian Era until some two or three centuries after it, there were in Britain, Europe, the Near East, and Egypt a large number of organizations which are now called Ancient Mysteries, or Mystery Cults. It is now impossible to discover how many there were, because many were small, or local, or temporary, and some were too secret to leave any records behind them, but the total number must have amounted to some hundreds. Among the most famous of them were the ones called The Eleusinia (Greater and Lesser), Mithraism, Samothrace, Magna Mater, Isis, Osiris, Serapis, Orpheus; many of the old stories, and much of the mythology which in later centuries passed into art, and especially into poetry, plays, and fiction and which have been described as "classical" are not classical because they did not come from the Greek and Roman classics but from the Mystery Cults. Those Cults were somewhat like a modern fraternity, and at the same time were similar to a modern religious sect or denomination. They were secret, admitted members by initiation, were organized in local bodies with officers, used rites and symbolism, had many ceremonies, and had fraternalism, fellowship, and relief among their purposes. They were destroyed by the Church, many of them being so completely obliterated that their very names were forgotten until recovered by archeologists. Many attempts were made in the Nineteenth Century to show that some one or two of them had survived, and been preserved in the form of Freemasonry, but the gap in time is too wide, and no evidence of any historical connection between the last Mystery and the earliest Lodges has ever been discovered —and scholars do not expect that one will ever be discovered because in spite of superficial resemblances Freemasonry is in principles, Landmarks, and purposes unlike any Ancient Mystery about which we have any knowledge.

During the whole of Ancient Times each craft, profession, art, trade and calling had an organization of its own. Among Latin-speaking peoples they were called *collegia* (from which we have our word "college"); in other languages they had similar names. They were somewhat like Medieval gilds, and also somewhat similar to modern trade unions. Each *collegium* had a local town or parish as its jurisdiction; met in a room of its own; had its own officers; governed its members by its own rules and regulations; and gave members much fraternalism, sociability, and charity. The collegia of architects in Rome were called *Collegia fabrorum* ("fabric" is an old name for a building); it was once hoped that an historical connection between them and the first Lodge of Freemasons could be found, but that hope was not realized.

Astrology was never confined to an organization, or to one people, or country, but always was a loose name for a collection of popular beliefs about stars—as far back as the most ancient times there were many astrologies and astrologers but there never was *the* astrology, or *the* astrologers. Modern astronomers know that a star or a planet (there are many millions of planets, large and small) is a material body composed of materials of the same kind as are in the earth or the sun or moon—stars are nothing but stars. But before the period of modern astronomy it was almost impossible for men to believe that stars are bodies of the same kind as the earth. If they were lumps of matter in space, why did they not fall? If they moved, what pulled or pushed them around? What kept them alive with light and color? Although they are far off, they have observable effects on the earth and on us; see what happens when the sun rises? see how the moon pulls the tide along without the use of visible means! It was argued that the stars and planets must have a life of their own, and be possessed of supernatural powers, and that through these powers they influenced or settled the fate of men. This was the doctrine of astrology. To foresee these influences, or to control them, or to protect themselves against them, astrologers invented horoscopes, charms, incantations, the zodiac, etc., and accumulated a mass of facts about the heavens—many of these facts were taken over bodily by the science of astronomy. In their books and charts astrologers used many signs, emblems, symbols—as when a point within a circle was used as an emblem of the sun—and a number of these were so similar to Masonic emblems and symbols that a few writers propounded the theory that Freemasonry had an astrological origin. At its best this theory rested at no time on anything stronger than a few points of similarity, which always is a weak foundation for a theory. At no place or time during the past eight centuries have Lodges or Grand Lodges been composed of, or been influenced by astrologers.

The peculiar form of occultism which is called Kabbalism contained some astrology, but cannot be included under that head because it was a distinctive and separate movement with its own literature. The Hebrew word "Kabbala" (or cabala, or Kabbalah, etc.) means an official collection of writings, a canon; it came into general use as the name for some four or five books written by a circle of Spanish Jews in the Thirteenth Century, and when correctly used denotes that collection of writings only. In them were a strange assortment of speculations on mysticism black and white magic, secrets of the Jewish religions, and they employed many emblems and symbols. They were little read outside of a small group in Spain and would have been forgotten had not a few leaders in the Protestant Reformation chanced to become interested in them. After the Reformation almost any form of occultism was called "Kabbalism." Since a small number of the emblems and symbols used in this "Kabbalism" were very similar to a few Masonic emblems and symbols a number of writers set up the theory that Freemasonry had originated in Kabbalism; but even if the theory had possessed two or three times as many of these similarities it would have been impossible because the Masonic Fraternity had been in existence centuries before the original Kabbalistic books were written.

Alchemy, like astrology, with which it was often combined, is difficult to describe because it was never organized, had no books of its own, and floated about at large taking many forms. The name might be applied to the search for an elixir of perpetual youth, or to the secret of turning metals into gold, or to some secret knowledge which would be the key to all knowledge; or it might be used as the name for medicine (medical physicians were often called alchemists), or for chemistry, or for laboratory physics. Since alchemy was forbidden by both church and civil laws, it was carried on under-ground, and alchemistic writings took the form of emblems, symbols, codes, and other disguises. Here again a few of these devices and symbols were similar to Masonic symbols, and it was once a somewhat popular theory to assert that Freemasonry itself was a form of alchemy. There is nothing in the buildings left behind by the Freemasons, or in the *Old Charges,* or in the *Book of Constitutions,* or in the Ritual to show that the Masons in any period were alchemists, or were ever even interested in it.

A gentle-minded and religiously devout German named John Valentine Andrea published a book entitled *Fama Fraternitatis* in 1615 A.D. In this short, extraordinary, and for a long time little-known volume, he tells a story about a character named Christian Rosencreuz which in some of its passages reminds a reader of one of the old saints' legends, and in others resembles Bunyan's *Pilgrim's Progress.* It is neither biography nor history, but a mystical tale, and its author may have intended it to be an allegory. According to the tale Rosencreuz was a seer or mystic possessed of supernatural powers, and when he died did not actually die but remained miraculously present at the center of his small circle of apostles who were sometimes called the Brotherhood of Rosicrucianism, and sometimes the Brothers of the Rosy Cross. This was not the first telling of a tale about a Rosy Cross, or Rose Croix; on the contrary it was one of the last and it may be that it won a certain fame for itself for that reason. There is no evidence that any Society of Rosicrucianism was ever organized with that name until a Masonic Side Order was set up in England late in the Nineteenth Century: it never consisted of anything except a book, and the tale told about Rosencreuz. Nevertheless it came to have a certain popularity in both Britain and America in the Eighteenth Century, and because there was neither an organization nor an official literature to hold it in check, the name ran loose and came to denote any one of eight or ten different theories or movements; it was the name for Andrea's own followers; one of the names used for both chemistry and alchemy; the name for a form of communistic socialism; the name for almost any form of occultism; and so on forth. A number of writers have tried to show that it was the origin of Freemasonry but theirs has been an even more hopeless attempt than had been that on behalf of Kabbalists and alchemists because the Masonic Fraternity was already centuries old when Andrea wrote his book.

Godfrey Higgins was one of those men whom we believe to be impossible until he arrives in flesh and blood, because it will always appear impossible for any man to read as much as Higgins did, in countless volumes of erudition, and remember as much of it as he did. In 1836 A.D. he published a work entitled *Anacalypsis*. It was as ponderous as Burton's *Anatomy of Melancholy*, as erudite as Dr. Francis Drake's *Eboracum,* and as startlingly unorthodox as Darwin's *Origin of Species.* In it he packed away endless histories of tribes and peoples whom everybody else had forgotten, and dead religions, and queer religions, and philologies and etymologies, and occultisms, and biographies, the whole of it ranging at large over Europe, Asia, and the Americas. There is, however, a key, or a master-trail, into the otherwise impenetrable jungles. Higgins himself believed this to be the key, or master-trail, to the whole meaning and history of the world. This was Higgins' theory: that ever since the Creation there has been in the world a single, true religion; that this religion has always kept underground, or gone disguised, or masked itself behind temporary and only half-true religions; that it has always been secret because only adepts can understand it; that it has always had such adepts, working behind the scenes; that these adepts, one after another, working from behind the scenes and adapting themselves to circumstances, were the real founders of such religions as Brahminism, Buddhism, Judaism, Christianity, Mohammedanism, the Ancient Mysteries, and thousands of primitive and now-forgotten cults. Higgins then went on to argue that these adepts also were the fathers and organizers of Freemasonry, and that the ancient British Druidism, a religion in England and Ireland before Christianity arrived, had been Freemasonry in its earliest form.

This Higgins theory can serve as the specimen or type for a number of theories of a like kind, for a description of the rest of which there is no space. Among these are such *anacalyptic* theories as that our Ritual is a survival of primitive initiation ceremonies; that Freemasonry originated with the Druses, an occult religion in the Lebanon Mountains; that it is a "cultural survival" of the "mysteries" of the "Maya Indians" of 20,000 years ago; that the Brahma priests of India invented it; that it originally was the secret cult of the Assassins in the Syrian Mountains, brought to Europe by the Crusaders; that it was set up for purposes of their own by a circle of "Great Masters" who live hidden away in Thibet, who created and rule the world, and never die; that the Masonic Lodge is a perpetuation of the "Mens' Home" of tribes in Africa and the Pacific Islands; that in generation after generation a few mystics have known and understood the "secrets of all things"; have maintained a "Hidden Church" and perpetuated their secrets by means of the "Secret Tradition" and that Freemasonry is a disguise for their teachings.

There are the equally numerous theories that Freemasonry was founded by some one great man, in Ancient, or in Medieval, or in Modern times, to carry out a purpose of his own, and such theories have named Adam, Noah, Pythagoras, Athelstan, Charlemagne, Francis Bacon, Oliver Cromwell, Ignatius Loyola, etc., etc.; and there are theories that it began as a secret science in Egypt when the Pyramids were built, or as an heretical church, such as the Bulgars or the Huguenots or the Anabaptists, or as a political party such as the Jacobites.

Though they differ among themselves to the very extremes of difference, though there have been hundreds of them, they one and all have in common the one point, *that they ask a Freemason to believe that Freemasonry was never itself but always was something else in disguise!* It is because they make this impossible demand on our credulity that none of these theories can be true. The whole story of the origin of our Fraternity can be told in a sentence of six words: *Freemasonry was founded by the Freemasons.* The Freemasons who erected the Abbey Church of St. Denis at Paris, or Cologne Cathedral, or York Minster were Freemasons *and they themselves knew it;* they knew that they were not Crusaders or Assassins, or Maya Indians in disguise. The Brethren who sat in the first permanent Lodges under authority of the *Old Charges* knew that they had taken the Masonic obligation, and not a Brahmin or a Druidic obligation. Nowhere in the records embodied in the Fabric Rolls, or the Borough Records, or old Minutes, or in the Proceedings of the first Grand Lodges are references anywhere made to alchemy, or Kabbalism, or astrology, or Rosicrucianism but they invariably are Masonic records. We ourselves who now belong to the Fraternity know who and what we are, and it would never cross our minds that we could be Druses, or Crusaders, or Jesuits without knowing it. It would be possible for a small number of men to call themselves by a name and to carry on ostensible practices as a cover for activities of another kind but it would be impossible for Freemasonry to do it, because it has always been too large, too public, too open to inspection, and is at work in too many countries. For centuries the Operative Freemasons used the Fraternity for operative purposes; when the Fraternity passed into the keeping of non-Operatives those non-Operatives did not turn the old Craft into a secret or occult cult but preserved it as it was, and though they used it for non-Operative purposes they did everything possible to keep it unchanged. We have now a great mass of documents and other records, and the mass is growing rapidly; nowhere in the whole of it is there a hint that at any time in its long history the Fraternity has ever been anything more or anything other than the Fraternity of Freemasonry.

CHAPTER II

# The Regius and Cooke Mss.

A SEVENTEENTH CENTURY English book collector owned a vellum manuscript book of about four by five inches in size which Bernard listed in his Catalog at Oxford in 1697 A.D. It was purchased for the King and was included by David Casley in his *Catalogue of the Manuscripts of the Royal Library* (1734 A.D.) under the title (possibly chosen by himself) *A Poem of Moral Duties*. King George II included it when he made a present of the Royal Library to the British Museum in 1757 (the Grand Lodge was then forty years old), and for that reason the *MS.* was christened (by R. F. Gould, and others) the *Regius MS*. It lay unnoted until J. O. Halliwell, a non-Mason, chanced to discover that it was not a poem, though written in doggerel verse; and was not on moral duties, but a document which had been written for an old Lodge of Freemasons. He discussed it in a paper read to the Society of Antiquarians in 1838–9 A.D., under the head of "On the Introduction of Freemasonry Into England." After his marriage he hyphenated his name to Halliwell-Phillipps; the MS. is often called by that name.

This was the most important single discovery ever made in Masonic scholarship, which in its modern, professional sense may be said to be dated from it, and which stands in sharp contrast to the guesswork of the earlier writers of whom the Rev. George Oliver was the most conspicuous example. It proved by documentary evidence that permanent Lodges of Freemasons had existed before 1400 A.D.; that Freemasons were in a class apart from other Masons; and that our Fraternity had not grown out of the building craft in general, but out of a highly specialized branch of it. Experts at first dated the *MS.* at 1390 A.D., but it is now believed that it was written at about 1400 A.D. Other written records in Fabric Rolls and Borough Records are older but they are not *Freemasonic* and cover only such details of building work as the dates of construction, names of workmen, wages, etc., etc., whereas the *Regius* belonged to an organized body of architects, of peculiar and specialized skill, with traditions, usages, and rules belonging exclusively to themselves. It is our Fraternity's oldest written historical record.

There are only 64 pages in the little book, with about fourteen lines to a page. Its title is also the first line of the text: *"Here begin the constitutiones of the art of Geometry according to Euclid."* The author states that he found the story of how Euclid came to constitute it "written in an old book," possibly a *polychronicon*. According to this "old book" a number of lords and ladies were in poverty and had no heritage to leave to their children; Euclid arranged for these "children" to learn "Geometry," or architecture, because it was a fine and highly-respected art suitable to their breeding. "He that would learn best" Euclid would "pass"; those that rose highest should teach "the simplest of wit"; "And so each one shall teach the other, and live together as sister and brother."

In this Craft there is to be a "Master"; "So that he were most worshipped, [honored] then should he be so called"; but within the Craft Masons should not call each other "subject nor servant," but "my dear brother." Euclid found geometry in Egypt, and from there taught it "full wide, in divers lands on every side." It, and by geometry was meant Masonry, or architecture—was brought into England in "good King Athelstan's day." "This good lord loved the Craft full well," so much so that to clear it of some faults and abuses which hindered it he called "all the Masons of the Craft" into a general assembly at York, with "divers lords, dukes, earls, and barons also" to decide "How they might govern it." These last statements show that in the eyes of the writer, and presumably of the Lodge for which he was writing, the rules and regulations of the Craft had *civil authority* behind them, which were laws in a full, true sense; they also show that the authority possessed by the Master and the Lodge to enforce discipline, to hold courts, and to assess penalties was a *dele-*

## The Regius and Cooke Mss.

*gated authority,* delegated, that is, by the King and his Counsellors, the ultimate source of the Civil law, to Craft Officers.

Without further preamble the scribe gives those rules whereby "they might govern it" in fifteen articles and fifteen points:

I. The Master must be steadfast; must see that Craftsmen are well fed and housed; is to be of no faction, and is to accept no bribe from "lord or fellow"; and must be an upright judge.

II. Unless a Master is ill, or has not been notified, or has any other reasonable excuse, he must represent his Lodge in the "general congregation."

III. No Master Mason should take as an apprentice any youth not willing to give seven years to training.

IV. A Master Mason should not "make" a bondsman an apprentice; he must be free; and the scribe inserts on his own opinion that he ought to be "of gentle kind."

V. The apprentice must not be deformed, but must "have his limbs whole."

VI. This article is obscure, but the general sense of it is that no apprentice shall be dealt with differently from others.

VII. In this is a peculiarly Medieval rule that a Lodge shall not be a place of sanctuary for thieves or murderers.

VIII. If any craftsman proves to be inefficient the Master has full authority to discharge him and to employ another in his place.

IX. A Master of Masons should not undertake a building unless he sees his way clear to completing it, for to abandon a work, half-finished is a great injustice to the employers; neither should a Master of Masons scamp or hurry his work.

X. If a Master Mason agrees to undertake a work, and is at work on it, no other Mason may by guile ease him out of it, or supplant him.

XI. This article ordains that "no mason shall work by night."

XII. If one Master Mason is asked about the ability of another, he shall not "run down the other": "he shall not his fellows' work deprave."

XIII. A Master may not neglect any part of his apprentice training.

XIV. Unless a Master is free and able to give an apprentice complete training he is not to have apprentices.

XV. No Master can tolerate false oaths, or sins, or other wrongdoings among craftsmen, for gain or for any other reason.

The Fifteen Points, the scribe says, were also ordained at King Athelstane's Assembly; he entitles them *"Plures Constituciones,"* or additional or Plural Constitutions:

1. A Mason must "love well God and holy church" and his fellows.

2. If Masons expect to be paid for holy days when they do not work, each must work "on the work day, as truly as he can or may."

3. Apprentices must reveal no secrets or counsels of either their Masters or the Lodge, even if they are among great lords and bodies who may believe themselves to have the right to command information.

4. "No man to his Craft be false"; he shall not maintain his errors against the Craft, nor do it "prejudice."

5. A Mason must accept his pay as agreed on; if a Master will not need him more he must "warn him lawfully before noon."

6. A warning against rancors caused by "great debate," or the interruption of work because of disagreements.

7. A rule of chastity among Masons and their families is enjoined.

8. Each Mason ought to be "a true mediator" among his "fellows free" to maintain peace and harmony.

9. Stewards who prepare and serve Lodge feasts should do it cheerfully and the fellows should serve as stewards in turn; and great care should be taken that everything is fully and promptly paid for.

10. No Mason should slander another.

11. If another Mason is doing his work "wrongly" teach him easily to amend.

12. Masons are subject to the laws as are other men; if any one of them "any strife against them make," he shall go into the hands of the sheriff.

13. Thievery of any form or degree is not tolerated.

## The Regius and Cooke Mss.

14. A Mason must swear "the oath of the Masons" to observe these points, and to be "true also, to all their ordinances, wheresoever he go, and to his liege lord the King."

15. Any Mason who violates the ordinances made at the general assembly is to be expelled from the Craft.

At this point the writer inserts another general ordinance which calls for general assemblies at fixed times and places, a rule which prepared the way for, and in after centuries ultimately led to, the founding of the Grand Lodge System. Immediately afterwards he inserts a long version of the old legend of the Four Crowned Martyrs, whether because it was at that time a living tradition in the Lodges or as a contribution made by himself it is impossible to learn from the context, but in any event it reads as if written by a priest because it is concerned with worship and theology, and homilies on good behavior written around the Medieval text, "Manners make a man." Much of the material at the end is obviously either quoted or paraphrased from a book.

The second oldest of existing versions of the *Old Charges* (also called Ancient MSS., Old Constitutions, etc.) was written ten to twenty years after the *Regius*, but internal evidence (and internal evidence is frequently the most solid kind of evidence) shows it to have been based on a "version of the *Old Charges*" older than the version which was used by the author of the *Regius;* since the *content* of the younger MS. is the older, it has the greater importance for historians. It was purchased for the British National Collection in 1859 A.D., was edited by Matthew Cooke, was published by R. Spencer, London, in 1861 A.D., and was named the *Cooke MS.* after its editor.

The writing of the original text of the *Old Charges* was not an event of importance in the history of the building Craft in general; it was more important but not in any sense epoch-making in the history of architecture, which is the branch of the Craft devoted to building as a fine art; but it was of the greatest importance in the history of the Fraternity of those architects, or Freemasons, because out of that general, Operative Fraternity there could never have developed the Fraternity of Speculative Freemasonry without the *Old Charges,* and without the new steps taken by Freemasons here and there which is marked by the writing of the *Old Charges*.

Before the middle of the Fourteenth Century a Lodge of Freemasons was temporary. Any given Lodge lasted only as long as a sufficient group of Freemasons continued to work together in a given place; once they completed that work they dissolved their Lodge, and its members divided, each one going his own way to seek employment elsewhere. If Lodges had thus continued to be temporary no Speculative Freemasonry would ever have developed out of them; it was because they were documents used to constitute *permanent* Lodges that the *Old Charges* are a continental divide across our history; it is in those permanent Lodges, not from the building Craft in general, or even from Operative Freemasonry in general, that the history of our own Speculative Fraternity properly begins.

When the first permanent Lodges were established we do not know, because no records have survived; it could have been at York, or at Westminster, or some fifty or sixty miles south of London because conditions in any one of those centers were favorable, and internal evidences in the *Old Charges* themselves incline scholars to that belief; it may be, as is most likely, that permanent Lodges were established within a few years of each other in all three centers.

When a Lodge became permanent it became in that instant in the eyes of Medieval law a corporation (or "body") and as such was required to have a charter; this charter could be issued by the church, or by a borough or city or county, or by the King; it had to be of required form, it could be granted only for a fee (oftentimes a large one), it had to satisfy certain conditions, and it had to be legally authorized and registered by the competent civil authority. Without such authority a body holding meetings under its own officers and for its own purposes was deemed to violate the civil laws governing assemblies, its oaths were unlawful, and if it was a gild of craftsmen it was stigmatized as an adulterine gild and its members were subject to severe penalties. The *Old Charges* carry on their face the marks of having been used for the purposes of a charter by the first permanent Lodges;

this is borne out by the fact that subsequent permanent Lodges had to secure a copy before they could constitute themselves.

Once they are seen to have been used for charter purposes the *Old Charges,* as they stand, and without explaining anything away, become intelligible. If the *Cooke MS.* (or any later version) is taken as history it is full of absurdities from beginning to end, and no amount of special pleading or learned pedantry can explain those absurdities away; if they were never intended to be histories, but were composed solely for charter purposes, the absurdities themselves (from an historical point of view) cease to be absurdities and become reasonable. It is even possible that when the author of the *Cooke MS.* quoted from a number of non-Masonic books instead of setting down Freemasonry's own traditions it is because he was writing for the non-Masonic eyes of the civil authorities.

A body of men petitioning for a charter had to have *grounds* on which to base their plea, these grounds being that such a body as theirs was needed, that it was honorable, would engage in no conspiracies, and would loyally keep the Ordinances of Religion and the King's laws. The petition for a charter then went on to set down a statement of its purposes, of the rules and regulations by which it would govern itself, its offices, and the territory or jurisdiction to which it would confine itself. The *Old Charges* follow this usual form of petitioning for a charter *except* that they claim that a *Royal Charter* had been granted to the Craft in the Tenth Century by King Athelstan and that its rules and regulations had been drawn up and approved at that time; they are in reality not a petition for a new charter but a petition to have an old charter officially recognized; their claim was allowed.

The *Cooke MS.* follows this outline. It is so composed that if the Lodge's claim to having charter authority already and, is disallowed, the claim can in that event (and at the same time) act as a petition for a new charter. The first part of the *MS.* lays down the *grounds* upon which the claim is made. Freemasons practice an art, called geometry or architecture, which is as old as the world; it was founded by the same patriarchs who had founded the other ancient arts and crafts. It has been patronized and approved by a long succession of kings and princes, and upon its introduction into England was not only approved but was headed by Athelstan, the first great English king. During its history it has been practiced or developed by many of the greatest and most famous of men, among them being Hermes, Moses, Adam, Noah, Tubalcain, Solomon, Euclid, Pythagoras. In France it had a glorious career. The art truly had been handed down from the beginning by apprenticeship and oral tradition, it never countenanced secret or occult practices, and could not work to the detriment of Church or State.

In the middle portion of the *Cooke MS.* it claims that in the Tenth Century King Athelstan called together at York an assembly of Freemasons themselves, and also, to meet with them, a large number of great lords; he gave the Freemasons a Royal Charter; and between them the Freemasons and the great lords of government agreed upon rules and laws for the government of Freemasons. Prince Edwin, who in the *Cooke MS.,* and in the old Saxon Chronicles, both, is described as Athelstan's son, became head of the Craft; That Royal Charter continues to be active, and any Lodge of Freemasons can act under it. Modern historians may doubt if Athelstan had a son, but the fact is neither here nor there; the Freemasons of (about) 1350 A.D., did not doubt it, nor did the civil authorities.

The third and last portion of the *Cooke MS.* consists of the charges, points, offices, rules and regulations by which the Lodge would govern itself, or any other Lodge under the same constituting document. These rules and regulations are wholly unlike modern club rules; they are not even the work-rules of day laborers, although they contain work-rules; they are a composite portrait of a Fraternity, and there was as much of what we now call 'Speculative" in them as there was "Operative." They show that Freemasons were not merely building laborers but were architects, and practicing a fine art. They show that the organization included families and homes and religion and sociability as well as labor, and that Freemasons comprised a community; that new members were *made* Masons before being received as members; that members were in the grades of Apprentices and Fellows, and that Officers had a status of their own (they were responsible to civil authorities as well as to craftsmen); that Freemasons lived and worked according to their own laws, within their own obligations, under their own lawful and official oaths, and that the only penalties were reprimands, fines, suspension, and expulsion. The work consisted not only of stone-cutting but was an assemblage of many arts and sciences, and skills, and therefore Freemasons had to be men of intelligence, education, and character who could live and work together in peace and harmony.

The *Old Charges* therefore were a *legal document*—not historical or ritualistic—and they were legal, as it were, at each end, in the eyes of the Craft itself and at the same time in the eyes of the civil law. It is this legal character that they have borne through the chances and changes of the Fraternity ever since. They were a constitution, and no permanent Lodge could be legally and regularly constituted without them—hence the multiplication of copies and versions, of which there must have been at least 1200 over a period of two or three centuries. They were used when a Candidate took his oath; they were kept in the Lodge; the first *Book of Constitutions* was a Grand Lodge version of them; and in the Eighteenth Century they became the Volume of Law on the Altar, and the Charter on the wall.

CHAPTER III

## *The Polychronicon*

ALTHOUGH THE WORD *polychronicon* is English, and the document to which it gave its name was the most important writing in a period of about two centuries, the word is almost never used, and the writing is seldom mentioned in histories of English literature. For all that, the Polychronicon is a subject with which we Freemasons must familiarize ourselves, because it was one of our principal origins; because without a knowledge of it we can understand neither the history of our Fraternity nor our Ritual; and the *Old Charges* would be a sealed book without it.

Ranulf Higdon (also spelled Higden) a Benedictine Monk, lived in a monastery in Chester for sixty-four years, and died, it is believed, in 1363 A.D.; he therefore could not have been born later than 1299 A.D. He spent the largest number of those years in compiling a chronicle of which the complete title was, loosely translated, "A Polychronicon from the Beginning of the World to the Reign of Edward III, in seven Books," by "Ranulphi Castrensis Cognomine Higdon." The original work was written in Latin. After Higdon's death, it was carried on by two other compilers. The first of the translations made into English was done by John of Trevisa, in 1387, and became so famous that the book is often called by his name. Caxton printed it in 1482 A.D., ten years before Columbus discovered America—and there is reason to believe that Columbus's own teacher in geography and navigation had read it. More than 100 copies of the *Polychronicon* are now in existence. One of them was published by the British Government in the Rolls Series as No. 41, edited by Babington and Lumby.

The word *Polychronicon* defines itself, the *poly* meaning "many

## The Polychronicon

or inclusive," the *chronicon* meaning "chronicle, or writing of, or history"; a polychronicon was a collection of many paragraphs, or many articles or chapters, on many subjects, of many kinds, and was therefore roughly comparable to a modern encyclopedia, or *omnium gatherum*. The compiler gathered into his net whatever he could find, from far or near, ancient or modern, events out of history, old stories, tales of adventure, accounts of marvels, bits and fragments of Ancient or of Medieval sciences, antiquarian gossip, or what not. He did not weigh or criticize his sources, or care much what his sources were, and helped himself to whatever suited his fancy or might interest a reader. He left behind him a huge scrap-book, in the miscellany of which are things possible and impossible, credible and incredible, all jumbled together. Works of this kind were immensely popular and might have any one of a dozen titles, but for the most part they were called *polychronicons*. Higdon's was probably the best of any of them, certainly it was the best written, and it was the best of the great specimens to be produced before the invention of printing. This also was a source book for the earliest writers in Modern English, and any number of its traditions and ideas passed into general literature, so that we all carry about in our minds more than one work or thought which we owe to a book which we have never read, by an author of whom we have never heard.

When in the middle of the Fourteenth Century the first permanent Lodge found the need to have a written charter, or constitution, they had a now unknown scribe prepare for them a document which ever since has been known generally as the *Old Charges*. The oldest existing specimen is the *Regius MS.*, written at about 1392 A.D. to 1400 A.D.; the second oldest is the *Cooke MS.*, written some twenty or thirty years later. Each of these is a version of an original which either was lost or remains undiscovered; it is not believed that either the writer of the *Regius MS.*, or of the *Cooke MS.*, had the original before him but that he worked from a copy; and it is believed that the *Cooke* is from an older version and the more important historically.

Beginning at line 132 of the *Cooke MS.*, the author states frankly that what he is setting down about the history of Freemasonry, which he also calls Geometry, he has taken from a number of old books among them a *polychronicon*. Freely transliterated, his lines read: "You shall understand that among all the crafts of the world men's Masonry has the most notable and largest part of this science of geometry, as it is noted and stated in Stories (Histories) and in the Bible, and in the Master of Stories. And in the stories that are named Beda. And in *Polychronicon*, a chronicle *preuyd* (which means, authoritative); *De Imagine mundi* & *Isorodorus ethomolegeriaum, Methodius episcopus* & *martyr,* and many others."

The polychronicon is more likely to have been Higdon's than not, but if it was not Higdon's it was one very similar to it. "The Master of Stories" was Peter Comestor, a Frenchman, who was nicknamed "the bookworm," who became chancellor of Notre Dame in Paris, while there wrote his famous *Historia Scholastica,* and died at some unknown date between 1178 A.D. and 1189 A.D. "Beda" was the chief ecclesiastical chronicler; he wrote his *Ecclesiastical History of the English Nation* in 731 A.D. *De Imagine* was written by a Frenchman, believed to have been a bishop, and may have written his book within some years after 1100 A.D.

Isidorus was the noted Isidore, Bishop of Seville, who lived between 570 A.D. and 636 A.D., and whose *Sentences,* a sort of theological dictionary, was for centuries a standard work scarcely less reverenced than the Bible.

Methodius was a Fourth Century Bishop, who suffered martyrdom in 312 A.D. and won remembrance as the theological opponent of the great "Origen."

The writer of the *Cooke MS.* may have had these books before him but it is more reasonable to believe that he found them quoted in his *polychronicon:* the jostling of many writers together, of different periods of time orthodox and heretical, was one of the characteristics of the *polychronicon.*

It is interesting to compare two passages from Higdon's *Polychronicon* with parallel lines from the *Cooke MS.* Higdon tells the story of Jubal, Tubalcain, etc., as very loosely transliterated:

"This Lamech took two wives, Ada and Silla, and had two sons; of Ada was born Jabel, that was father of them that wander in tents and pavilions. And Tubal that was inventor of organs and harps. And of Silla was born Tubalcain, a smith who worked with a hammer; and his sister Naamah, inventor of the craft of weaving.

"Tubalcain founded first the smith's craft, and when Tubalcain wrought in his smithy, Tubal had great liking to hear the hammers sound, and he found proportions and harmony of melody in the hammers, and so they used them much in the accord of melody but he was not the inventor of the instruments of music, for they were invented long afterwards."

The author goes on to say that they were invented by Pythagoras. At another place he tells the story of the two pillars; "The time men knew, so Adam had said, that they should be destroyed. by fire or by water, therefore the books that they had made by great travail and study would be destroyed. They enclosed them in two great pillars of marble and of tile. In a pillar of marble for water, and in a pillar of tile for fire, in order to save them for the help of mankind."

The *Cooke MS.*, beginning at line 159, and at various places in the text following it, says (loosely transliterated): "In Adam's line lineally descending down the seven ages before Noah's Flood there was a man that was called Lamech; he had two wives, one called Ada, and another called Sella. By the first wife he begot two sons, one called Jabel and the other called Jubal." He goes on to say that the elder son discovered geometry and Masonry, and made houses; he was a Master of Masons, and built the first city. And his brother Jubal, or Tubal, was fonder of music and song, as Pythagoras is represented as saying in the *Polychronicon*. And he goes on to say "that he found that science by the sound of ponderations of his brother's hammers. . . ." "Tubalcain was fonder of the smith's craft, and his sister 'Neemah' was the discoverer of weaving, and this third brother aforesaid had knowledge that God would take vengeance for sin either by fire or by water." They took counsel as to how to save the arts and sciences. "There were two kinds of stone of such quality that one will never burn, and it is called marble. And the other stone will not sink in water and is named *Cacerus:* And so they devised to write all the sciences that they had found in the two stones." So they made two pillars, and because they did Noah and his wife, and their sons and their wives, eight in all, had the arts and sciences to use to build the world over again "after all the world was drowned."

In one form or another, and to one degree or another, the succeeding versions of the *Old Charges* repeated these old stories.

When the Mother Grand Lodge came to collect these "old manuscripts" and to compare them in order to prepare the *Book of Constitutions* in 1722 A.D., they did not quote the *Old Charges* verbatim but they at least preserved something of them, as witness the paragraph on page 2, including its footnote: "No doubt Adam taught his sons geometry, and the use of it, in the several Arts and Crafts convenient, at least, for those early Times; for Cain, we find, built a city . . . and becoming the Prince of the one-half of Mankind, his Posterity would imitate his Royal Example in improving both the noble Science and the useful Art." After this follows a foot-note: "As other Arts were improved by them, viz., working in Metal by Tubal Cain, Music by Jubal, Pastorage and Tent-making by Jabel, which last is good Architecture." The author of the *Old Charges* lifted materials out of the *Polychronicon* almost bodily; the author of these sentences from the *Book of Constitutions* did not quote those materials verbatim but unquestionably he had the *Old Charges* in front of him.

The author of the original text of the *Old Charges* wrote his document in some unknown year represented by the decade 1350 A.D.–1360 A.D. The *Cooke MS.*, is undoubtedly a very close version of it. He wrote his document for a permanent Lodge of Freemasons; they would read or recite it to a Candidate, and either then or not long afterwards would keep a copy of it on a pedestal in front of the Master, as one of the most revered objects in the Lodge Room; and the Masons at that time, with few exceptions, were Operatives; it is very important therefore to note in the *Old Charges* what it was that those Operative Freemasons were most interested in, and most concerned with, and deemed to be most essential to their Fraternity. From the *Cooke MS.*, we learn that they were concerned with such subjects as these: architecture and its history; geometry; the Liberal Arts and Sciences; the originators or founders of the arts used in architecture; how the art of geometry or architecture was brought to England; and how the Fraternity came to be honored by receiving a Royal Charter. This picture of the Masonic mind as thus mirrored in the *Old Charges* proves that the Freemasons at that early date, even in Lodges wholly Operative, were not merely stone-cutters or stone-masons.

Why did the author of the original version of the *Old Charges* turn to the *Polychronicon?* First, because everywhere it was, as he himself noted, a source approved by the scholars of that age. Second because there was no other source to which he could go for the materials he needed. The Old Testament was available to few men, and probably was available to the writer of the *Old Charges,* for he refers to it as to a familiar book, but there was in it no history of either geometry of architecture and very little history except of the Jews. The *Polychronicons* were everywhere in use, as encyclopedias are now; in drawing upon one of them he was doing what any other writer would have done, therefore his doing so was neither peculiar nor questionable.

The author of the *Old Charges* set down what was needed by the Lodge for which he prepared his document, and like any writer now he utilized the best materials then available; he would have been surprised out of his breath could he have looked ahead six hundred years to see some three or four million Masons in the world using a Ritual for which his own document helped to prepare the way, and which would incorporate in itself much of his document. Ranulf Higdon, if, as is probable, it was his *Polychronicon* that was used, would have been even more astounded, Benedictine monk that he was, could he have looked forward seven hundred years to see a few passages or paragraphs of his own embedded in that Ritual because of the accident of their having been quoted or used in the *Old Charges.* Such, however, is the fact, and in the whole scope of Masonic history few other facts are more revealing, or more romantic.

For after the Lodges had used the *Old Charges* for generations to obligate and admit their Candidates, and after their membership had become increasingly Speculative, they began to cut down the time required for initiation (a very significant fact) by reducing the first third of the *Old Charges* to a set of figures, or pictures or diagrams which they drew on a black-board or floor-cloth with chalk, or painted on a board, or represented by models and other objects set out on a trestle. It was in this manner that a number of symbols and emblems came into use, the Forty-Seventh Proposition, the Letter G, the Ark, the Two Pillars, the Mosaic Floor, etc., most of them from the *Old Charges* themselves, and of these a number ultimately derived from the *Polychronicon* and the other similar learned books on which the author of the *Old Charges* had drawn. Without the *Polychronicon* we should probably have never had those particular symbols, and in the oral portions of the Ritual would probably have never had Euclid, Pythagoras, Jubal, Tubal, Cain, etc., nor a good half of the Lectures and Emblems. The *Polychronicon* was therefore one of the origins of the Ritual of the Freemasonry which we now have; to say so is not a far-fetched theory but is a statement of fact based on written and official documents of unquestioned authenticity.

This use of a *Polychronicon* by the author of the original version of the *Old Charges* brings to the front one of the most perplexing problems with which Masonic scholars must wrestle, and historians and specialists in historical research in particular. Any Mason who studies Masonry not as a professional scholar but for his own satisfaction also encounters it, and if he is thoroughgoing must wrestle with it. This is the problem of *Masonic tradition*. The *Old Charges* themselves raise the question because in their original version they drew so much upon some one or more *polychronicons,* and every *polychronicon,* Higdon's as much as any other, and as stated above, drew largely from traditions. They also raised the question a second time when they introduced a tradition not taken from a *polychronicon* in the form of their account of an assembly of Masons called by King Athelstan almost 500 years before the original version was written. What is a *Masonic tradition?* Is a Mason expected to accept it at its face value whether or no, because it is *Masonic?* Is it a chapter of history, differing from other history only by its being not written? Or is it a mere tale, repeated generation after generation, possessing no historical weight? And what of the other terms closely associated with it in our nomenclature, such as legend, myth, and oral transmission?

There is in our own language, as in every other, a peculiar set of words which some etymologist, perhaps such as the late Logan Pearsall Smith, once described as "somersault words," because at some point in their history they suddenly turned upside down, and began to mean the opposite of what they had always meant before. The word "hell" once carried the connotation of something made extinct, brought to a complete end; it now connotes something endless. In early Anglo-Saxon, "read" was used of a man who received reports or advices because he could not read. "Story," which now denotes a piece of fiction, and "history" the opposite of fiction, once were the same word. The constellation of words which centers in the word "tradition" belong, many of them, to that class of odd and surprising terms. "Tradition" itself is a Latin compound adopted into English; the *trans* here shortened to *tra* means "over" in the sense of across; the *dition* is an elaboration of *do*, which meant "give"; a tradition meant "to hand over," but it became confined to the simple use of a set of facts which must be preserved and therefore must "be passed along." The picture is easy to see; some man or set of men learned something so important, or knew something so weighty, that it must not be lost, therefore it was passed on, or passed over, or made to hand along to some other set of men, or to the next generation; it was preserved not only because it was *true,* but also because it was importantly true; in that sense a "tradition" was accepted as reliable, true beyond question, *because* it was tradition. Then, perhaps during the latter part of the Middle Ages, the word turned a somersault and came to denote a narrative or story without any reliability in it—at least it did so in one of its most common uses.

A *myth* was originally a piece of knowledge, but it was known only to a few, and the path of its early history intersects at a common point the paths of *secret,* and of mystery; a myth was knowledge, but it was secret knowledge. Then, and because so much of what many cults and priesthoods advertised as secret knowledge turned out to be tall tales about gods, devils, heroes, monsters, *et al.* which nobody could accept literally, the word turned a somersault, and a myth became the least secret of things, and the farthest removed from knowledge. *Legend* meant something read, as when a teacher read a book or a man in public office read a report; then it turned upside down to mean something not written as a record, something of the same kind as our modern fictional stories. These are etymologic notes, and normally can have no place in a book about Freemasonry, but they may be of help to a student of Masonic traditions because they warn him that he is dealing with slippery words, and remind him that before he makes up his mind about anything purporting to be, or said to be, a *Masonic* legend, myth, story, or tradition he must make an unusually cautious examination to see whether it is true or not true—as, in example, the Rite H.A., is not a *legend,* yet the two greatest and most complete *Histories* of Freemasonry call it a *legend,* and discuss it as if it were one.

A list of suggestions will give a Mason an armory to have in his mind ready-made when he undertakes his study of Masonic traditions; or, to state it otherwise, that in Freemasonry which is traditional; how these suggestions reflect back upon the *Old Charges* and the Polychronicon they themselves will make clear.

1. If "tradition" is taken in its very oldest and most literal sense of "go over" or "send over to the next generation," then the whole of Freemasonry is traditional, and that is one of the stupendous facts about it; for twenty-five or thirty generations Freemasons have been handing it over, or passing it on, to each succeeding generation.

2. Before reading, writing, and printing were in general use specialists were employed to learn by heart long histories, biographies, genealogies, technical knowledge, etc.; practitioners of it were tested at intervals of every year or so to make sure that their memories had not been at fault on so much as one word. This was called Oral Transmission; modern writers, when referring back to it, and especially if they are careless, usually call it tradition. If we have anything in Freemasonry which was preserved by Oral

## The Polychronicon

Transmission we can treat it as we could treat a written document, even if it is now called a tradition.

3. Before writing and printing, a story might be preserved by the people and without Oral Transmission, because it was a good story, or because it had a place in their holidays, or fetes, or feasts, etc. Such a story might or might not be a true story, but ususally if it had been a true story to begin with "the story would gain by telling"; if such a story is called a tradition, the historian will try to recover the original facts and free them from the accretions of fiction. The stories about King Arthur are a case in point. If a Masonic Tradition be a tradition of that sort no Masonic historian is absolved, merely because he is a Mason, of separating the fact in it from the fiction in it, and his Brethren ought not to be shocked when he does so, because it is his moral duty.

4. Some traditions in Freemasonry are things we Masons do for no other reason than that Masons have always done them, generation after generation, century after century. If any iconoclast asks us if we have no better reason for continuing to do them we can answer that no better reason can be found anywhere for doing anything. "Keep the young generation in hail," cried George Meredith to his contemporaries; in a traditional custom we are keeping the old generation in hail, and that also is a satisfying thing to do. Why do we celebrate the St. Johns Days? We Masons have no patron saints. It is because we have always done so. It is a tradition.

5. Finally—and perhaps this is the most useful of these suggestions—when we come upon an historical tradition in Freemasonry there are two things to do about it. The account of the Assembly at York called by King Athelstan is an example of a number of such traditions. If we examine it as historians, and as historians decide against its historicity because sufficient evidence is lacking, we can rule it in whole or in part out of history and preserve it as non-historical tradition.

Nevertheless and at the same time it is an easily proved fact that Masons possessed such a tradition as King Athelstan in the Middle of the Fourteenth Century and presumably before that date; it is also a fact that both the Masons themselves and the civil authorities *believed* it to be true; and it is also easily proved that they acted in good faith upon that belief. The *content* of that tradition may in part be non-historical; but even if an iconoclast avers that it is wholly non-historical it still remains true that few other facts or events have had a larger part in the history of our Fraternity than that of tradition.

CHAPTER IV

# *The Book of Constitutions*

(Anderson)

A CONSTITUTION IS A DOCUMENT or instrument with inherent authority used as the means by which an organized body of men is brought into existence with a name and identity of its own, and on the understanding that the body thus formed, or erected, or organized, or constituted will thereafter continue to be governed by that document or instrument as its own law. The first Lodges to be made permanent soon discovered the need for such an instrument and drew up the written version of the *Old Charges* to satisfy it. Almost immediately after it was begun in 1717 A.D., the Mother Grand Lodge began to feel that same need; to satisfy it the Grand Lodge prepared a version of the *Old Charges* for its own use, and in 1723 A.D., published it in a written volume entitled *The Book of Constitutions*. To make sure that this important task would be soundly and regularly done the Grand Lodge appointed a Committee with Rev. Dr. James Anderson as chairman, called a number of the oldest and best-informed Master Masons into conference, and collected as many versions of the *Old Charges* and other time-honored documents as it could find and analyzed, compared, and collated them. After the Book was read to Grand Lodge and was officially approved it was turned over to Dr. Anderson for publication, and for that reason has since been often called the "Anderson Constitutions," though to call it so is incorrect because Dr. Anderson was not its author—the Grand Lodge was its author.

The book consists of 91 pages, 8¾ x 11¼ inches in size. Its title page reads: "The Constitutions of the Free-Masons. Containing the History, Charges, Regulations, etc., of that most Ancient and Right Worshipful Fraternity. For the use of the

Lodges, London: Printed by William Hunter, for John Senex, at the Globe, and John Hooke at the Flower-de-luce over-against St. Dunstan's Church, in Fleet-street. In the Year of Masonry—5723. Anno Domini—1723."

The full-page Frontispiece is a line drawing believed to represent the Grand Master the Duke of Montagu presenting the Roll of the Constitutions to his successor, the Duke of Wharton, with their officers behind them; it was engraved by John Pine.

The first four pages of the body of the Book consist of a dedication "To His Grace the Duke of Montagu," signed by his Deputy Grand Master, J. T. Desaguliers.

Except for seven lines of reading text at the bottom the page numbered 1 is at one stroke title and an introduction: "The Constitution, History, Laws, Charges, Orders, Regulations, and Usages, of the Right Worshipful Fraternity of Accepted Free Masons; Collected From their general Records, and their faithful Traditions of many Ages. To be read At the Admission of a New Brother, when the Master or Warden shall begin, or order some other Brother to read as follows: etc."

From the bottom of page 1 to page 48 inclusive the book consists of a loose and rapid summary of the story of the art of Masonry, or architecture, as that story had been first narrated in the Fourteenth Century, and with the addition of enough facts to bring it down to date in 1723 A.D. This section is not signed.

Page 49 consists of a title, introduction, and table of contents for a second section, reading in full: "The Charges of a Free-Mason, extracted from The ancient Records of Lodges beyond Sea, and of those in England, Scotland, and Ireland, for the Use of the Lodges in London: To be Read At the making of New Brethren, or when the Master shall order it. The General Heads, viz.—

    I. Of God and Religion.
   II. Of the Civil Magistrate supreme and subordinate.
  III. Of Lodges.
  IV. Of Masters, Wardens, Fellows, and Apprentices.
   V. Of the Management of the Craft in working.
  VI. Of Behaviour, viz.—

*The Book of Constitutions*

1. In the Lodge while constituted.
2. After the Lodge is over and the Brethren not gone.
3. When Brethren meet without Strangers, but not in a Lodge.
4. In Presence of Strangers not Masons.
5. At Home, and in the Neighbourhood.
6. Towards a strange Brother.

This section ends on page 56 with an "Amen so mote it be." Page 57 consists of a long foot-note, entitled "Postscript," in the form of a quotation from Lord Coke to the effect that a statute against Masons by Henry VI had been repealed by Elizabeth.

The section from page 58 to page 70 inclusive has another long, combination title-introduction: "General Regulations, Compiled first by Mr. George Payne, Anno 1720, when he was Grand-Master, and approved by the Grand Lodge on St. John Baptist's Day, Anno 1721, at Stationers'-Hall, London; when the most noble Prince John Duke of Montagu was unanimously chosen our Grand-Master for the Year ensuing; who chose John Beal M.D., his Deputy Grand-Master; and Mr. Josiah Villeneau and Mr. Thomas Morris, Jr., were chosen by the Lodge Grand Wardens. And now, by the Command of our said Right Worshipful Grand-Master Montagu, the Author of this Book has compar'd them with, and reduc'd them to the ancient Records and immemorial Usages of the Fraternity, and digested them into this new Method, with several proper Explications, for the Usage of the Lodges in and about London and Westminster."

A Postscript on pages 71 and 72 gives the "Manner of Constituting a New Lodge, as Practis'd by his Grace the Duke of Wharton, the present Right Worshipful Grand-Master, according to the ancient Usages of Masons."

Pages 73 and 74 consist of an "Approbation," which was in fact a Grand Lodge official action, signed by Grand-Master Wharton, Deputy Grand-Master J. T. Desaguliers, two Grand-Wardens, and the Masters and Wardens of twenty "particular Lodges."

The section from page 75 to 90 inclusive consists of songs: The Master's Song, or the History of Masonry; in five parts. The Warden's Song; in thirteen stanzas. The Fellow-Craft's Song;

The Enter'd Prentice's Song; By "our late Brother Mr. Matthew Birkhead, deceas'd."

On page 92 is an official authorization for the printing of the Book signed by Philip Duke of Wharton, Grand-Master, and J. T. Desaguliers, Deputy Grand-Master.

An unnumbered last page consists of a detailed advertisement for "Some Books Printed for J. Senex, and J. Hooke."

It will be noted that no name of either an author or an editor is given in any of the title-pages, yet at some three or four pages in the text the writer refers to himself as "the author." It has been presupposed, but without certainty, that "The author" was Dr. James Anderson; on the other hand it may have been used for whoever may have been writing the page in which it occurs, after the fashion of the "editorial we"; in any event the word could not have been used in the present day sense of "sole writer of this book" but in the early Eighteenth Century sense of "editor"—the records of Aberdeen Lodge in which Dr. Anderson is believed to have been a Mason used it in that same sense of editor. The phrase on page 58 which reads "digested then with this new method" does not mean that a new practice is being introduced into the Lodges; the word "method" is here used in its old literary sense, and means that George Payne's text has been revised.

In the first paragraph of the long section which is called "History" God is described as the Architect of the Universe, and geometry is made synonymous with architecture. Adam must have taught the builders' art to his sons because Cain built a city, and Seth made many "curious works," and in a foot-note it is said that according to "some vestiges of Antiquity" that Enoch "erected his two large Pillars" "the one of stone, and the other of Brick, whereon were engraven the Liberal Sciences, etc.," to preserve the latter from the Flood.

Noah and his three sons were cognizant of the art else they could not have devised so wonderful a vessel as the Ark. Then for about 131 years after the Flood Noah's descendants, "a large number of them" worked at building a Tower (among other wonders) in the Valley Shimar; God confounded their speech,

## The Book of Constitutions 35

and for that reason the populaces separated, and this explains why there have been so many nations and languages ever since. Nimrod was the mightiest of Ancient architects because he built so "many splendid cities." From him and his generation the Chaldes and the Magi "preserved the good Science, Geometry, as the Kings and great men encouraged the Royal Art."

Mizraim, the second son of Ham, six years after Babel, brought a colony down to Egypt and in his irrigation systems "caused an improvement in Geometry." The "great sons of Canaan" erected many "stately cities." Even into Asia the art was carried, for Abram, after the Confusion of Babel about 268 years, was called out of Ur of the Chaldees, where he learned Geometry. "From him it passed on to the twelve Patriarchs of the Hebrews."

The Israelites, "at their leaving Egypt, were a whole Kingdom of Masons" and Moses was their Grand Master, "who often marshalled them into a regular and general Lodge while in the Wilderness" and before many years they erected a Temple in Jerusalem "to the Amazement of all the World," and 183,600 men were employed on it. "Hiram, or Huram," was "the most accomplished Mason on Earth."

Nebuchadneza's city of Babylon was "the Third of the Seven Wonders of the World." Then architecture was carried down into Greece. Miletus was the first to have "any considerable knowledge in Geometry," but it was his scholar Pythagoras who was the author of the "47th Proposition of Euclid's fifth Book, which, if duly observed, is the foundation of all Masonry, sacred, civil, and military." After him Geometry "became the Darling study of Greece," and it was the Greek Euclid who gathered "up the scattered Elements of Geometry" and "digested them into a Method that was never yet mended." And thus the art of architecture was carried triumphantly from land to land, and in Rome it was finally made illustrious by "the great Vitruvius, the Father of all true architects to this Day."

After following the introduction of architecture into Gaul, Britain, the Lowlands, and even into the Gothic north, the "history" then pauses to quote from an old MS. "written in the Reign of King Edward IV, in which it is told that King Athelstan was "a mighty Architect," called expert Masters of Masons out from France, reconstituted the Craft, and created many towns and buildings. His youngest son, Prince Edwin, who had been obligated in a Lodge, "purchased a free Charter of King Athelstan his Father, which empowered Freemasons "to hold a yearly Communication and General Assembly." Acting upon it Edwin called a General Assembly at York.

After telling the story of the Craft in England, the "history" turns to Scotland, where the Kings were "often the Grand Masters." When James of Scotland became King of England he introduced the Augustan (or neo-classical) style; in describing this, many famous architects and Grand Masters are named, Palladio, Inigo Jones, and Sir Christopher Wren. The long excursion through this story of the Masons' art reaches its conclusion in a peroration genuinely eloquent:

"And now the Freeborn British Nations, disentangled from foreign and civil Wars, and enjoying the good Fruits of Peace and Liberty, having of late much indulged their happy years for Masonry of every sort, and reviewed the drooping Lodges of London, their fair Metropolis flourisheth, as well as other Parts, with several worthy particular Lodges, that have a Quarterly Communication, and an Annual Grand Assembly, wherein the Forms and Usages of the most ancient and worshipful Fraternity are widely propagated, and the Royal Art duly cultivated, and the Cement of the Brotherhood preserved; so that the whole Body resembles a well built Arch; several Noblemen and Gentlemen of the best Rank, with Clergymen and learned scholars of most Professions and Denominations, having frankly joined and submitted to take the Charges, and to wear the Badges of a Free and Accepted Mason, under our present worthy Grand-Master, the most noble Prince John Duke of Montagu."

The "Manner of Constituting a New Lodge" on page 71 is especially worth a thorough study by a student of Masonic history because it shows so clearly two fundamental facts about the first, or Mother, Grand Lodge. First, the Grand Lodge took itself to be a *Lodge* in every sense of the word, except that where a local Lodge has individual Masons as its members, the Grand

Lodge has Lodges; this is shown by the Officers of the new Lodge being described as "Candidates"; the new Lodge itself is a "Candidate" in the eyes of the Grand Lodge. Second, it is for the Grand Master *himself* to constitute a new Lodge: "A new Lodge, for avoiding many Irregularities, should be solemnly constituted by the Grand Master," and it is the Grand Master, not the Grand Lodge, who decides whether a new Lodge is to be founded or not; afterwards this power was transferred to the Grand Lodge, where it has remained ever since. When the Grand Master himself constituted Lodges he issued a letter, or Warrant, authorizing the action; when Grand Lodge took over the power of forming Lodges it issued Charters. A Charter is a *Grand Lodge* document, and it is only because it is one that it possesses inherent authority.

Pages 73 and 74 are unique among the contents of the book because they do not belong to the text of the book itself, but are a statement about the book. The material in the two pages is entitled "Approbation." Since this material is strictly official, and is itself an act of the Grand Lodge in 1723 A.D., it is unfortunate that it has not been more carefully studied, because if it had been fewer inaccurate statements would have been published about the First Edition of the *Book of Constitutions.* In this Approbation Dr. James Anderson is described as "Author of this Book" but this can only mean that he acted as scribe, or secretary, or amanuensis; the text itself makes it plain that he did not himself originate the materials. Grand Lodge itself was the true author.

The Approbation states that because of wars "the Freemasons twice thought it necessary to correct their Constitutions . . .", once by Athelstan, the second time under Edward IV. But since through the passage of time many errors crept in, it is now deemed necessary to correct, or to revise, them a third time. The Grand Master, the Duke of Montagu, "ordered the author to peruse, convert and to digest into a new and better method." This new version was carefully studied by Grand Lodge, the Lodges, and many learned Masons, and it is now fully and officially approved. The Grand Master, the Duke of Wharton, who is speaking, ends by saying: "And we ordain that there be reviewed in every particular Lodge under our Cognizance, as the ONLY CONSTITUTION of Free and Accepted Masons amongst us, to be read at the making of new Brethren, or when the Master shall think fit: and which the new Brethren should peruse before they are made." The Approbation is signed by the Grand Master, Deputy Grand Master, Grand Wardens, and twenty Lodges—among the then Worshipful Masters of these Lodges were George Payne, Matthew Birkhead, the Earl of Dalkeith, and James Anderson. These twenty were in London and Westminster; no "county Lodges," or Lodges outside of London, were added to the List until the following year.

On page 70 Regulation No. XXXIX (the last one) states: "Every Annual Grand Lodge has an inherent Power and Authority to make new Regulations, or to alter these, for the real Benefit of their ancient Fraternity; Provided always that the Old Landmarks be carefully preserved . . ." The Grand Lodge itself acted upon this inherent right to such an extent that in 1738 A.D. it published a Second Edition, and this work of revision has been carried on ever since. But though the body of Constitutional Law now printed in the Code of any Grand Lodge is scarcely to be recognized as the same *Book* as that of 1723 A.D., it nevertheless is a direct descendant of that Book. When the Grand Lodges of Ireland, Scotland, the Antient Grand Lodge, and, later, American Grand Lodges adopted a Book of Constitutions it was on that volume of 1723 A.D., that they patterned it; and since that *Book* itself, as the official Approbation is at so much pains to state, is a revision of yet older laws, and which it does not hesitate to describe as ancient, Masonic constitutional law is very old indeed.

CHAPTER V

# History of Masonry in the United States

John Skene of Aberdeen, Scotland, was a member of the Aberdeen Lodge, as we know from the "Lodge Book" which it published in 1670 A.D.—in all probability it was the Lodge in which James Anderson was made a Mason. With a number of other Aberdoenians, five or six of whom were Masons, Skene came to what is now New Jersey to work for a large company which owned much of that territory and was Deputy Governor of East Jersey from 1685 A.D., until his death five years later. The other Masons returned to Scotland after short stays. Jonathan Belcher, a Governor of Massachusetts, was a wealthy land-owner, and otherwise one of the leading men in that vast Province; also he was an officer in an English corporation having large American holdings in which company Christopher Wren was a member of the Board. On a business voyage to London in 1704 A.D., he was made a Mason, possibly by Sir Christopher Wren himself, who was a member of Antiquity Lodge, and had been what the Book of Constitutions described as "Grand Master." Skene and Belcher were the earliest Masons in America of whom any record remains.

This means that Masonry came at a very early date indeed, because the settlement at Plymouth was only sixty-five years old when Skene arrived; it means that there was Masonry here, and in all probability a few Lodges, *before* the first Grand Lodge was erected in England in 1717 A.D.; and it also means that Freemasonry did not begin here in germinal form, crude and undeveloped (as a number of British writers have assumed), but was full-fledged and complete; there were Lodges in Britain centuries before there were Lodges in America but the *Masonry* in those American Lodges was itself as old as the Masonry in any British

Lodge because it was the same Masonry. Furthermore it means that Americans did not invent anything which could be called American Masonry; they could have done so, as men had done in France, because they could have invented a new kind of fraternity and *called* it Masonry; but they did not, from the first Mason and the first Lodge their Masonry was self-same with the Masonry in Britain, and the history here is not a history of Freemasonry *in* America. Masons insisted in the beginning, as they continue to insist now, that there cannot be a number of different Freemasonries scattered about among the nations but that there is but one Fraternity of regular Freemasonry, and it is the same the world over.

The oldest existing written *Lodge* record is that of a Lodge in Philadelphia which was at work as early as 1729 A.D.; Benjamin Franklin was made a Mason in it, became an officer, was an officer when he published his edition of the Book of Constitutions in 1734 A.D.; this Lodge, called St. John's acted as a Mother Lodge and in 1734 A.D., must have turned itself into a Grand Lodge because in that year Franklin was "elected" Grand Master. It has been argued that this Philadelphia Masonry was not duly constituted because St. John's Lodge had no charter from the Grand Lodge of London, and Franklin was not appointed by the Grand Master of that Grand Lodge. It is true that according to rules later adopted that every Philadelphia Lodge and its daughter Lodges were not "duly constituted" but the fact tells nothing against their legitimacy as Lodges or the regularity of their Masonry: 1) a large number of regular but independent Lodges in Britain were not on the Grand Lodge List yet were recognized by it; 2) at that date Charters were not required; 3) the Grand Lodge at London did not have exclusive Territorial Jurisdiction of North America, and never did have; before 1717 A.D., each and every Lodge was *self-constituted;* it was not until many years after 1717 A.D., that self-constitution made a Lodge irregular; 4) after the Grand Lodge at London had set up Provincial Grand Lodges here, they recognized the legitimacy of the Lodges in Pennsylvania.

It is unfortunate that the young Grand Lodge at Philadelphia did not stick by its guns, and that Lodges in other Colonies did not do likewise, because if they had we should have possessed such independent Grand Lodges as did Ireland and Scotland, and they would have been preferable on every count to the ill-adjusted, creaky, feeble Provincial Grand Lodges which were set up instead. There was too much private ownership by individuals, families, or companies of whole "Colonies" or parts of colonies here for anything to be as it should have been. Before the Revolution America suffered as much from the incalculable evils of absentee landlordism as did Ireland, and Freemasonry suffered along with it. American Masons administered Provincial Grand Lodges with only a tenuous and intermittent supervision or assistance from Britain; they just as easily could have administered their own independent, sovereign Grand Lodges.

But not for half a century was that to be. In 1733 A.D., Henry Price, who was in literal fact one of "the makers of Masonry in America," returned from London with a written deputation from the Grand Lodge there to constitute a Lodge in Boston, and to establish a Provincial Grand Lodge with himself as Provincial Grand Master; his deputation was for the whole of "North America" (that included Canada); this did not mean that he was to have exclusive jurisdiction at that period—but only that he could issue warrants to Lodges anywhere in North America. Later other Provincial Grand Masters were appointed with the same right. This was the first Lodge and the first American Provincial Grand Lodge to be constituted by *written* authorization from the Grand Lodge at London, and of whose uninterrupted activity a written record exists. Three years before, in 1730 A.D., Daniel Coxe, of New Jersey, was appointed Provincial Grand Master of New York, New Jersey, etc., but though he remained in residence in New Jersey, where he had a large place in public affairs, there is no record to show that he ever acted upon his Masonic authority. From the period 1730–1733 A.D., and until the eve of the Revolution one Provincial Grand Lodge after another was constituted by the London Grand Lodge of 1717 A.D., the Antient Grand Lodge of 1751 A.D., the Grand Lodge of Ireland, the Grand Lodge of Scotland, and in a number of instances Lodges were constituted on authority from France and from the West Indies.

In any given country, during any given period, Freemasonry is there, and then, what the Lodges in their hundreds, or the members in their thousands, or their millions, are making of it. The few histories thus far published of Freemasonry in America before the Revolution describe it, with few exceptions, in the form of a history of the Provincial Grand Lodge and thereby mis-describe it, for the planting of Freemasonry in what is now the United States was not done by those Provincial Grand Lodges except to a minute extent, but by thousands of individual Masons and by a few hundred local Lodges. The Minute Books of the earliest Lodges here show that in some instances Lodges did not know what Provincial Grand Lodge they belonged to, and few of them ever saw a Provincial Grand Master. It was done, that planting, by the rank and file of ordinary Masons, and since it was done by them then great glory is due to them, because in the long history of the Fraternity there is no chapter so large, no achievement so magnificent, as the setting up without fanfare or assistance of the undivided and undivisible, magnificent, simple Masonic Fraternity from New York to San Francisco, from Duluth to New Orleans, and all within only a century of time! Consider this catena of facts.

1. No Officer, Committee, Board or group of Masons came here from abroad with any directions or plans for the Fraternity in America; it established itself, and acted out of its own nature.

2. No place was chosen for its capital, or center, or headquarters, or base; it had no London or Dublin to act as its center of gravity but the Craft planted a Lodge wherever it found a place for one, and members carried their Masonry wherever they wished. This fact helps to explain why we did not constitute one Grand Lodge for the whole nation; we doubtless would have done so if in its formative period the Fraternity had possessed a Masonic London, or Dublin, or Paris.

3. Thousands of sailors and hundreds of sea captains either lived in our port cities or spent a part of their time there; thousands of men came to work as employees of the large companies

or families which owned so large a part of the Colonies; settlers, trappers, explorers, adventurers, traders, soldiers and sailors came by the tens of thousands; among them was a Mason here and there, and a number of regiments and ships brought their own Lodges with them. By using ambulatory warrants (a travelling warrant) they set up Lodges, some transitory and some permanent, wherever a sufficient number of Masons might chance to settle in some new community. Freemasonry then entrusted itself to that uneven and unpredictable flood of men, making no attempt to set either limits or conditions to its own extension, and it therefore went wherever the first Americans went, and arrived there at the same time.

4. What kind of Masonry did these men have? The kind called for by the warrants (or charters) they carried. This in itself is a decisive fact which crops up in any history, one which is so easily overlooked because it appears to be a small fact—too small to identify with the breadth and vastness of its consequences.

On the one side was the almost boundless, vasty, yeasty uncontrolled, undirected movement of peoples which populated this country, itself almost as large as a world, in the extraordinary short period of only two centuries—it had taken 1500 years to fill permanently and with an organized citizenship each and every area of the Island of England! Carried about and tossed about in that flood, Freemasonry might easily have been twisted out of all recognition. On the other side, and explaining why it was not so twisted, was the fact, which above was described as apparently a small fact, that wherever these restless and ever-moving settlers and soldiers carried Freemasonry with them they carried a *warrant* with it; it was that warrant which prevented the twisting out of recognition and caused Lodges, even in the Wild West, to adhere to the Ancient Landmarks. Some measure of how much Freemasonry might have been changed from its original form is furnished by a contrast of American denominationalism in 1800 A.D., with the parent church in England and Scotland as of that same year; the use of warrants and charters saved us from being divided into a congeries of Masonic denominations and sects; and it is at the same time another eloquent testimony to the truth that the extreme of unity can be attained in the center of the extreme of diversity by means other than force, compulsion, or despotism.

5. If the Lodges constituted from about 1730 A.D., to about 1853 A.D., are marked on an outline map of the United States, a dot and a date for each Lodge, and if a line is drawn from each Lodge to its mother Lodge or Grand Lodge, the story of the planting of Freemasonry here can be visualized; among the dots which bear dates prior to about 1788 A.D., every Lodge had a Charter from the Modern or Antient Grand Lodges in England, from those of Ireland, Scotland, the West Indies, or France; if the Lodges and their connecting lines chartered by any one of these sources are put down in one color, the Lodges from another source in a second color, etc., the proportionate share of each of those Grand Lodges in the planting of American Masonry would also be visualized.

If a complete map of this sort were made (it has been made in part) it would lay bare to the eye some four or five of the largest facts about American Masonry which are not easy to see among the multitudinous details of a written history. The most important cities in the earliest period were Philadelphia, Boston, and New York; other cities and Masonic centers in succeeding periods were Albany, Norfolk, Louisville, Cincinnati, New Orleans, St. Louis, Cedar Rapids, Santa Fe, and San Francisco—a Masonic history of those and a few other cities would be almost a history of the Fraternity in the United States. Port cities and towns, almost without exception, were early local centers because of the number of Masons among soldiers and sailors.

Freemasonry did not advance steadily and evenly westward across a north-south frontier line but in the form of thrusts or currents—a map of the *movement* of the Fraternity would look like a weather map. Different currents passed through Philadelphia, Boston, New York, and Norfolk; a large current came southwest out of Canada into the Mississippi Valley, another flowed westward out of New England, a third moved from North Carolina and Virginia toward Cincinnati through the Cumberland gap; the largest current flowed westward out of St. Louis and then divided into three, one each toward the South West, the Far West, and the North West. Another one consisted of a large number of Lodges brought to the West Coast by ships from Atlantic ports. The main current from France came first to the West Indies, and then divided, one up the Atlantic Coast as far as Philadelphia, the other entering the Deep South through New Orleans.

The map would show that in the histories of the Fraternity in America, which are either local histories or chapters or parts in general histories (for a reason too mysterious to guess *no* complete history of Masonry in America has ever been published), there are gaps and hiatuses. They usually ignore the *Masonic* consequences of the French-Indian War; the part played by Canada in New England Masonry; the peculiarity of New England Masonry; the part played by Lodges in the settlement of the West, South West, and North West; the effect of the Mormon Empire on Masonry in the Mountain States; the part played by Lodges in the settlement of the Republic of Texas; the leadership of Masonry in establishing the Public School System; and almost without exception they ignore the large role of the West Indies in the planting of Lodges; and few of the accounts have anything to say about the militant and destructive Anti-Masonry of the Roman Catholic Church in the deep south, especially in Florida and in Louisiana.

If the same Masonic map were to be interpreted in the same manner with which a field commander interprets a military map, it would also show (this is written without prejudice!) that the larger number of our writers have misinterpreted the part of Masonry in the Revolutionary War, and the story of the attempt to set up a National (or General) Grand Lodge. Freemasonry as a single Fraternity was *not* on the side of the Patriots in the Revolution as a body; it never takes sides in any war; there were as many Lodges and Masons in the British army and navy as in the American, and they fraternized across the lines—General Washington himself visited a British military Lodge under a flag of truce and received a degree in it (probably the Mark Degree). The Masons who early in the war started a movement for a National Grand Lodge expected, like the majority of Americans, to see a single government take the place of thirteen separate governments, and they therefore expected to see a single Masonic government for the same reasons—a compromise, hybrid system of one Federal Government plus forty-eight sovereign State Governments was something they could not even picture at the time.

The main reason for the failure to set up a National Grand Lodge was the formation of those independent and sovereign States; the secondary reason was that in spite of the Revolution, and for some years after it in some cases, American Provincial Grand Lodges refused to believe that the Revolution had had anything to do with Freemasonry therefore they continued to keep their Masonic connections with Britain as long as they could in order to make sure of violating no Landmarks; in a few instances British Grand Lodges themselves took the initiative in persuading American Grand Lodges to become sovereign and independent.

Next only after the general planting and establishing of the Fraternity in the United States the most epochal event was the setting up and perfecting of that which now everywhere is called The American System. Royal Arch Masonry was brought over before 1750 A.D.; Templarism, the Cryptic Rite, and the Scottish Rite were brought over (in pieces, as it were) between that date and about 1800 A.D. When these High Grades began to constitute Grand Bodies and local Chapters, Encampments, Lodges, and Councils of their own the question, of whether each Rite was to function independently was posed to the Craft, or if one Rite should absorb the other four; the question was answered by declaring Freemasonry to consist of these five Rites and of no others, and then by forming them into a single Fraternity by means of a system of Comity.

Among Masons as among the people at large events or movements occur which are dramatic and therefore remain long in the national memory, or are of national importance; general historians devote separate chapters to events or movements of that kind, and Masonic historians do the same for like reasons. Among the subjects for those chapters in American Masonic history are such as these: The New England Anti-Masonic Movement of 1800 A.D., the Morgan Affair and the Anti-Masonic crusade which began in 1826 A.D.; the "Degree Peddler" evil, and the movement to establish Uniform Work; the Mormon Anti-Masonic campaign; Freemasonry in camps and covered wagons in the trek of westward immigration; Freemasonry in the Civil War; the establishing of a number of academies and colleges by Masons; Freemasonry in the two World Wars; the Masonic Educational movement which began about 1915 A.D.; the extraordinary craze for new Temples between the World Wars; the rise and prosperity of Side Orders, especially of the Shrine, the Grotto and of the Eastern Star; the present powerful movement toward a general co-operation among the 49 Grand Lodges; etc., etc.

CHAPTER VI

## History of Masonry in Other Lands

*France.* THE FRENCH REVOLUTION came close on the heels of the American Revolution and was both fired and inspired by it, but unlike the American Revolution it was brought to a dead stop when only half completed. Ever since, there have been two Frances, one of them royalistic, aristocratic, with a hierarchy of generals, Cardinals, bankers and great landlords leading it, the other one (Civil France) republican, bourgeoise with farmers in it, functionaries, small tradesmen, etc. The two Frances have been at war with each other ever since, at a few periods they have been in a civil war with each other, but they did not fall completely apart until World War II when aristocratic France openly sided with the Germans at Vichy, and republican France went underground as the Resistance.

The history of Freemasonry in France since the establishment of the first Lodges in 1725–1730 A.D. has been the story of the Fraternity's attempt to overcome within itself this national division; it has never wholly succeeded. The first Lodges were warranted by the Grand Lodge of England and were therefore regular and duly constituted according to the Landmarks and therefore recognized no social castes, and the Degrees used were inherited from the Operative Masons, but in a few years French aristocrats began to refuse to sit in Lodge with farmers, tradesmen, and artisans, and to avoid this meeting on the level they began to design "lodges" of a new kind, and broke away not only from the Ancient Landmarks but from Masonic history. They invented the legend that Freemasonry had not been founded by Medieval workmen but by Medieval Knights, especially by the Knights Templar, and that the earliest leaders had not been Masters of Masons but Emperors, Kings, and Princes, and to accomplish their purpose they fabricated many new degrees. Until the Revolution (about 1770 A.D.) the French Masonry was predominantly aristocratic. But immediately they had won half freedom in the Revolution "the rank and file of ordinary men" (by which were meant non-aristocrats) began to set up Lodges of their own, and which were as close to the Ancient Landmarks as they could make them; their purpose was to be democratic, tolerant, non-Roman Catholic, and they worked for public schools, free speech, free thought. This internal rivalry between the so-called "French Masonry" of the aristocrats, and equalitarian "republican Masonry," complicated by political invasions from without, as by the Jacobites and the Fascists, could not be grasped by the American Mason even in a work of three volumes in which each detail was explained because so much of it involves questions which have always remained outside his ken. But Freemasonry does not permit itself to be dismembered to suit political diversions, and no Grand Lodge is "foreign" to another; French Masons might be Masons in France but that fact was of secondary importance; the fact of primary importance was that they belonged first of all to the one family of World Masonry. It is intolerable for one national government to interfere with another national government; but Grand Lodges are not national governments, and if one Grand Lodge joins in some form of work with another it is not interfering. During the 1920's and 1930's British and American Grand Lodges were assisting French Lodges to overcome their division, and to restore themselves to the Ancient Landmarks and to Masonic history; World War II halted that work, but it will be resumed, and in due time it will succeed.

*Italy.* Lodges deriving their authority from the Mother Grand Lodge in London were constituted in Italy in the 1730's—the decade of world-wide expansion—and would have flourished quietly and have multiplied prosperously had not the Pope issued his Bull of Excommunication in 1738 A.D. From that time on, the history of the Fraternity in Italy may be summarized by saying that it continued, but continued now under ground and now above ground. Italy is the home of the Vatican; the Vatican is Italian to the bone and the large majority of Popes and Cardinals have been Italian, yet the Vatican has also always been international, and it has always been able to use the full force of its great political and financial power against its foes at home; that force took the form of religious and educational monopoly, restraint, restriction, censorship, suppression, the denial of the right of free association, the use of excommunication. The Italian has always been as likely to disbelieve the Vatican's creed as any other man—he is not *born* a Roman Catholic; no man is—; and he is as certain to resent repression, despotism, the loss of freedom, as any other man.

*Britain and northern Europe.* In Britain and northern Europe the rebellion against the Vatican took the form of Protestantism and set up a new theology to replace the old; in Italy the rebellion took first the form of the Renaissance, in which free men exercised their freedom in thought and in art, and second (in the Nineteenth Century) it took a political form. But since until the middle of the Nineteenth Century Italy was cut up into fifteen or sixteen separate nations, opposition to the Vatican was always divided. And since for a long time the Vatican could call in French military power to crush opposition in Italy, and at a later period could call in Austrian military power (and often did), Italian opponents of the Vatican could set up neither an army nor a church but had to work by means of conspiracy. Conspiracy works in secrecy; its typical form of organization is a secret society (such as the Carbonari); such a society often preserved its secrecy by camouflaging itself as something else and by calling itself by a name belonging to other societies. In consequence there came a time when there were many political conspirational groups which called themselves Masonic Lodges but were not, and there were Grand Bodies which professed to be doing Masonic work but were in reality doing political work. In Italy as in France regular Grand Lodges from outside came to the assistance of regular Masons inside Italy to clear away the confusion; by the 1920's they were beginning to succeed; but they were cut short by Mussolini who ordered Freemasonry obliterated.

*Germany.* In Germany early Freemasonry took its cue not from the Mother Grand Lodge in England but from France, and especially from the French "High Grades," the resounding and glittering mysticism of which appealed to the dukes and princes and electors and kings who ruled the fifty or sixty tiny German states. But where the French aristocracy was social the German aristocracy tended to be religious, and for a number of generations religion was a keyword of German Masonry; even the long refusal to accept Jews into membership was more theological than racial. But here also, by the 1920's, a powerful movement began to draw an increasing number of Lodges back into the Ancient Landmarks, and it is possible to estimate that by the time Hitler ordered Freemasonry abolished the number of regular Lodges almost equalled the number who still refused to accept the *Old Charges.*

*Scandinavian countries.* Freemasonry in Scandinavian countries has always gone a way of its own unlike that of any other. Behind it has always been the religion of Lutheranism in the form of a state church, but the determining factor in it has always been the king, who in most instances in Denmark and Sweden has been Grand Master by virtue of being king. But Scandinavian monarchy has always been in principle almost the opposite of monarchy in France, Italy, and Germany, for where in the latter countries the monarch has always represented the greatest possible distance between the ruler and the people ruled, in Scandinavia it has always represented the closest possible union between the ruler and the people; it is as if the people ruled themselves by means of a king instead of by means of a parliament. Scandinavian Freemasonry has followed the same pattern; at the head of it stands royalty, but the body of membership is as democratic as American membership.

*Britain is the homeland of Freemasonry.* There was always as much Operative Freemasonry in Europe as there, but Freemasonry as a Fraternity of Speculative Masons began in London, and from that center spread around the world. But the Mother Grand Lodge of 1717 A.D. was never a Masonic Vatican; it claimed no supreme authority; from the beginning it was but one among other Grand Lodges. The fact that Operative Freemasonry began in England did not make it English nor did English Masons ever claim Freemasonry to be their private property. As soon as any regular Grand Lodge was erected anywhere in the world it instantly had the same sovereignty as the Mother Grand Lodge. English Freemasonry has therefore always been characterized by a double feeling: "England is the homeland of Speculative Freemasonry, and we are very proud that it is. But we are humble enough to know that it is not our private or our national property." Freemasonry is in Britain, but it is not "British Freemasonry."

Italian Lodges have always been confronted by the Vatican itself—they must look the Pope in the eye. French Lodges and Spanish Lodges have always been confronted by the Catholic Hierarchy; their conflict has been with Cardinals and Bishops, and these latter have been backed and supported by the great landlords.

*Latin America.* In the Latin Countries of Mexico, Central America, and South America Lodges have always been confronted by the priesthood. The cornerstone of Latin-American priestcraft, as the priests themselves understand clearly, is their hold on the woman, and through her, on the children; the man will be drawn in, according to this polity, by using his marriage to the woman as a cable tow, and by using his fatherhood of the children as a threat. Nevertheless the Latin-American man is no more a Roman Catholic "naturally" than any other man, and he often rebels against it—the great Mexican Revolution under Juarez was a men's rebellion against priests, and secondarily against the landlords of whom the priests were the servants. In consequence of this history Latin Masonry has always been full of inner self-contradictions and paradoxes; it flourishes, and yet it languishes; it is powerful as a tide, and yet as weak as water; it now flies off to the extremes of Masonic orthodoxy, and then to the opposite extremes, and even sets up Lodges full of women. It is because the Fraternity represents the schisms and unbalance inside the family; the most religiously and political revolutionary of men are likely to have a wife in love with priestcraft, and she holds the children as hostages for his good behavior. The great universal in Latin countries is neither the church nor the state but a polished and perfected etiquette, which holds together what would otherwise fly into pieces, and smooths over what would otherwise be too rough to walk upon. If our American Grand Lodges were to find a common ground in this realm of courtesies, and stay on it, and let other things stand, they would cease to deal with our Latin Brethren with such ineptitude, and would be less guilty of what Latin America takes to be our gaucheries, and would find a *via media* along which we and they could walk together.

*Asia Minor—Middle East.* The Grand characteristic of Freemasonry in the *Levant,* in *Iraq, Turkey, Iran, Arabia, Palestine,* and *Egypt* is that it is *Town Masonry,* because you cannot set up Lodges on the desert, nor erect temples among the millions who live in tents; the grand characteristic of Near Eastern towns is their extraordinarily polyglot population, and since that is true a Lodge in such a town will have in it a polyglot membership. Among its forty members, if it have that many, will be twenty races, nations, colors, languages; it is a mosaic in which no two pieces are the same in shape or color. A New York Grand Master who visited a Lodge in Syria found seven languages being spoken in it; a Kentucky Grand Master who visited a Grand Lodge in Cairo found five different volumes of the Sacred Law on its altar. The note of it is therefore Masonic universality, not in its geographic sense but in its cultural and social sense. The ends of the earth meet in it, and not only meet but mingle, and Freemasonry's great significance in those strife-torn lands is this proof that they who were born foes can be born again as friends.

*Asia—Far East.* Asiatic Masonry, including the vast populations of *India, Burma, China, Japan, Korea, Manchuria, Malaya,* the *Philippines, Indo-China, Siam,* and the *East Indies* (three-quarters of the world's population) is two hundred years old. The determining factor in it, the key to it, has been colonization—the planting of colonies of population, of commerce, of religion, of armies, of education. The majority of Lodges have been set up in such colonies; they have therefore begun as a foreign importation; in their early history their membership has consisted of colonizers;

and since these colonizers almost always drew a hard line between themselves and the "natives" (a disgraceful word!), the Lodges remained on the White, or European, side of the line. But not even a Britisher or an American can draw up a line against "natives" and make it stick for ever, and therefore the great Masonic movement in Asia since about 1900 A.D. has been a steady increase in the number of regular Lodges with members drawn from the local population; it is as yet in its first, faint beginnings, but the movement will grow, and as the centuries pass will grow to vast proportions; we ourselves contributed all that we are able to when we made it possible for Filipinos to have Lodges and Grand Lodges of their own, free from any control by ourselves; they have already established many regular Lodges in China for Chinese members.

It is, however, in the English-speaking countries of the *United States, Canada, Great Britain, South Africa, Australia* and *New Zealand* that Speculative Freemasonry has had its longest and most remarkable history, and reached the highest pitch of power and of membership; nor is it a mystery why it has done so because the explanation can be stated in one sentence: *Churches and Governments in English-speaking countries have left Freemasonry alone.* If those governments which are anti-Masonic, such as Soviet Russia and Phalangist Spain, and those governments which are afraid of it, such as Portugal and the Argentine, only understood the Fraternity better, they would know that it cannot, and therefore would not, interfere with or embarrass any government which gave it the freedom to exist. It could not, because of its own nature. For the same Freemasonry which is self-constituting and therefore brings itself into existence, is also, and by the same token, self-regulating; and the same Fraternity which will not tolerate interference *by* churches, governments, or *their* agencies will not tolerate interference *with* churches or governments by *its* own members. What do churches and governments have to do with it? Nothing. If it is left at peace, if it is left free, if it is left to do its own work and in its own way, it can be itself and do its own work in any country in the world without disturbing that country's religion, government, or society.

*Part Two*
MORE ABOUT MASONRY

## CHAPTER VII

# *Grand Lodges*

WHERE IS GRAND LODGE? In the chapter on the subject of Grand Lodge which is included in each of the many books on Masonic Jurisprudence this question is never asked, but it ought to be because it is always arising among Masons, and in one form or another it is one which a Worshipful Master is always asking himself. The answer is like the Servant in the House in Charles Rann Kennedy's play of that name who when he tries to describe what the builders do, says "it is not easy to describe" and "you must look at it in a certain way." A Grand Lodge has a set of Grand Officers but a Grand Lodge is not where they are because they may live anywhere in its Grand Jurisdiction. It may have its own hall or Temple or permanent headquarters where the Grand Secretary and the Grand Master have offices but the headquarters cannot be a Grand Lodge's *where* because they are in one city only. It is not where the Grand Communication meets because it may meet anywhere in its own Grand Jurisdiction. Even a Grand Jurisdiction is not its *where* in Freemasonry in America because some four or five Grand Lodges have Lodges in other countries. "You must look at it in a certain way," because the secret of the question lies in the fact that a Grand Lodge is many kinds of things at once, and the answer depends on which one of the many a questioner has in mind when he asks his question; but on the whole and in the rough, the answer is that a Grand Lodge is *where* its Lodges and their members are. It is omnipresent within its own Jurisdiction. It has no residence, no post-office address.

*When is Grand Lodge?* The question also is deceptively illusive, and is passed over by the books on Jurisprudence. A Grand Lodge has a regular Grand Communication once a year (in a few Grand Lodges, two or four times a year) and it may hold Called (or Emergent) Grand Communications when the Grand Master summons it, but this is not a Grand Lodge's *when*, it is only the *when* of its assemblies. It itself has no *when* because it is on duty twenty-four hours a day, 365 days a year, keeps no holidays, does not stop for Sundays, never, as it were, shuts its doors or closes shop. It would be a curiously interesting book if one of our historians were to write a history of our Grand Lodges in the terms of chronology; a number of events occurred, but *when*, on what day of the week or year, and at what time of the day? If such a book were prepared, and if a sufficient number of Grand Lodges were included, it would show that somewhere a Grand Lodge is taking action on something at each minute of the day, and each day of the year. A Grand Lodge has no *when*, unless by a *when* is meant the whole of time; it never slumbers or sleeps.

*What is a Grand Lodge?* Here again "you must look at it in a certain way," because the *what* is just one thing and then another, and some of those things are hard to see. A grand Lodge has its own members, those officers and delegates who sit in its Assemblies with a voice and a vote, but those members take no action *as members* except when summoned to do so. Moreover, a Worshipful Master who is a member is not one in his own person, but as a representative of his Lodge. Therefore it falls out that *Lodges* are members, and for that reason are called constituents of a Grand Lodge. Yet at the same time a Grand Lodge is not only something more than its Lodges combined but also is something other. It has a complete complement of Grand Officers, and it is they who carry on much of its work between Annual Communications, but it is obvious that no Grand Lodge could consist solely of its own Officers. A Grand Lodge has a printed Book of Constitutions and a set of general laws but these are not its *what;* else it would exist only on paper. Its concern is with the Grand Jurisdiction as a whole and as a unit and with the Lodges severally and collectively as wholes and units; its *what* therefore is whatever Freemasonry has in it with which to deal with such concerns, therefore while the *what* is fixed and crystallized at the

*Grand Lodges* 59

core of it, its edges (as it were) are not fixed and crystallized but are living and fluid—if its duties make it necessary for it to take on a new function it can do so, or it can discontinue a function if conditions demand it. The Fraternity has a certain number of Grand Lodge Landmarks and whatever they are a Grand Lodge is and has to be, but otherwise the Fraternity is not dogmatic about a Grand Lodge's *what* but permits it to have a living flexibility—as we know in the United States, where a Grand Lodge may be carrying on a kind of work or have a department of its own which a neighbor Grand Lodge neither does nor has.

*Why is a Grand Lodge?* To this question Masonic history gives a summary answer: The Fraternity of Speculative Freemasonry could not exist without Grand Lodges. It tried to do so, but it failed. There were Lodges, Speculative or partly so, for more than a century before the first Grand Lodge was constituted (1717 A.D.), and there were many regular Lodges, perhaps 200 of them, which tried to work outside the Grand Lodge after it was constituted, but they did not succeed. In any given geographical area, as in one of our own States, events occur, or questions arise, or something must be done, which affects the whole Fraternity within it; unless the Fraternity could act as a whole, as a unit, it ultimately would break down, and that is why it needs a Grand Lodge, for any Grand Lodge is nothing other than the organized means by which Freemasonry in any Grand Jurisdiction can act as a unit, and by which a Lodge can act as a body, and the Lodges can act together. In almost any other fraternity, society, or association a Grand Body could take any one of many forms, and as a matter of known fact they have often done so, but in Freemasonry it was impossible for a general governing and directing agency to be anything other than that which a Grand Lodge is: to exist, the Fraternity not only must have a Grand Body but it must be just that particular kind of Grand Body we now have— no other form of Grand Body, organized differently, could have served. The first Grand Lodge was not constituted because some leader persuaded the Craft to erect it, nor was it designed according to the blue-prints of any leader's theory; it came into existence because it was needed, when it was needed, and where it was needed; and its Constitutions, laws, and offices were each and every one required in order to satisfy some need in the Fraternity itself.

The Fraternity as a whole in a Grand Jurisdiction must act in a body and as a unit to carry on a number of activities; these activities vary among themselves in kind, and the organs, agencies, officers, etc., of a Grand Lodge are designed, each one, to carry on one of those activities; this answer to the *Why a Grand Lodge?* contains also the answer to the question of why Grand Lodges are not exact duplicates of each other. The variations express unlike needs and dissimilar circumstances. In a large Grand Lodge the Lodges are represented only by the Masters because there is not seating space for more, a small Grand Lodge can seat Masters and both Wardens. One Grand Lodge can transact its annual business in a single Grand Communication; another must hold four Grand Communications a year. A Grand Lodge in a thinly populated Grand Jurisdiction may have ten Grand Lodge Committees, a Grand Lodge in a Jurisdiction crowded with towns and cities may have fifty; and in the same instances the one may have only twenty-five Appointive Grand Officers, the other may have two hundred. History in actual practice often takes the form of customs, usages and traditions, and each of these is itself necessary; one Grand Lodge in consequence is unlike another (Louisiana and Pennsylvania are striking examples) because their history is so different. In some Grand Jurisdictions a task is best performed by the Grand Lodges; in another by the Lodges. Also, there are justifiable and rational differences of thought among the Grand Jurisdictions as to what is proper for a Grand Lodge to do (instead of Lodges or their members) and what is not allowable. The axiom that "new occasions teach new duties" is equally valid when it reads that "new occasions teach new methods"; it will always be impossible (and will never be desirable) to abolish the different theories of Grand Lodge functions, the very act of abolishing them would breed a new set of conflicting theories.

Nevertheless there is a set of Grand Lodge Landmarks, and in respect of it every regular Grand Lodge is in the exact dupli-

## Grand Lodges

cate of every other one. In the United States a Grand Lodge has a Grand Jurisdiction which lies within the boundaries of a State (including the District of Columbia); over it the Grand Lodge has exclusive territorial jurisdiction. Each regular Lodge in such a Grand Jurisdiction is on the List of the Grand Lodge and can owe neither obedience nor allegiance to any Grand Body in a Rite other than Ancient Craft Masonry; nor can any regular Grand Lodge permit any Grand Body other than itself to have any voice in its affairs or in any one of its Lodges. The Principal Officers are elected at a Grand Communication, usually for a term of one year. Their duties are defined by their constitutions, but they are answerable for the performance of them to the Grand Master. Appointive Officers are appointed by the Grand Master for a term of one year; their duties are assigned to them by the Grand Master—in some Grand Lodges they are called the Grand Master's Staff. A Grand Lodge has its own Constitution, statutes, by-laws and general laws. It must hold a Grand Communication for the transaction of business at least once a year, deciding for itself the place and date for it. The membership of a Grand Lodge consists of its Grand Officers and of Lodge representatives; only members are entitled to a voice, a vote, and to hold office. Insofar as Lodges help to constitute a Grand Lodge they are called Constituent: insofar as they must obey Grand Lodge rules and orders they are said to be Subordinate—there can be no "hold-outs," or "loyal opposition," or any "minority" in a Grand Lodge; if it enacts a law each and every Lodge on its List must without exception or excuse obey that law, even if a Lodge was not in favor of it, and its representative voted against it; it is this which is meant by saying that a Grand Lodge is sovereign. A Grand Lodge collects dues and fees from Lodges, and its appropriate Officers may attend or inspect a Lodge. At least once a year each Lodge must send a written report ("Annual Returns") to the Grand Secretary. A Grand Lodge may have Standing Committees and Special Committees; their members usually are appointed for one year, but may be for longer, and though the larger number of Committees are appointed by the Grand Master they may also be appointed by Grand Lodge—in a few cases where a Committees' composition is defined by the Constitution or a law (as that it shall consist of Past Grand Masters) the law creating the Committee virtually names its members. Non-members of a Grand Lodge are entitled to seek to visit it under the same terms and conditions as visiting in a Lodge. A Grand Lodge can own property, and can own and administer homes, schools, hospitals, etc.

Ever since William Hutchinson, the sagest of the philosophers and interpreters of the Craft have known that almost nothing in Freemasonry is a definition for a man to learn, or a doctrine for a man to believe, but is a subject presented to the mind for a man to think about. It is one of the consequences of that fact that the Ritual does not do his thinking for the Candidate and a Lodge does not do his thinking for a Mason; each one must do his thinking for himself, and that includes his thinking about Grand Lodge. Another consequence is less easy to state because it has to do with a certain complexity or subtlety, almost a mystery, in each theme or subject in the Craft. A man can take the dimensions of a table with a yardstick; he can take the dimensions of a house with a tapeline; he can even take the dimensions of the earth with geometric calculations; but no man can take the dimensions of a Grand Lodge because so much in it is either multi-dimensional or non-dimensional; it has so many aspects, it contains within itself so many things of different kinds, that "you have to look at it in a certain way"; just when we think we have run down some question or subject in it and have followed it almost out to the end we find that it does not come to an end but merges into something else—it is an illustration of William James' phrase "ever not quite."

These observations hold true of what we may safely take to be the essence of a Grand Lodge. It is itself a Lodge, it has a Lodge form of organization, and yet it is not a single Lodge standing among other Lodges. It is a Lodge of Lodges: is constituted by 50 or 100, or 500, or even 1000 Lodges, yet it is both more and other than these Lodges combined. It is more nearly a pooling, a throwing together, of the Lodges, their members, their money, their work, their wisdom, abilities, and talents; and no sooner are all these resources pooled together than that the whole pool of them is made fully available to each and every Lodge. A Lodge has its own Room, its own members, its own funds, and the measure of them is the apparent measure of its strength; yet at the same time that one local Lodge might almost be the same as the whole Grand Jurisdiction because everything which belongs to Freemasonry in that Grand Jurisdiction belongs also to that Lodge, is available to it, is accessible to it, and is so without restraint. Because of the Grand Lodge system each Lodge and each Lodge member is strong with the strength of the whole Grand Jurisdiction.

Because these things are true we can lay down a fundamental axiom in Masonic Jurisprudence; *Any Lodge is to its Grand Lodge what the Grand Lodge is to itself.* This axiom instantly blows away the confused and foolish notion that Grand Lodge is there to act as if it were a "boss," or that if it enters a Lodge it does so as an intruder, or that Grand Lodge discipline is an arbitrary device for using force, and seeks only to penalize. The whole spirit and purpose of a Grand Lodge's concern with one of its own Lodges is the opposite; its concern is *for* and on behalf of a Lodge, it is on the Lodge's side, if a Lodge is in trouble its aim is to save the Lodge from self-destruction; the whole spirit of it is unselfish service.

CHAPTER VIII

# *The Grand Mastership*

"THE MAN WHO" is the phrase provided in the English language to denote the fact of agency. A physician is *the man who* remedies our illnesses or diseases. A lawyer is *the man who* counsels us in matters of law. The teacher is *the man who* schools us. The auto mechanic is *the man who* repairs our automobile. The grocer is *the man who* provides us with food. The rain falls of itself and ragweeds grow up in the empty field without our aid, but to have foods, medicines, laws, clothing, education we must produce them by work, and when doing so the production, distributing, or administering of each kind of thing can be done only by a man with a special knowledge of it, or skill, or experience, or equipment, and the rest of us are dependent on him. If he fails us we perish, because any one man can provide by his own efforts only one, or two, or three of the things needed by himself and his family. In each of the peoples of the world there is a net-work of *men who*, and ultimately each and every man must himself be a *man who* at some point or station is in the scheme of things. *Who* is one of those few words which are to language what the numbers from 1 to 10 are to arithmetic. *The man who* denotes the universal and eternal fact of agency, of office, of delegation. Unless we have him we can obtain nothing or produce nothing. *Office* is built into the nature of things like time, or space, or gravity. It means nothing that the word is used only in government and in organized bodies or societies; it is the same fact and function in them that it is elsewhere, though elsewhere it has other forms and is called by other names.

When commenting on the fact that Shakespeare seldom used what we call common men as the principal characters in his plays

Richard Green Moulton explained that Shakespeare did so of his own choice, but not because of snobbishness. One man was as large as another in his eyes, but he was a dramatist and needed characters in whom the qualities and fates common to us all are heightened and highly colored. A king, a statesman, a hero is a *man who,* no more so than any other, but his role in things is such that he must live at a high tension, in which his powers are strained, and in which the penalty for failure is most tragical; he is a common man blown up into a picture large enough to fill the sky where every man can see it, the agent or officer for a role as heavy as the world. There is a sense in which Caesar is Rome, and if he fails Rome falls—as it did, for when he fell his empire was for years ravaged by civil wars. This is the fatefulness, and it may be the tragedy, of being a captain at any point, for he carries in his hands the welfare of not himself only but of thousands of others.

In Freemasonry, in which every member is a *man who* at some place or station, and which has in it first and last so many offices of so many kinds, the Grand Mastership is the Shakespearean Office; it is all that any other office is, and much more beside; it is Masonic office writ large, filling half the sky; the incumbent of it is captain of all other Officers; he is the *man who* carries responsibility not for one Lodge, but for a whole Grand Jurisdiction. He is what the Third Degree describes him to be, a Hiram Abiff in strict and literal fact, and if he falls or fails the whole Craft is brought to a standstill.

A Grand Lodge is connected with a local Lodge, its Grand Officers have functions in a local Lodge; to cut a local Lodge off wholly from its Grand Lodge would be to destroy it; a local Lodge in turn is constitutive of Grand Lodge, its Worshipful Master acts in Grand Lodge and helps to make its laws; yet in spite of this connectedness and conjunction the two Bodies are separate and distinct from each other. Similarly a Grand Lodge can give instructions to the Grand Master, reviews his work, receives his report, accepts or refuses to confirm his edicts and decisions; a Grand Master in turn is an officer of Grand Lodge, presides over it, addresses it upon its duties, lays proposed legislation before it, yet for all this interelation and combination the Grand Master's Department and the Grand Lodge are separate and distinct. He is not the Grand Lodge's servant or agent, he is not the Grand Master of the Grand Lodge but the Grand Master of Masons. There are two spheres, one belonging to the one, one belonging to the other, which intersect but do not coincide; within his own sphere the Grand Master has original sovereignty, and possesses power and authority which inhere in his Station; the Grand Lodge also has original sovereignty in its own sphere, but it is not the same as the Grand Master's. At the head of a Grand Jurisdiction is not a single sovereign authority but two, one as original and as ancient as the other; each is under its own Landmarks, and in fundamentals they are not like each other. For these reasons it is inaccurate to use the name "office of Grand Master"; it should be called the Grand Mastership.

When the thirty or forty Brethren from four old Lodges in London constituted the Mother Grand Lodge in 1717 A.D. their procedure in doing so reveals the theory on which they acted. The office of the Worshipful Master with a copy of the *Old Charges* in its possession had theretofore been the means (the machinery) by which a new Lodge was constituted; the Brethren of 1717 A.D. made use of that office in the same way, for they began by electing a Master with two Wardens to assist him, and left it to him to appoint other officers and to complete the new Body and to set it to work; but they used the old offices for a new purpose; a Worshipful Master presided over individual Masons, their new Master was to preside over Lodges, and as the old Master made Masons this new Master was to make Lodges; to signalize the difference they gave him the new title of Grand Master—the "Grand" meaning head, or chief.

Because of this procedure the majority of Masonic historical writers have ever since dated the office of the Grand Master from 1717 A.D., and have therefore necessarily classified it as "modern"; and at the same time they have assumed that the modern office of Worshipful Master is the lineal descendant or perpetuation of the ancient Operative office of Master of Masons. It is as difficult to indict a whole body of writers as it was for Edmund Burke to indict a nation, but in this case (as in Burke's) it must be done. It is not true to say that the Office of Grand Master is modern, and the Office of Worshipful Master is ancient. The Operative Office of Master of Masons was the origin of *both* the Grand Mastership and the local Mastership; the office of the local Mastership inherits *only a part* of the Ancient Operative Office, the Grand Mastership is the heir of the other part; one is as old as the other; or, to state it in another form, using our present-day nomenclature, the Operative Master of Masons of centuries ago was both Grand Master and Worshipful Master at one and the same time. That which was one office for centuries, has been two offices since 1717 A.D.

The ancient Master of Masons directed the craftsmen when at work, and presided over the Lodge, but these were only two out of his many authorities, powers, and prerogatives. Far more important than any of these at the time was his headship over the whole Masonic Community, and this was so as much by night as by day. He employed and discharged workmen; he made the contract with the lord or administration or body for whom the building was to be erected; he was responsible in person to the lords of state who delegated to him his authority to rule and govern; in Assemblies he was his Lodge's or his Craft's spokesman and delegate; he had final authority over the whole Craft where they were at work, and was superintendent of the whole building on which they were at work. His authority was far greater than a modern Worshipful Master's, was exercised over a much larger scope or jurisdiction, and in many fundamentals was different in kind—he could, to give one example only, summon a Lodge into existence, and could, when the work was completed, dissolve it at will, an authority possessed now by no Worshipful Master.

But the authorities and powers which the Brethren of 1717 A.D. invested in the office of Grand Master were not drawn, each and every one of them, from the old Office of Master of Masons; a certain number of them had been exercised by the Craft at large, by individual Masons, by Masons in Assemblies, by single Lodges, or by groups of Lodges. A group of individual Masons could secure a copy of the *Old Charges,* could constitute themselves a Lodge, and then could secure recognition from other Lodges. A member from one Lodge could visit in or demit to another Lodge, or could hold membership in as many Lodges as he wished, and at one and the same time. A Lodge could constitute one or more "daughter Lodges"—as occurred at Derby, London, York, Edinburgh, etc. There was nowhere a Grand Lodge but many of the functions of a Grand Lodge were being performed, and under such circumstances a Master often performed functions which are now reserved to a Grand Master—a fact which explains the otherwise puzzling history of the first Lodge in Philadelphia (1729 A.D.) which was Lodge and Grand Lodge at one and the same time, and was headed by an officer who acted as Master and also Grand Master. (American Lodges were slow to learn and to practice the new Grand Lodge rules.)

For these, and for the reasons also given in the second paragraph above, the new Grand Mastership was not as great a novelty as it appeared to be. The Brethren who established it in 1717 A.D., and their Lodges as well, were cautious, conservative, and they took seriously the oath they had taken not to alter the old usages. The fact that the Grand Master would rule and govern *Lodges* instead of, as a Worshipful Master did, individual Masons, was in their eyes their only departure; and this fact explains why it was that in their *Book of Constitutions* which they had ready to print in 1721 A.D. they did not debate their new departure, nor defend themselves against innovations, but took it for granted that they had done nothing more than to revive the old General Assemblies and recover the good and ancient custom of the Quarterly Feast. The Grand Mastership was not in their eyes anything new but only a new use of something old.

No government, state or national, can function unless it can come down to any individual citizen in it, at any place, or on any day. It may be as small as the government of Luxemburg, or as large as the government of Great Britain, but unless it has a way to reach any given man in it, anywhere in the world, it cannot actually govern—nothing could be more of a delusion than the notion that as a government grows larger it necessarily grows more impersonal; for unless a government has a way down to

## The Grand Mastership

each man, woman, or child in it it can make no arrests, or levy any taxes or conscript an army, or deliver a letter, or cast a vote. No government ever governs any such thing as an "all"; it governs "each and every." The fact holds as true of Freemasonry as of general government (or any other large organization or society or corporation); and it is in this fact that we can find the central secret, or root principle, of the Grand Mastership. It could not be better defined than to say of it, that it is the agency or the means by which the World Fraternity as a whole can come down to each individual Mason, or to any individual Mason; for that reason the correct title of the Grand Master is not Grand Master of the Grand Lodge, or the Grand Master of a Grand Jurisdiction, but the Grand Master of Masons.

A Grand Lodge holds each year a Grand Communication (in some Grand Jurisdictions it holds four) at a fixed time and place, and are called by such names as Annual, or Regular, or Fixed Communications. It also may convene at other times, for Special occasions or in an emergency, and when it does it is known as a Special, or Emergent, or Called Grand Communication, and the Grand Master calls or summons it as an Emergent Grand Communication—a technically correct description is to say that he presides *in* Grand Lodge over the Grand Communication; it is also technically correct to say that he presides as *Grand Master,* for he continues to exercise the same powers, authorities, prerogatives, and privileges inherent in his office when sitting in a Grand Communication as when not sitting in one.

It is stated in books on Jurisprudence as an old rule that the Grand Master "has the right to visit any Lodge at any time," if within his Grand Jurisdiction, but the word "visit" is an error. Like any other member of the Craft he has the inherent right to visit when doing so in his private capacity as a Mason, but when he goes to a Lodge in his capacity as Grand Master he does not visit but *enters;* when he does so he does not need to ask consent, or to announce himself, or to wait the Master's pleasure, but walks in at will, and when he enters it is for the Master immediately to have him conducted to the East and to present the gavel to him. He can then "enter" a Lodge at any time, without word or warning, whether it is in Communication or not; he can summon the Master to convene the Lodge; and he can summon the Lodge Officers to appear before him; he can inspect the records and books, and can demand information; he can order charges to be brought against any member, or he can suspend a Lodge's Charter for cause; and he takes precedence over any other Mason present. When he thus enters or acts it is not as if he were a potentate arrived from a distant or an alien government, or as if he ought to have a central office and transact his business in it; the whole Grand Jurisdiction is his office, and he can "open for business" wherever he needs to.

In any Grand Lodge there are from 50 to 150 appointive officers; the Grand Master himself appoints them and has them installed and gives them his instructions. In addition, he can create temporary offices, can set up his own committees, and can appoint members to both. He has also a very wide discretion and ample power or deputation and delegation, and can appoint either an Officer or any Mason of his choice to represent him or to act or speak for him; this power is infinitely flexible—the Grand Master is not present everywhere and at all times at once throughout his Grand Jurisdiction but his authority is.

Similarly he has an equally wide and flexible authority to issue dispensations, the difference being that where in using his deputizing power he sends men to represent or act for him, in his dispensing power he sends documents. A document carrying his seal and signature has the same weight as his personal presence; and only men who are active in Grand Lodge office or who are close students of Jurisprudence realize how important and how large are the functions of dispensations in any year of the work in a Grand Jurisdiction; they are for many purposes, to constitute a new Lodge, to lay a corner stone, to hold special meetings, etc., etc.

A Grand Master has authority to issue Edicts. There is much discussion among the Grand Lodges as to what, exactly, an edict is; how much authority it carries; how permanent it is; some Grand Lodges take them to be of temporary importance and of only some special or local application. other Grand Lodges accept

## The Grand Mastership

them as a species of Masonic law; it is a peculiarly provocative subject because it raises the question as to where the line is to be drawn between the Grand Master's jurisdiction and the Grand Lodge's jurisdiction. Can a Grand Master enact a law for a Grand Jurisdiction? If he can, an Edict is a law; (the general rule is that edicts and decisions of a Grand Master expire with his term of office unless confirmed and adopted by his Grand Lodge) if he cannot, then an Edict is a pronouncement which for some given time or place has the force of law, but is not permanently a law.

A yet more provocative subject is the question whether a Grand Master can "Make a Mason at Sight," that is, can he Raise a Candidate from the time of his first entrance to the Sublime Degree of Master Mason at one sitting? Some Grand Lodges insist that a Grand Master possesses such a prerogative as a Landmark, and can exercise it at will; other Grand Lodges grant him the prerogative but expect him to use it only in extreme emergency; yet other Grand Lodges refuse to admit that he possesses the prerogative in any form. Behind this question lies a long history which is curious and yet at the same time may contain the answer to the question. Until about 1740–1750 A.D. Lodges conferred only two Degrees (a third was conferred in a few Master's Lodges); this under normal circumstances would mean that the Lodge took two evenings to make a Mason, but the Minute Books of the early Lodges show that in (roughly) half the cases they hurried up the ceremonies and conferred both Degrees in one Communication; and even after they all began the use of Three Degrees many Lodges now and then conferred the three in one evening, and made various excuses for doing so. This telescoping of the Degrees became such an evil that to eradicate it the waiving of the regular time between Degrees was made illegal, and such emergencies as might appear to justify it were turned over to the discretion of the Grand Master. It follows that if a Grand Master exercises the prerogative of Making at Sight it is not because he had in the past, and out of some imagined lust for power, usurped the prerogative; he was given the exclusive power of Making at Sight to put a stop to the abuse of that power by Lodges.

The Grand Mastership is exacting and responsible. In it a man has but small play for private and personal decisions or for ambition, because it is grounded in Landmarks and hedged about by them. His powers are defined by law, and a Grand Master does not own his office but is only an incumbent of it. It is possible for a Grand Master to loaf his way through his year, but it is not too easy to do so because the demands made on him so often are urgent. Much traveling is obligatory, and his mail is heavy. In the larger jurisdictions the office may absorb the whole of a man's time. The panoply of his prerogatives is a wide one but it is equated by an equally wide panoply of duties. Grand Lodges appropriate funds for his expenses but the amount is almost never large enough, and the majority of incumbents are out of pocket at the end of the year. If he is given honors and titles he earns them—there is nothing else to earn because he receives no salary. If in our forty-nine Grand Jurisdictions the Fraternity can find men to assume that burden each year who have the efficiency to manage the offices of a Grand Jurisdiction and the fortitude to confront its difficulties, it is yet another tribute which Masons must lay at the feet of their Fraternity, another testimony to the hold which it has upon the hearts of its members.

## CHAPTER IX

# *Lodge Offices*

IN A FRAGMENT OF A POEM written before the time of King Alfred, a knight is described as riding forth "to win his worship"; he was a young soldier, and untried, he had labored through years of apprenticeship, he had only recently been dubbed a knight, and he was now setting forth to win a name for himself. The fragment proves that in its earliest usage the word already meant what it has continued to mean ever since. The Anglo-Saxon term *weorth* meant worth; the suffix *ship* meant to possess, to belong to; a man was entitled "worshipful" because honor, rank, position belonged to him. The word became a salutation of respect, and the early Operative Freemasons used it because it was in use everywhere.

The word *master* as now used in English is in reality three or four words, spelled and pronounced alike; as used in "Worshipful Master" it is derived from the same origin as "magistrate," and means "one who has complete authority," the *mag* having the sense of largest, chief, first; judges are called "magistrates," and a member of a special court may be described as "Master in Chancery." "Worshipful Master" is a title, not the name of an office; as such it means, "you are entitled to respect and honor because you are chief, or head, or magistrate of the Lodge."

The correct name for the Office itself is "Master of Masons," and not merely "Master." A Master Mason was so called because in his seven years of apprenticeship he had mastered his art, and when thus used it had the same meaning as the Latin word "doctor," which connotes professional competency. But the phrase "Worshipful Master" comes not from that origin but from the other origin, which means head, chief, magistrate. He is addressed as Worshipful Master in recognition of the Office he holds, not because he has mastered the art—the salutation appropriate to the latter is "Brother," which also is a title. In the third person the magistrate or administrative chief of the Lodge is referred to as Worshipful Master; in the second person he should be addressed as "Worshipful Sir."

The Worshipful Master of Masons has always been a *constitutional officer* because he has always been a *constituting officer historically*, and disregarding modern jurisprudence, the function of his Office in Freemasonry may be technically described as the means by which a Lodge of Freemasons is brought into existence, and maintained in existence—it has always been *constitutive*, a word which means to organize, to set up, to establish. In the Middle Ages a lord or the government first set up an administration; the latter then selected and employed a Master of Masons —many other titles and names were used at one time or another, but of these only "Master of Masons" has persisted because it is linquistically most correct. This Master of Masons sent out a call for craftsmen, employed such of the respondents as he chose, and organized these employed craftsmen into a Lodge with himself as its head. Much of this ancient constitutive, or constitutional authority continues in power at the center of the Office of Worshipful Master; he opens and closes his Lodge; calls it into special Communication; can summon his members; appoint Officers; preside over the Lodge, and superintend the work.

In any body of men consisting of a large number of members, and more especially if it belongs to a net-work of similar bodies, it is always a problem to find a means to come to a final decision binding on all without giving the means used too much power. If no such means is found the body becomes a victim of that "fallacy of action" which is called "elusive responsibility" where one man evades responsibility by passing it on to a second, and he to a third, etc., until the last man has evaded it; such a body of men can do nothing because it has no means to decide what to do. Centuries ago Freemasonry avoided this merry-go-round of elusive responsibility by making the Office of Master of Masons *sovereign* as well as first. When a decision comes to his office he makes it; when he has made it, it is final; neither he nor any

## Lodge Offices

member can return it to the floor to start over again, a futile circle of endless discussion, nor can any member evade the Master's sovereignty by appealing from him to the lodge. These decisions which come up to be made by the Worshipful Master always, directly or by implication or in principle, *are such as concern the Lodge as a whole*. In his eyes the Lodge is an entity, an *it;* he is responsible for the *it;* if any appeal is made from his decision it is to the Grand Master or to the Grand Lodge, and the appeal is made by the Lodge itself.

*Warden* is of such ancient usage in the Fraternity that it is doubtful if any other term in the whole nomenclature is older, or as old. It was the root from which we have guard, guardian, ward, ward off, warder, etc. The Senior and Junior Wardens are *executive officers,* which means that in principle they assist the Worshipful Master *to rule and govern* his Lodge. Any other Officer or all the other Officers, may assist the Master; if he orders them to, then they must perforce do so; but no other officer assists him to *rule and govern*—the Wardens are, as it were, deputy Masters, or Vice-Masters, and when the Worshipful Master is prevented from attending to his duties, the Lodge naturally looks to the Senior Warden to act for him; nevertheless, if the Senior Warden does so act he acts only as a deputy for the Master, not as Master for the time being, because the Master is responsible for what is done in his name whether he is present or absent. For this reason the two Wardens also are *constitutional* offices because they have a share in the work of *constituting;* it is because this is true that for centuries Lodges have deemed terms in the offices of the Wardens to be the best training for the Mastership, hence that elective custom which is called "the Lodge Line; only a Warden can be elected a Master."

The office of Secretary is *constitutional* in the sense that the Lodge could not *continue* to exist without it—it is also constitutional in the sense that the Grand Lodge Constitution provides for it, but the sense as just given is the more important: it also is the more revealing, for unless it is understood the office of Secretary cannot be understood. A Communication is the means by which the Freemasons in a given Jurisdiction act together as a body, and do so officially; when a Lodge thus acts it often *acts for the future;* therefore the Lodge's action, any time, is binding on the Lodge a year from then, or ten years from then, and binding in the same sense as a law. Since that is true the Communication of tonight does not come to an end when the Master closes the Lodge but is transferred to the Minutes, where it will continue to be active and alive through the future. It is the function of the Secretary to transfer all the acts of a Communication to the Minutes, and to act as the custodian of the Minutes. He may read letters, write letters, file letters, keep books; he may perform the functions which Secretaries in other societies perform; but in a Masonic Lodge his chief function is to see that the records of a given Communication are transferred to the Minutes, and that it is there preserved without alteration or tampering, because the Minutes of any given Communication continue to be binding on the Lodge for years afterwards.

When the Secretary thus acts as the custodian of those past Communications which are never dead and done with, he is acting *for the Lodge* as a body, as a unit—to do so is one of the meanings of "constitutional office."

The Treasurership of the Lodge is a constitutional office for like reasons; the Treasurer acts for the Lodge, he never acts for himself, and he is far more than a bookkeeper. In the oldest Lodge Minutes the monies of a Lodge are never spoken of as the "treasury," but always as "the box," and in some of them the custodian of it is called "the box-master"—many American organizations called their treasurer "box-master" as late as the middle of the Nineteenth Century. This box was kept in open Lodge; in it the members deposited dues, fees, fines, and gifts. In many Lodges it was used as a repository for membership cards (the members did not carry their cards about with them), and since the membership was often thought of as "the Lodge" this custom may have given its name to that odd piece of furniture used in Consecration Ceremonies which is still called "the Lodge"—it is a material emblem of the membership. Lodge monies were not banked, but boxed. That is, they were put into a receptacle and nothing was done with them except to keep charge of them. The

## Lodge Offices

Lodge was not in business; it did not buy or sell; it made no profits, interest, or dividends. Its money, in short, was a fund, and from the moment of deposit each dollar was earmarked for some fixed expenditure.

The Lodge Treasurer has therefore two fundamental and constitutional functions; first, he is the official custodian of these funds, and as such his first thought is for their safety; second, he is to see that no money is taken from the funds *except by action of the Lodge;* and this action must prove the authenticity of any requisition or warrant made on him for any part of the funds. He is therefore not the Lodge's financial manager, or its financial agent; the Lodge is its own financial manager.

*Deacon* was a Greek word, and originally meant "messenger." The earliest Speculative Lodges had only one Deacon. The reason for having two is not made wholly clear by early Lodge records, but such of the data as can be pieced together indicate that a second Deacon (Junior) was made necessary by changes in the office of Tiler. At one time the Tiler had a number of duties inside the Lodge Room; he might conduct the Candidate; he drew designs on a floor-cloth, and then rubbed them off; he cared for the regalia, and handed it about; he was inner guard as well as outer guard. When the office of Tiler was shorn of all duties inside the Lodge Room, and he became wholly an *outside* officer, a vacuum was left, and to fill it Lodges began to appoint a second Deacon, giving the two the titles of Senior and Junior. But while their titles are thus modern, as well as some details of their function, the office of Deacon is as old as Freemasonry. The need for them arises from the fact that the Principal Officers of the Lodge occupy Stations. Neither the Master nor his Wardens are supposed to leave their stations except at fixed times and on fixed occasions; whenever unexpected or unpredictable calls are made on the Master or Wardens to go elsewhere, to act away from their Stations, the Deacons are there to go or come as they command, to escort visitors or members, to take or bring messages, etc. (It is not good form for a Master to move at will about his Lodge Room.)

*Steward* is one of the very oldest words in our language, or in any language. In it or behind it is the picture of provisions stored up against the future, animals, fruits, grains, with a man standing guard over them. In Freemasonry also it is an ancient term, and the office has belonged to the Craft from the first; there are paragraphs about it among the rules and regulations of the *Regius MS*. It is a constitutional office because feasts, bread and meat and drink, have always been one of the necessary functions of a Lodge—in the Lodge for which the *Regius Ms* was written feasts must have been held monthly because the members are advised to take turn in acting as Steward, and the Lodge is urged to pay its feast bills promptly. Sociability is requisite of a Lodge; the Junior Warden, with the Stewards to assist him, is custodian, guard, arranger, and administrator of those sociabilities.

The word *tiler* is a mystery to philologists, Masonic and non-Masonic. For centuries the gild of tilers who cut and laid tiles of stone, clay, and slate on roofs was an organized branch of the building craft; it may be that the Outer Guard is named after them because he closes in, or shuts in, the Lodge. Historians of literature believe that the word came into use as the name for the doorkeepers of clubs, inns, and taverns who kept the hats of the guests. The word had been used as the name for a covering, as of a box, or pot, or jar, and from that had passed into usage as the name of head covering—such phrases as "the Master remained covered" supports this latter theory. It is also possible, and is very probable, that both these meanings and usages converged—*tiler* would not be the first word to have two or more origins.

In Operative Freemasonry the Tiler was openly and frankly an armed guard, who remained outside the Lodge door or the Lodge building to ward off intruders, cowans, eavesdroppers; in many Eighteenth Century Lodges the office carried the title of Outer Guard. The Masons' Company of London called him beadle. In Lodges he was also called "the servant" or "the officer"; he was supposed to belong to the lower social orders—as it has been said "he represented the presence of the servant class in early Lodge organization"; the humbleness of his position was also emphasized by giving him gifts, fees and tips. But this class status was inherently contradictory to the spirit and tenets of Freemasonry, and the Speculative Fraternity had been at work barely a half century when the standing as well as the duties of the Tiler began to be changed. When Lodges began to fee their Secretaries it took the curse off Tiler's fees; a number of his duties were turned over to the Junior Deacon; after the post-office came in he no longer delivered Lodge summons by hand; after the towns had their armed police forces his own sword (or poignard—"the sharp instrument") became merely a symbolic weapon.

The Tiler is one of the most colorful of the officers of the Lodge—partly because of his sword, partly because he is on guard, and often because he is likely to develop idiosyncrasies if he remains many years at his post—as many Tilers do; he has been the subject of immeasurable pictures, songs, poems, stories, and jokes. Much of the colorfulness is an inheritance from the past; in future centuries this office is likely to increase in dignity and probably will take on more functions—it is not impossible that a Department of the Outer Precincts ("the Porch") may develop, with the Tiler as its head, assisted by a standing examining committee and an officer in charge of the Preparation Room. He is the only officer who remains *outside* the Room, who has not so much a place as a *post,* and he is the link between the Lodge and the outside ("profane") world, and the representative of the Lodge's hospitality as he is the first to receive and greet guests, visitors, and strangers. As indicative of Freemasonry's inherent Democracy, some Lodges elect the retiring Master to be Tiler, tho he does not serve as such.

In Anti-Masonic literature it was once a favorite charge that a Lodge is not only secret and secretive, that it hides itself from view, and conceals itself behind Chinese walls of silence; the office of the Tiler was always a standing contradiction of that charge. He is not a closed gate between the Lodge and the outside world but a link between the two, or a bridge, and he stands in plain view, though an officer of the Lodge; any stranger, any non-Mason can knock at the outer door of his Ante-Room. There is no street door to a Lodge room; between the Lodge Room and the outside world is the Tiler; in a very complete sense the Lodge Room itself is inviolable; but what is it that cannot violate it? Only that which cannot enter it *lawfully*. It does not say in the Landmarks of Inviolability that *none shall pass;* it says that none shall pass or repass except *the duly qualified.* The Tiler's sword is never lifted against any man, Mason or non-Mason, who has lawful business with the Lodge. There are many bridges between the Lodge and the world outside; the fact is both signalized and proved by the number of Masonic assemblies which are not Tiled.

The word *marshal* is in American general usage most often the "officer of the day" who keeps order in military parades, and hence has a military connotation; that connotation is strengthened by the similarity of sound as between *marshal* and *martial*. Also the word is widely used as the name for a peace officer, the town marshal, who is the local policeman, and this again links it with the use of armed force. But there is no necessary connection between *marshal* and *martial*. The word came to us from the French in which it was spelled *mareschal,* and in which it had less application with *mars,* than with *mark,* or *margo,* which is preserved in *landmark,* and means boundary, limits, fixed lines. A marshal is not concerned with things and objects; he has nothing to say as to why men assemble and move or march; his one and only function is to see that they keep order and remain in the line of march or according to the rules of decorum. Many Lodges do not have the office, perhaps because it sounds military, and would appear to be out of place in a Lodge Room. In Lodges which have it the Marshal's duty is to maintain order, and to supervise the movements of the members when they move together in a body.

Similarly, some Lodges have the Office of Chaplain, and others do not; each Lodge however has in it the functions which belong to the office and they are performed by the Master, or by any Brother deputized by him. Originally a Chaplain was a priest in control of a chapel, and when so it was he, and not the worshippers, who had authority over the services and observances; but a Masonic Lodge never makes over any control of its own actions to any but its own installed officers, therefore the religious usages are as much in the Master's keeping as any other, and if a Lodge has a Chaplain he acts under the Master's direction, and he may be a clergyman or a layman whomever the Master may appoint.

Anti-Masonic writers, a number of them, have made use of the fact that Lodges have an office of Chaplain to argue that Freemasonry is a religion. This ignored the fact that governments, legislatures, courts, the army, the navy, and many societies and clubs have chaplains—even a private family may have a chaplain as is often done in Britain or Europe; but it ignores (or misses) the more fundamental fact that the office of Chaplain proves the opposite, for in a Lodge a Chaplain *always acts for the Lodge and never acts as the spokesman, priest, or official of any church, religion or theology.*

CHAPTER X

## *Masonic Jurisdiction*

IF ANYTHING IS TO COME into existence or is to be born or is to begin it can do so only if it is some particular plant or animal or material thing. A philosopher would describe this in the shorthand of his own profession as *the principle of individualism.* There is nowhere in the world any mere flux, or chaos, or void. Each thing is always "a this particular thing." Aristotle stated the fact in his own shorthand in his treatise on logic by saying that a thing is either A or it is B; it cannot be A and yet not be A, neither can it be A and B at the same time. Any thinking of any sort must take it for granted that this is true; no man can think about nothing in particular, he can think only when he has some given, identifiable, knowable thing to think about; you can say that a horse has four legs but you cannot say that X has four legs because you do not know what X is.

This principle of individualism is as true of the largest things there are as it is of the smallest; the universe itself is a "this particular thing" as surely as a leaf is; so is the earth! so is the sun; so is space; so is time. There is no such thing as climate in the large, in the abstract, but only a number of particular climates in the earth which can be counted, placed, and described; even weather, which is climate as it is in some one area, is never weather in the abstract but always is a definite kind of weather and is determined by the particular climate to which it belongs. The surface of the earth has an anatomy; an ocean is confined to its own basin and does not go wandering about at random; a river runs in its own bed, and does not wander loose everywhere; a valley has its own margins, a plain extends only so far, even a wilderness though its name is a synonym for indefiniteness has its own frontiers; before ever a people occupy a country the country already has its boundaries laid down by geology, and if a people's political boundaries do not coincide with its natural boundaries the people will always have trouble with them.

The principle of individualism is as true of any other kind of facts and things as it is of material things. You cannot say that something in general is true, you can only say that what this particular man says in a particular statement is true. If anything is beautiful it must be a something, there can be no beauty where there is nothing to be beautiful. We have the three institutions of the home, school, and government; work has in itself some fifty-odd separate and distinct "forms of work"; we have separate, individual crafts, trades, arts, professions, callings, and each one has its own particular subject-matter, that subject-matter lies inside its own limits or boundaries, consists of its own entities, and a man who masters any one of them must do it by the process of mastering each entity, step, degree, one after the other. To know invariably means to know "this particular thing"; nobody can know nothing in particular, or everything at once.

Every government is *a* government, not government in general. It is an institution which a people establishes because they will suffer unless they do, and its purpose is to put the great world of law to their use and to set it in practice. In a government the principle of individualism takes a form of dividing the work of governing into areas which are called jurisdictions. Any government has jurisdiction only over that territory which lies within a people's political boundaries, and only over such people as live inside them. Its own subject-matter is the law, and it has no authority outside that subject-matter. The government used by the people in the United States has stupendous power at its disposal, but even it cannot tell a man how many spoons of sugar to put in his coffee, nor could it arrest a kitten north of the Canadian boundary nor trap a mouse south of the Rio Grande because such matters lie outside its jurisdiction. Any government which makes use of the force at its command beyond that jurisdiction is at war with other peoples. A government does not find and declare and enact law in general but always particular laws;

each law has jurisdiction over certain actions only—the law of contracts has no jurisdiction over a case of manslaughter. Each court has its own jurisdiction; a sheriff has his county; a policeman has his beat. A people should be implacably firm in seeing to it that the government makes full use of its awesome weight of force against crime; it should also implacably forbid its government to take one step outside of its own jurisdiction to do what is never a government's business to do.

"Jurisdiction" has been one of the most beautiful and majestic words in the languages of Western Man for more than three thousand years. It is composed of *jus*, which means the law, added to *dico*, which means to speak forth, to say and, to give voice to; jurisdiction is therefore "the voice of the law." It is the law which the voice carries; the boundaries of a nation are the area over which the voice carries.

The jurisdictions provided for in the rules of Freemasonry are in principle and purpose, either the same as jurisdictions in civil government or are similar to them. Freemasonry, like the United States itself, is not something "in the air," vague, or abstract, or a flux, or "in men's minds," but is the name for an actual and visible fraternity with flesh-and-blood members who work in visible Lodges which are housed in material rooms or buildings; but like the government of the United States, and for organizational purposes, its rules are specific and determinant, and it divides itself and its activities into jurisdictions, wherever it is present at all it establishes itself in a village or city in the form of a Masonic Community which centers in a Lodge; this Lodge has authority over Masons and their Masonic activities within fixed boundaries, called a local jurisdiction, and the Lodges of any given state are combined under a Grand Lodge which has those combined local jurisdictions as its Grand Jurisdiction.

This principle of jurisdiction is as old as the Fraternity itself; and, by a kind of paradox, it may be said to be even older, because the Fraternity grew up out of the early Medieval gild system, and jurisdiction was one of the cornerstones of that system. Each craft, art, or profession was organized and had its own rules and regulations but it had authority over only its own work and

## Masonic Jurisdiction

workers. Any particular gild was in turn divided into local gilds each of which had authority over its own local work and workers inside a fixed boundary, and no neighboring local gild of the same craft was permitted to trespass across those boundaries. This was true also of any Lodge of Operative Freemasons.

When the first Grand Lodge of Speculative Freemasonry was erected in London in 1717 A.D., it began by extending its jurisdiction as far as Westminster, which meant an area with a radius of about ten miles from the center of the city. Outside of that area it was "open country" therefore when a Grand Lodge was Constituted at York in about 1725 A.D., and another was set up in London in 1751 A.D., neither one violated the jurisdiction of the first Grand Lodge; it was not until 1813 A.D. that England became the exclusive Grand Jurisdiction of the present United Grand Lodge of England. Before 1717 A.D. none of the Speculative Lodges had claimed territorial jurisdiction but each one had had full jurisdiction over its own members; it was only after the Grand Lodge System had become permanently established that local Lodges were given local territorial jurisdiction.

In the United States a local Lodge has exclusive authority over its own members and their Masonic activities, within an area of which the boundaries are fixed by Grand Lodge enactment; if no other Lodge is working within those boundaries the Lodge is said to have Exclusive Local Territorial Jurisdiction. If two or more Lodges are at work within the same boundaries, as in a city, the Lodges are said to have Concurrent Local Territorial Jurisdiction. A Grand Lodge has jurisdiction over its state, and over the regular Lodges and Masons in the state; this is said to be Exclusive Territorial Grand Jurisdiction. If an American Grand Lodge has Lodges in foreign countries (as in China, Panama, the Near East, etc.) those Lodges belong to its jurisdiction but they are necessarily in "open country" (not inside the Exclusive Territorial Jurisdiction of any other Grand Lodge) and hence are not in its own Exclusive Territorial Jurisdiction. A Lodge or Grand Lodge has jurisdiction over only Ancient Craft Lodges and their members; Bodies and Grand Bodies of the other Rites have their own jurisdiction.

In addition to these local and Grand Jurisdictions and the jurisdiction of each Rite over its own members and territories there is also a form of jurisdiction which cannot be so definitely described; it may be for convenience called partial jurisdiction, or joint jurisdiction, and comes into play when a Mason, or his acts, are necessarily under more than one jurisdiction at one time. If the Mason resides in one Lodge jurisdiction but holds his membership in another, he is under the partial jurisdiction of his own home Lodge and Grand Lodge and at the same time is under the partial jurisdiction of the nearest Lodge and its Grand Lodge—otherwise a Mason could put himself beyond the reach of Freemasonry's "voice of the law" by moving or visiting outside his home jurisdiction, and for him to be so would be a violation of the Landmarks. Any Mason who is away from his home jurisdiction, who introduces himself as a Mason to other Masons, or who asks for Masonic favors or privileges or relief, or seeks to visit a Lodge, is while doing so answerable to the nearest Lodge or to the Lodge he visits. If when doing so a question arises which is not easily answered by the rules the case is then discussed and decided by *Masonic Correspondence* between the nearest Lodge and his home Lodge, or between the nearest Lodge and his Grand Master. Wherever a Mason goes, even though it be in the countries farthest away, or in a country without Lodges of its own, he is never beyond the reach of *some* Masonic body of competent authority; nor does it follow that this is true only in questions of Masonic discipline because jurisdiction is not solely for legal purposes but may equally well operate for purposes of Masonic fellowship and relief. It is always a mistake to take jurisdiction to be a legal principle only; for it is the *whole* of Freemasonry which operates within each jurisdiction, and it is for the sake of the whole of it that it operates.

This fact that jurisdiction includes boundaries in space and yet includes many other things because it is the whole of Freemasonry that is jurisdictionalized ought to be the point of departure for the national debate over the question as to how large (or how small) a Lodge ought to be. Which is better, a large Lodge, or a small one? In the lean year of 1939 A.D. the Lodges in the District of Columbia averaged 434 members, Rhode Island averaged 342 members, and Massachusetts averaged 316 members; at the opposite end of the scale Alabama and South Carolina averaged 61 members per Lodge, and Arkansas averaged 55; Wyoming and Minnesota coincided with the national average, which was 163.

Each of these Lodges had its own jurisdiction, but because a jurisdiction is a unit containing everything which belongs to Freemasonry, the word "size" manifestly cannot be reduced to the terms of size in space or membership. A Lodge of fifty members may easily be "bigger" Masonically than one of 500; it confers as many Degrees, it omits nothing from any Degree, it has as much room for each member as a large Lodge, it carries out the same Masonic purposes; and—this is said as a plain statement of fact, not as a sentimental exaggeration—if the Lodge of 50 members has more fellowship, more sociability, more friendship, more help, aid and assistance, more brotherly love then the Lodge of 50 is *Masonically* larger than the Lodge of 500; it is the amount of Masonry, not the number of members, which ultimately decides the "size" of a Lodge jurisdiction. Freemasonry is a life to be lived, not a set of observances, nor a mere system of duties, nor a code of doctrines; the motto of a Lodge now is "Let there be light" but a Lodge could as rightly take for its motto "I have come that you shall have life, and that you shall have it more abundantly"; the Masonic Community cannot be measured in the terms of miles, or number of members, or number of dollars, but must be measured by the amount of the Masonic life in it; and though its geographical area remains fixed whether it is a dead Lodge or a living Lodge the true size of its jurisdiction is the richness and the abundance of the Masonic life in it.

What, then, is it which in the long run and over the terms of generations decides how much geographic space a Lodge needs, and where its boundaries are to be fixed? The amount of life, and vigor, and activity which it has in it. *It should have as much space as it needs.* Therefore the boundaries of a jurisdiction are not only laid down *for* Masonry, but are also laid down *within it,* and *by* it. It is Freemasonry alone, out of itself, and for its own purposes, which decides them. And it is because this is true that the jurisdictional boundaries of a Lodge often do not coincide with the political boundaries of the city, or the state, or the nation. What do they have to do with Freemasonry? What difference does it make to Masons where political boundaries are drawn? If you live in Indiana and I live in Illinois what is that to us *as Masons?* If you live on one side of the U.S.-Canadian boundary and I live on the other, does the boundary divide us? *As Masons* we ignore its existence. Lodge and Grand Lodge jurisdictional boundaries are *organizational conveniences* which separate us into many families in order that we may throughout the world be one family, and are not Grand Canyons or Chinese Walls which pen us up apart from each other in small parochial separateness, each one with a Freemasonry of its own; for Freemasonry is a seamless robe; it stretches without let, or division, or hindrance around the earth, simple and whole, in an embracing unity, and jurisdictions are not obstructions to that unity but are the means to maintain it.

CHAPTER XI

# *Masonic Monies*
# *Masonic Lodge Funds*

THERE ARE MEN HERE AND THERE who look down their noses on those who must work to earn money. There are others who consider the subject of money to lie below them, and deem it too vulgar to mention at the dinner table. There are others of a supposedly spiritual sort, mystical, or metaphysical, or other-worldly, who condemn money because they look upon it as something crassly materialistic. Such men should never petition for the Degrees, because if they do they will be shocked by the Fraternity's frank and open acceptance of money, the need for it, its high place in men's lives, the honorableness of it; and not money in any Pickwickian, or evasive, or make-believe, or occult sense but actual money, dollars, half-dollars, quarters, dimes, and pennies. They will find that the subject of wages is chock-ablock at the center of the Ritual, one of its great themes, and becomes as big as a mountain; and they will discover that the very *sanctum sanctorum* is nothing other than the place where a young Craftsman has ceased to be an Apprentice, working for nothing, and has become a Fellow of the Craft who can now earn wages. Freemasonry is neither backward nor abashed by the subject of money, but accepts it wholeheartedly with full frankness and an above-board enthusiasm.

If a man must have belongings, such as his hat, his clothes, his shoes, his handkerchief, and what he carries in his pocket, it is because he would perish without them—especially in winter. If he needs many possessions, furniture, utensils, tools, an automobile, etc., it is because he could not have a home or make a living without them. He is so made that without food, sleep, rest, remedies, and what not he will be unmade, but if he is to sleep he must have a bed, if he is to rest he must have a chair, if he is to eat he must have groceries and a cook stove, if he is to recover from his illness he must have medicine, if he is not to be rendered helpless by ignorance he must have schools, and if he is to retain his possessions and be able to continue to work he must have government. If such things are material, or physical, or external he cannot hate them or hold them in contempt or despise them without hating or despising himself, because they are as much a part of him as his own hands and feet.

There are hundreds of such things of many kinds and sorts; to make or produce almost any one of them is impossible without materials, equipment, special knowledge, or special skill—consider that a man must spend four years in college, four years in medical school, and two years as an interne before the law will permit him to feel your pulse or prescribe an aspirin tablet for your cold! Any given man is incapable of making or growing more than three or four of the things which he must have to live; it is for that reason that a man needs money. He must have it to trade with. Since he can make only a few of the things he must have, then he must be able to trade what he himself makes or grows for the many things which he cannot make or grow. He must include money itself among the many things which he owns or he can own nothing; he uses his shoes to wear on his feet, and his hat to wear on his head; he must use money for a similarly necessary purpose, because without it he cannot trade for the necessaries which he cannot produce.

Through a long process of trial and error men have found that to date the best material for use as money is gold and silver, and more especially gold. These metals are convenient, durable, and everywhere in demand; they cannot easily be counterfeited (as other metals can), and they may be used in high units of value without bulk—sooner or later all usable money must be pocket money. The Latin term from which we derived our word "money" meant "to mint," and it is this minting which distinguishes gold money from gold. To mint money a government fixes a standard quantity of a standard fineness of metal; stamps it into a fixed shape, which in modern times is always a disc; mills the edges to prevent clipping; and stamps on both sides the denomination, its seal, the name of the government, etc.; and then declares it to be official and compels every citizen to accept it as valid money.

It is a prevalent theory that every man who works desires to have what he produces, and is entitled to it in justice; in actual practice the world over a man seldom wants what he produces. If you have potatoes in the ground which are worth $40.00 where they lie, but you are not able to dig them, you can make an agreement with me to dig them for you; if after I have dug and sacked them the potatoes are worth $50.00 it is obvious that I now own one-fifth of those potatoes, or, say, ten bags. I could take these ten bags of potatoes home with me because they belong to me; but I already have more potatoes than I need, therefore you trade me ten dollars for them; or if you do not need them I can trade them to a third man for the ten dollars, and I can then in turn trade the dollars for things I do need. If you pay me the money instead of leaving me in possession of my potatoes that money is called wages, which is money paid for work. There are two very curious and illuminating facts about the wages you pay me—they *must* be curious, because it has always been so difficult for men to see them, they *must* be illuminating because as soon as they are seen they clear up a thousand questions about wages. One of the facts is that you do not *give* me the ten dollars, still less do the ten dollars belong to you; the ten dollars are my property and when you "pay" them you are giving me something which already belongs to me—*you* are not out the ten dollars because the ten dollars did not belong to you; if you give me the ten dollars it is not because I have forced you to, or have taken from you something which was yours; they are mine, and you have lost nothing by turning over, to me, what is mine. The other fact is that there can be no competition between you and me because my work was done by agreement between us both. *We both profit;* you have your own potatoes dug, and you are that much ahead; I have my potatoes or my money and I am ahead; we both are ahead but neither is ahead at the expense of the other. It is possible for me to cheat you by not doing as much work as I agreed to, or for you to cheat me by not turning over in the form of wages what belongs to me, but cheating has nothing to do with the system of wages. Wages are an everlasting method necessary in the nature of things because by no other possible method can a man who works through the year producing or making one or two or three kinds of things trade them for the hundreds of other things which he must have; and by the same token it can never be true that a man who has money he did not earn is superior socially or intellectually to a man who must earn every dollar he has.

Next to religion and politics money has always been the most prolific source of public follies. The mid-Twentieth Century American who has become dazzled by the merry-go-round of economic theories, and to whom socialism, communism, and fascism have come with an air of exciting surprise, cannot have read history; if he had, he would have known that those schemes have no newness except a new mask in this guise, and that in reality they are as old as the hills, and far less exciting than most of our American hills; history is a record of endless experiment with such economic theories. But nowhere in history have theories multiplied so rapidly, or taken so lunatic a form, or gone to such extremes of folly, as during that long period in Britain in the Middle Ages when Operative Freemasonry arose, and in which it took the form which our Speculative Fraternity inherited. This Medieval ignorance was most dense on the subject of money. Governments, such as they were, did not understand even the A B C's of it; they could see no difference between money and barter; they fixed costs, prices, and wages by arbitrary and rigid law; if a king waged war he clipped his own coinage to steal the gold or silver out of it; they struck it out in awkward shapes and sizes; they farmed out the coining of it to private firms; and the honesty of governments was so rudimentary (honesty is what money means to character) that it took a microscope to find it—even Joan of Arc connived with her French king to clip his coin in order to pay her army.

No government understood wages, either, as is proved by the stupidity of the laws enacted to regulate them, for they took it that a workman's wages were largess, or a form of charity, paid

## Masonic Monies—Masonic Lodge Funds

by the employer out of his own pocket. The Church was even more unenlightened. Wycliff was only one of the great divines who thundered at workmen for being greedy enough to accept the wages they had earned; and he and all the other divines for a thousand years firmly believed that work is a curse, that money is a low-down thing because it is "material," and that wage-earners were low-down men, belonging to the lowest castes of society. Employers were superior to employees even in God's eyes, and a rich man was more certain to go into heaven than a poor one because his riches were a proof in this world of God's favor, and therefore a warrant of God's approval in the world to come. The worst and most disastrous of the church's stupidities was its identifying interest with usury; you could let a man have the use of a $5,000 house for $30.00 rent a month, but to charge him rent on the use of $5,000 in money was a sin as well as a crime—this was the tap-root out of which grew the hatred of the Jews, because Judaism permitted the charging of interest; and if Roman Catholics practiced their doctrine of the infallibility of the Pope not one of them would ever lend money at interest because for centuries one Pope after another issued thundering condemnations of it in a long succession of Papal Bulls. As for Operative Freemasonry itself it taught no economic doctrines, either orthodox or heretical, and came unscathed and unmarked through centuries of Utopian schemes about money, and "revolutionary" transformations; the whole history of Freemasonry's own economic theory may be told in the three words, "It has none."

Freemasons no longer work for wages. The member of a Lodge may work in it one, or two, or four nights a month but is never paid for his time. That system of wages which Operative Freemasons laid down as one of the cornerstones of their craft, and from which they always refused to budge, come Church anathemas or Royal thunders, is no longer practiced by Freemasons; they use it symbolically only. But their using it symbolically does not mean that they have turned money itself into make-believe, or have dissolved it into mystical or into occult dreams; on the contrary wages in the Ritual continue to be real wages, literal wages, wages earned by work and therefore belonging to the worker; the dollar is an actual dollar; the only difference between the use of money and wages by Speculative Masons and their Operative Masonic forbears is that Speculative Masons aver that what the Operative Masons knew, and taught, and understood about money and wages is true of money and wages everywhere. Instead of having a money theory peculiarly its own the Fraternity affirms that its money theory belongs to everybody.

Money has been described as that subject about which no two of its own experts ever agree; it is because, of the four factors of which money is constituted, three can be predicted but the fourth cannot be; it is a variable, an X. But this is not a complete explanation of that sense of mystery which almost every man has, at least once in a while, about the function and nature of a dollar; for there is yet a fifth factor, which is not in money but about it, and it is the factor of its function. For like Aladdin with his lamp a man can turn a dollar into any one of countless things. There is a magic in it. He can at will turn it into two pounds of meat; or a bouquet of flowers; or (if he have enough of them) into a pair of shoes; or into medicine; or into a subscription to his church; or into a book; or into schooling; or into science. And as a man usually does not value the product of his own work merely for its own sake but for what he can get for it, so he does not value a coin for its own sake but because he can trade it for innumerable things or services which in themselves are wholly unlike gold or silver.

This complete freedom a man has of turning a dollar into whatever he may need, or want, or desire, or fancy is in a Masonic Lodge brought under a restriction; this restriction is that *Masonic funds can be expended only for Masonic Purposes;* these latter are broad, they ramify in many directions, they have in them a large number of potentialities, nevertheless they are defined by law, and the fact is a key to the Fraternity's use of money. Unless a Lodge owns property from which it collects rents, or receives gifts, or has an endowment on which it is paid interest, a Lodge, strangely enough, has no income, and even more strangely, it charges no admittance fee to the Lodge Room, charges no price for conferring the Degrees, and charges no price for membership.

## Masonic Monies—Masonic Lodge Funds

Yet if it is a true and living Lodge, and is at work in a community where it is needed, it is never without funds. The secret of it is that a Lodge pays out what monies are needed to carry out the purpose of a Lodge, adds up the expenditures, and has each man pay in his equal or his proportionate share. If he is a Candidate he pays his apportioned share, which means the sum apportioned to him as his share in meeting the expenses incurred while conferring the Degrees, and this is called his Initiation Fee—it is not a price of admission, and it is not a price at which the Degrees are sold, because no Lodge ever sells its Degrees, but is, to repeat, a share in Lodge expenses. During the year a Lodge must pay rent, must pay taxes, pays for light, heat, and janitor service, postage, equipment, entertainments, relief, and incidentals; the total is divided among the members each of whom pays an equal share, called Annual Dues; and since each member accepts responsibility for his share in a Lodge's fixed expenses in the act of becoming a member, and since appropriation for expenditures made through the year are made by vote, and he has a vote. Dues are not a tax levied upon him from without, but a charge assessed upon him by himself.

CHAPTER XII

# *Masonic Comity*

"COMITY" is not a familiar word, not even in Freemasonry where it has so large a use; it is not a friendly looking word, or a poetical word, and it is not a word that the rank and file of ordinary men will ever use in their daily speech because it sounds too stilted. It is all the more necessary, therefore, to become acquainted with this word itself, because in these studies it must stand up high and large and carry a heavy freight of meaning.

The Romans made much use of their prefix *com*, which they also wrote as *con*, because by it they denoted many words in that large family of terms which had the general meaning of association, of gathering together, or collectivity, or joint action. This prefix, along with many words formed from it, was transplanted into English, and it has there, as prefix or as root, fathered possibly 200 of our words. Thus, we combined *com*, together, with *mitto*, which meant to send, and produced *committee*, the name for a small group sent out, or told off, or set aside to act for a whole group. By combining it with *foedus*, to league together, to join up, we made our word *confederate*. If a man were to select out of English the large number of words with *con* or *com* in them, at first hand or at second, he would see a picture, as in a mirror, of what English-speaking people have always understood collective, or joint, or associative action to be. As a digression, the picture would show that English-speaking people are too individualistic to like associative action, and nearly always must be forced, or coaxed, or persuaded into it!

The sole purpose of this paragraph on *con*, or *com* is to say that in spite of both appearance and sound our Masonic word *comity* has no connection with it, even though in a very large

96

## Masonic Comity

and loose sense the meaning of the one is similar to the meaning of the other; and it is probable that our confusing comity with committee and other such words as are derived from *con* and *com* explains why Masonic comity is not as well understood as it ought to be. Comity is from the Latin *comes,*—not from it, but rather *is* it, for in this instance as in so many others a term was transferred bodily from Latin to English; *comes* meant kind, friendly, congenial, warm-hearted. A comity is a system, or set of usages, or an order of courtesies by which separate individuals or separate organizations can remain friends with each other. It will be instantly seen that instead of quashing out individuality in order to combine individuals, comity does the opposite; it presupposes that individuals will continue to be individuals, that independent organizations will continue to remain independent, but may nevertheless work together and be friends together.

It was of life-and-death importance for Freemasonry in the United States to find a system of comity at the beginning of the Nineteenth Century to keep American Freemasonry from destroying itself by pounding itself into separate pieces. Freemasonry in the United States found such a system, established it, universally accepted it, and has been successfully using it ever since; its ability to do so is the highest achievement of American Masonic statesmanship thus far.

From about 1730 A.D. until the Revolutionary War Lodges in the American Colonies were chartered by the Modern or Antient Grand Lodges of England, by the Grand Lodges of Scotland and of Ireland, and in a few instances by French Grand Bodies; had this process continued there would in time have been Lodges chartered by Italian, Dutch, Spanish, Swedish, etc., Grand Lodges. These charters were granted directly by Grand Lodges abroad, or indirectly through their Provincial Grand Lodges, in which they appointed the Provincial Grand Masters. It was a creaky, ill-formed, unsatisfactory system, and was so for reasons over most of which nobody had any control; Europe was far away, in both space and time; foreign Grand Masters could know little about the American scene; the Jurisdictions and the prerogatives of the Provincial Grand Lodges overlapped and were otherwise ill-defined; Provincial Grand Masters were given no clear directions or full authority. To complicate these difficulties Americans began to resent foreign overlordship as early as 1750 A.D., and the contempt with which Americans were treated after the fiasco of the French-Indian War added bitterness to that resentment. Masonic ties, like other ties, began to be strained before the Revolutionary War had begun.

During the War these ties were broken, not only with Britain but with Canada also, and for some six years American Lodges were adrift; their Provincial Grand Lodges functioned as well as they were able but they continued nevertheless to be provincial. Once the War was over, and indeed before it was over, a number of American Masons believed that all those Provincial Grand Lodges should be dissolved and that the thirteen new states (which thought of themselves as sovereign nations) should unite under one Grand Lodge. This demand was first made at a meeting of Masons in the army which was held at Morristown, New Jersey, on December 27, 1779 A.D., with General George Washington present; from then until the end of the Civil War meetings and conventions were held one after another for the same purpose (Henry Clay was one of the leaders) but without success. In reality the proposal for a National, or General, Grand Lodge did not at any time, even at the beginning, have any prospect of success, and for the same reasons that gave us in politics a union of sovereign states instead of a single national state. Since the Civil War Masonic constitutional law has been so much improved and strengthened that it would now be out of order to introduce a discussion of a National Grand Lodge on the floor of any Grand Communication—a Grand Lodge could not legally vote itself out of existence.

Nevertheless while the attempt to set up one National Grand Lodge failed, and failed for sound reasons, and could never have proved satisfactory in practice because no man could be Grand Master (except in name) of over three million Masons and over fifteen thousand Lodges, its champions had a well-grounded and wise fear of what would be the results if the Fraternity went to the opposite extreme. Those who stood at that opposite extreme championed a Masonic system which would have been as unworkable as a single Grand Lodge and would have been in practice even more disastrous, because they proposed that Lodges should be completely sovereign, and that Grand Lodges should be nothing more than an annual meeting of Lodges, and that each Grand Lodge, although it would be nothing but a phantom, should be absolutely independent of other Grand Lodges. This would have been a form of atomism. There are now five Masonic Rites in the United States: Ancient Craft Masonry, Capitular Masonry, Cryptic Masonry, Templarism, and the Scottish Rite; in Ancient Craft Masonry alone there are 49 Grand Lodges and over 15,000 Lodges, and in the other Rites, correspondingly to their membership, are an equally large number of local and state bodies; if the champions of localism and parochialism had won their way there would be not one Masonic Fraternity in the nation but there would have been thousands of separate Freemasonries.

In place of atomism on the one hand, with its localism and parochialism and separateness, and of a national Grand Lodge on the other hand which would not have given us Masonic unity, because it would have left nothing to unite, but would have given us a despotism, the American Craft solved the problem in a wholly different manner, and on another principle, by developing the system of Masonic Comity. It was not invented or devised by any one man or any one Grand Lodge or at any one time or place, nor was it discussed in conventions or voted on in Grand Communications but was built up and expanded and is now still in process of being completed, one step at a time, as wisdom and experience have dictated.

1. The forty-nine Grand Lodges and the corresponding number of Grand Bodies in the other four Rites are each one sovereign and independent, and the jurisdiction of each one, including the jurisdiction of each local body, is inviolable. The function of Comity is to maintain a unity among these many Bodies without invading the sovereignty of any one of them, so that in spite of many sovereignties there is in the United States not many Freemasonries but only one Freemasonry.

2. This Comity consists of *official* acts, agreements, and con-

ventions by Grand Bodies and by local Bodies; it is therefore not an aspiration only, or an unattainable ideal, but is a working system composed of actualities and realities; and it is now in operation. These official acts and agreements are not as between Bodies and Grand Bodies within one Rite only, but are also between Bodies and Grand Bodies from one Rite to another; they therefore constitute Masonic diplomacy, and since Freemasonry does not stop short at national political boundaries, these acts and agreements also are as between Bodies and Grand Bodies of one country with those in another country; Masonic diplomacy is therefore an international diplomacy. An agreement between a Grand Body in the United States and a Grand Body in Egypt is as binding as one between one American Grand Body and another.

3. By Recognition is meant an official declaration by one Grand Body that another Grand Body is regularly and duly constituted, and practices Freemasonry according to the Ancient Landmarks. If Grand Body A refuses to grant recognition to Grand Body B the former will carry on no official correspondence with the latter; its members cannot visit or demit to local Bodies under Grand Body B; as far as Grand Body A is concerned it is as if Grand Body B did not exist.

4. Grand Bodies themselves when in Grand Communication and their appropriate Grand Officers, at any other time, carry on correspondence with other Grand Bodies recognized by them.

5. Grand Bodies and Grand Officers and local Bodies and local Officers may visit in any recognized Masonic Body, personally or by deputy.

6. In its own published proceedings or transactions a Grand Body may review and discuss the proceedings published by any other recognized Grand Body. In Ancient Craft Masonry many such reviews are published and have been for more than a century; taken as a whole, and over that century of time, they have had an immense importance because they have served as a national Masonic forum, and as such have been a far better forum than a Grand Communication of a National Grand Lodge could have been. A large part of the unity of thought and practice

## Masonic Comity

among 49 Grand Jurisdictions is directly traceable to these reviews.

7. Masons and Masonic Bodies in one Rite or Grand Jurisdiction may extend Masonic relief to Masons in another Rite or Grand Body.

8. A Grand Body in one Rite may require of its own Candidates that they shall be members in good standing in a preceding Rite—thus, no man can become or remain a Royal Arch or a Scottish Rite Mason unless he already is a member in good standing in a regular Ancient Craft Lodge.

9. In periods of war, calamity, hurricanes, distress, famine, the Masonic Bodies of the states and Rites can act coöperatively or concurrently to extend relief.

10. There are, in conclusion, a large number of more or less unclassifiable practices in Comity which, though of a great variety, and independent in themselves, act to the same end, which is to knit the many Bodies and Rites into a single Fraternity; among these are: the holding of such conferences as the Grand Masters' Conference and the Grand Secretaries' Conference in Washington, D. C., each February; the exchange of literature; the publication of Masonic periodicals; the sharing of facilities; Masonic speakers; Masonic mass meetings; courtesy Degrees; etc., etc.

Comity itself is of two kinds: External, and Internal. External Comity consists of the above described practices as carried on between a Body or Grand Body in one Rite and other Bodies and Grand Bodies in the same Rite which are in other states or countries. Internal Comity consists of the same practices between a Grand Body and its own local Bodies. A Grand Body has many forms of relations with its own local Bodies; Comity is but one of them, but it is as official and as necessary as are any of the others.

It will be seen from the above descriptive notes (an exhaustive description would fill a large volume) that at each and every point Comity is strictly and rigorously *official,* either in the sense that it consists of actions taken by Masonic Bodies and Grand Bodies, or actions approved or permitted or allowed by tacit consent, and for that reason much interchange of Masonic thought and knowledge and many forms of sociability do not come within Comity though they may in their own way help to maintain a unity of thought and feeling throughout the Fraternity—thus, the publication of Masonic books, Masonic banquets, etc., etc., do not belong to Comity. Its practices are strictly organizational and official. Therefore while Comity is very large and is (Masonically) completely inclusive, and extends itself to the farthest bounds of the Fraternity, it extends itself so far but no farther, and does not go beyond those bounds. In the very act by which it fastens a universal unity within the wide reaches of Freemasonry it shuts Freemasonry up within itself, and shuts non-Masonic bodies out; if it did not do this Comity would defeat its own purpose because it would draw non-Masonry into Masonry, and instead of preserving the unity of Masonry would destroy it, because if just any body or society could go about calling itself Masonic nothing would in any real and true sense be Masonic.

Comity is one of the subjects in which a Mason ought to begin to take pride as soon as he is raised. We American Masons are proud of it, and without boasting or self-conceit. It solved a problem which good and wise men declared at one time to be unsolvable, and solved it in the grand style and on an imperial scale. It has bound together hundreds of Grand Bodies and thousands of local Bodies in a living and working unity and yet has done so without encroaching upon their sovereignty or trespassing upon their jurisdictions. Had it failed, Ancient Craft Masonry would itself have broken down into 49 separate Masonries; so, in turn, would each of the other four Rites; we should by now have hundreds or thousands of separate, atomistic, unrelated Freemasonries, which is a way of saying that we should have no Freemasonry at all.

CHAPTER XIII

## *Masonry and Ethics*

A MAN HAS IN HIS OWN BEING a number of ways of action which we call by the names truthfulness, goodness, honor, honesty, bravery, courage, purity, and righteousness; together, taken as a whole, they are called character. Character belongs to a man as a whole; it helps to constitute him, is born in him, and like seeing and hearing is inherent in men and women everywhere. Since it thus belongs to man, character is not entirely a set of habits, or a system of doctrines, is not learned at school, and it is for the same reason that the terms for character are found in every one of the more than two thousand languages in the world.

A man can maim himself; he can blind himself, as Hindu beggars sometimes do. He can destroy his hearing; he can cut off his own hands; he can refuse to think, or to speak, or to use his own mind until he finally loses the ability to do so. Similarly he can destroy character out of himself, and when he does he is described as criminal, or wicked, or sinful, or wrong, or unrighteous. Regardless of what he is called he is a mutilated man who lacks something in himself which belongs to every normal man or woman. By a convention of speech we say of a man who possesses normal character that he is *righteous,* or of a woman that she is *moral;* the two words mean the same thing; in either event it is no more a "struggle or painful endeavor for a normal and healthy man to be righteous than it is for him to see, or hear, or breathe.

A Man's own character is in himself and to himself and for himself what it is to others, and is so in toto, as a whole, and down to the last detail. To be truthful to himself and about himself differs not an iota from being truthful to others or about others. When a man is good to himself his goodness is identical with what it is when he is good to another. There is no such thing as "private" character, or "personal morality," still less is there any difference or conflict as between private ethics and public ethics—using the word ethics as a loose and large term for the whole realm of character.

Neither is it true that the external world in which we live and move about is "indifferent to character," or is "morally neutral," or is "non-moral" because the world as it is in itself, apart from a man, and independently of him, is such that if he is not righteous he will suffer and the world will see to it that he does. History is full of instances where whole peoples have perished because their men and women had destroyed character out of themselves.

That world is everywhere the self-same world—it would be a contradiction in terms to suppose that there could be many "worlds" because the word means "everything there is." Men are everywhere the same, they belong to Man, and it would be as impossible for more than one Man to be as it would for more than one world to be. By the same token character is everywhere self-same; it "does not alter when it alteration finds," or change with the seasons, or become one thing in one country, another thing in a different country. It would be as absurd to suppose that arithmetic is not the same today that it was ten thousand years ago, or to suppose that it is one thing in China and a different thing in the United States, or to suppose that truthfulness, goodness, honor, honesty, courage, bravery, purity, or righteousness are not the same everywhere. If they were not the same we could not travel from one country to another; one people could not understand another people; languages could not be translated into each other; one people's history would mean nothing to any other people; there could be no common civilization.

Does Freemasonry have "a system of ethics" peculiarly its own? It does not because no society *can* have one, any more than one people, or religion, or language can have one. What truthfulness is everywhere else is what truthfulness is in Masonry; its honor differs from no other man's honor because honor cannot differ. It takes character for granted and accepts it for what it is, just

## Masonry and Ethics

as it accepts manhood for what it is, or work, or geometry, and it has never fallen into the absurdity of fancying that a Mason might have a character invented by the Craft and peculiar to himself.

When a youth presented himself at the door of a Lodge of Operative Freemasons to petition for admittance into apprenticeship, its members made no more ethical demand on him than that he should be righteous, by which they meant normal in character. When they inquired to see if he was "under the tongue of good report" their only purpose was to discover if others, in the past, had found him to be righteous. If he was not righteous they refused to accept him, and that regardless of what talents he might appear to have, because their Craft was not a reformatory. It did not occur to them that character could be different inside the Lodge from outside it. Their work was trying and difficult therefore they had to have courage, it was hazardous and sometimes deadly therefore they had to have bravery, but they did not think of their own courage or bravery as being different from other men's. They knew that an apprentice would have to be loyal because they would entrust their lives and limbs to him, but there was nothing peculiar or occult in this loyalty.

Almost every Monitor in the United States quotes a definition of Freemasonry which has (and whether rightly or mistakenly) been accredited to Dr. Samuel Hemming, who had charge of the attempt to devise a uniform ritual when the Modern and Antient Grand Lodges in England united in 1813 A.D.; according to its familiar words "Freemasonry is a beautiful system of morality, veiled in allegories, and illustrated by symbols." The sentence possesses the quality of great literature because in it are verbal beauty and a high poetry, and it could without affront be incorporated in the text of the Holy Bible. But however beautiful it is, it suffers from a fatal defect: it is not true.

Freemasonry is a *fraternity,* not "a system of morality" (what could that mean?); it has never propounded a set of ethical doctrines, nor adopted an ethical code of its own; and a Lodge is a *lodge,* not a school of ethical culture, nor a school-room for ethical lectures; and instead of existing to make men righteous it demands that they shall be righteous before their admittance into it. Neither does Freemasonry "veil" anything belonging to character, nor does it disguise them in the form of "allegory" (what could that mean?), but states them in plain languages as forcefully and forthrightly as it is able, and without obscuration by fog or ambiguity; furthermore it states its demands for character over and over, in its questions to the Petitioner, in its questions to the Candidate (and his answers), in the Obligations, in the Landmarks, in the Rules and Regulations, and in the Lectures; if it states many of them in the form of symbols it is not to conceal them but to make them plain, and because a symbol often *says more* than words can. Neither does it "illustrate" its demands on character, but states them in their own terms, in plain words, without "beating about the bush"—if brotherly love, relief and truth are tenets it is they themselves that are presented, each in its own name, for its own sake; they are not presented in order to "illustrate" something other than themselves.

If there is therefore no such thing as "Masonic ethics" in the sense that character is (or could be) not what character is everywhere else, there is nevertheless another possible use for that phrase that leads in another direction which it is profitable to follow. Freemasonry is a world in itself; it has a field of its own, purposes of its own, activities of its own, its own forms of work, its own organization, and its own Landmarks. Wherever that is true, wherever men work in association, their needs require that certain things belonging to character shall be brought to the front, and emphasized, because they are especially needed. In a battle a man has a continual need for bravery, and he therefore emphasizes it to himself and keeps it in his consciousness, because his life as well as the outcome of the battle depend on it; when the same man is at home he has the same bravery in him but does not have the same need for it, but possibly may need to keep *goodness* to the front, and ever hold it in his consciousness. It would be difficult to think of a man as being in any set of circumstances, or in any form of work, or in any activity or place or association where he would not similarly be called upon to use one thing in character more than another. If this is true in Freemasonry it is not because Freemasonry differs from any other association, but because it does not; it is normal too if its members, being under its conditions and doing its work should, as men everywhere else do, bring to the front and lay more emphasis on some things belonging to character than others. These things of character which it thus especially needs, and therefore especially emphasizes, are the definition of a true use of the phrase "Masonic Ethics," and it is they which are the subject matter of the Masonic books that are classified under ethics.

It is interesting to note the point at which the Fraternity makes this emphasis. The point is nowhere in theory, and is nowhere in words; the Ritual does not ask of a Candidate, "Do you believe in righteousness? What is your opinion of it? How would you define this or that term in it?" Rather, it always raises the question as to what a man *does* about righteousness whenever he encounters something or must deal with something which raises a question about it. If you encounter a liar, what do you *do* with him? Do you come to grips with him there and then? If you come upon an act of dishonesty what action do you take? Of what good are thoughts, and theories, and doctrines when some given state of affairs calls not for your opinions and your theories but calls upon you to *act?* to *do?* If you encounter ruffians who are there and then engaged in assaulting a friend of yours do you content yourself with saying to yourself "I do not believe in crime," or do you attack them, or knock them down? Of what possible use is it to have the tenet of truth in the mind if when you see a crime being committed before you you back away, and let it work itself out? It is at this point, in this frame-work of *doing,* that a Masonic Lodge is very ethical—is, indeed, surcharged with it. For no Lodge ever asks a member that he shall pass an examination in any history of ethics or in ethical theory, or in the definition of ethical terms, but it insists to the limit of his power that whenever an ethical question arises in Lodge activity *he shall take action.* Disturbances and disharmony are wrong; every member present is expected to act on the spot to undo a wrong; quarreling is unrighteous, and few things are more so; the Lodge is not interested in a member's theory of quarreling or in his doctrine about evil but it is so much interested in having its members *act to put an end* to quarreling that if they fail to do so the charter will be withdrawn. It is this quality of ethical action rather than any concern with ethical doctrine or theory which marks the Degrees from beginning to end, and gives to them their feeling of reality and of manliness, because nothing is more unreal than the man whose head is full of powerful ideas about ethics but who is feeble in action. It is for this reason that the Lodge's own ethical life consists of conduct and behavior rather than of codes of doctrine or mere theory. It is not until a Mason sees this to be true that he can see how ethically sound is a Lodge and how ethically powerful are the Degrees, for in both the Lodge and the Degrees whenever evil or wrong is actually encountered they *act,* they are never false, they are never uncertain or mistaken, they never haggle or back down.

In the year 1581 A.D., which means that he was only seventeen years of age, and while he was watching a lamp swinging in the Cathedral of Pisa, the Italian Galileo Galilei saw that whatever the range of the oscillations of a pendulum might be, the oscillations are executed in equal times. Any man who sees the facts which Galileo was the first to point out, can see for himself that Galileo's statement was true because the facts are self-evident; since Galileo reported the facts as they are he was truthful, and his statement was therefore a truth. Galileo would have laughed if his father had said to him, "my son, you found out these facts, therefore your truth should be privately owned by you"; he would have laughed if the cardinals and bishops among his friends had said, "You are a Roman Catholic, therefore your truth ought to belong exclusively to your church"; he also would have laughed had a fellow Italian said, "You are an Italian, therefore your truth should belong to Italy." Galileo knew that his truth belonged to everybody; it had been a truth 10,000 years before he was born; it would continue to be a truth 10,000 years after; it is a truth in America, or China, or in Africa as much as in Italy. *No* truth, for such is the nature of truth itself, can be any man's private property, or be owned or monopolized by anybody; it is in its own essence something free, something which any man can have who desires to have it. No truth, this one stated by Galileo, or any other, and no matter what the truth is about, or who states it, or where he states it, or why, can be a Roman Catholic truth, or a Protestant one, or Jewish, or Confucianist, or ancient, or modern; it may be discovered by a scientist, or a theologian, or a statesman, but it does not matter who states it, or what party he belongs to, a truth is always a truth, and therefore is no one man's private property.

Truth is one of the three Principal Tenets of Freemasonry. They are "principal" because they are at the center of that in ethics in which Freemasonry is most interested; since they are, a man would expect Freemasons to be intensely interested in them, but for a mysterious reason they are not, as any man can learn for himself who reads Masonic books or periodicals, or looks through collections of Masonic speeches. They are an inactive spot in the Masonic mind. Why is that? It is because so many Masons have failed to see the point of why Freemasonry has these Tenets, and what it has to say about them.

Consider this Tenet of Truth. What point does the Ritual make about it? It is certain that the Ritual does not mean by "Truth" any one truth in particular, because if so, what is it? Or any collection of particular truths; if so, what are they? The point it makes is an ethical one, a moral one, it belongs to character, and the point it makes about truth is the same point that Galileo made; any truth, all the truths there are, are in their essence *free* truths, free to anybody, free to be known to anybody, free for anybody to use and without asking permission. There are many truths *in* Freemasonry, some of them were first discovered and stated by Freemasons, but not one of them is the exclusive property of Freemasonry, because *no* Truth can be anybody's private property; and the mere fact that a truth is found *in* Freemasonry cannot mean that it there differs from the same truth when found outside it; and if a truth is found outside Freemasonry, in any religion, in any science, in any country, Freemasons know themselves to be as free to know and to use it as they may desire to. Then Truth as one of the Principal Tenets is not a philosophic idea, or a scientific idea, but is an ethical idea, and this idea means that any righteous man will never try to make any truth his own property or the property of his own fraternity, or church, or party, will never lay hands on any truth to distort it or to misrepresent it to gain something for himself or his party, and will never try to prevent any other man from having any truth. This is what a righteous man does about truth; he will keep it wholly free, he will never do violence to it, he will never misrepresent it, and he will never try to keep any other man from having it.

*Part Three*
MORE ABOUT MASONRY

CHAPTER XIV

## *Civil Government—Politics*

ARISTOTLE was by profession a naturalist specializing in zoölogy who by offering payment for specimens turned Greece's whole merchant marine into a collecting agency, and who was able through his family and political connections to persuade scores of his friends to maintain private zoölogical and botanical gardens for him and who because he was a famous college professor was able to commandeer hundreds of students to conduct experiments and make notes for him. These notes he published, acres of them; and his must have been one of the best organizations ever devised because after 2500 years, so Professor Singer tells us, he has been found out in only four or five important errors. The secret of this amazing success in keeping thousands of individuals at work on one thing and of his being able to coördinate tens of thousands of findings was a system of classification which if he did not invent it he at least perfected it. He divided everything into kinds, animal, vegetable, mineral; animals and vegetables he divided into orders, families, genera, species, and varieties; it was a sort of vast filing system like the one employed by the Federal Bureau of Investigation for filing finger prints. To find any given plant or animal in it you only had to have the key.

This key was furnished by his system of classification which was built on the theory that each group of plants or animals has a set of properties or attributes peculiar to itself, animals with attributes A, B, C, D, E were put into the same group, or class, and this class was given a name. Those with attributes W, X, Y, Z were put into another class, etc. If within a class a number of animals had a set of special attributes peculiar to themselves they were a species or variety and given a secondary name. Any given specimen was identified and described by giving its family, genus, species, and variety.

It one day occurred to Aristotle in a blinding flash of imagination that the same system of classification could be applied to every kind of thing, even to our thoughts; the result was his preparation of that "organon," or system, to which he gave the name of logic; and by the time he died Aristotle had become convinced that he had hit upon the very system by which the mind itself works; he had found out, he was sure, "the science of thought"; since then, in Europe first and then in America, billions have agreed with him, because until a half century ago almost every man believed in Aristotle's logic as a matter of course, and the majority continue to do so. The theology of the Roman Catholic Church is one-half St. Augustine, and one-half Aristotle.

The largest and most illuminating fact about political theorizing from scholasticism until a few years ago was the almost unanimous use by the theorizers of Aristotle's method. Aristotle himself had taught them how to use the method when he and his students collected some hundreds of what he named "political constitutions" and analyzed and classified them as a naturalist would classify plants and animals; he and his colleagues believed that the largest and most important attributes of the politics of any people consisted of the form taken by its sovereignty; how, or by what means, does it enact its laws? how does it enforce them? how does it try criminals? how does it bring its laws home to its citizens? Where he found a number of states doing this in the same way, or at least approximately the same way, he put them into one class, and gave it one name. By use of this device he and his disciples after him produced a method of theorizing and of nomenclature which appeared to be impersonal, scientific, and almost infallible, and in consequence it has charmed generations of political thinkers ever since. How simple, how complete, it appeared to be! Such states as have kings he put into the class called monarchy; if a king inherits his crown, as in Great Britain, he belongs to the variety called hereditary monarchy, if he is elected, as Poland once practiced it, he belongs to an elective monarchy; etc.

## Civil Government—Politics

Thus it was that the old and familiar usage became fixed upon us. If a state is composed of a number of states, each with its own rules, it is an empire, and its head is an emperor. If its sovereignty is wielded by a small group of rulers it is an oligarchy. If it is ruled by its few richest or wealthiest men it is a plutocracy. If its citizens make their laws at first hand, while assembled for that purpose, as they did in Athens and as later was done by the Anglo-Saxons, it is a democracy. If they select representatives or delegates to make the laws it is a republic. If a people is divided into families or clans, if a woman is the ruler of each, and if there is a woman ruling those chieftainesses, it is a matriarchate. If one man seizes rule and holds it by violence he is a tyrant, or dictator. If a state is ruled by an hereditary ruling class (as in Medieval France) it is an aristocracy. If nobody rules because everybody rules, and one as much as another, and do so by an organization rather than by men, it is a commune, or is communistic. If it is ruled by a pope, or by its priests or preachers (as among the Aztecs), it is a theocracy. If it employs several methods at once it is a political syncretism.

Aristotelianism has been battered to pieces, bit by bit, until now nothing is left except the habit of it. Protestantism proved that it cannot be true in theology. Copernicus, Galileo, and Francis Bacon proved it false in the physical sciences, and whatever pieces remained were exposed in our own generation by Einstein, and the logicians and mathematicians in the middle of the Nineteenth Century, after Kant, Hegel, Bradley, and the French mathematico-logicians and the non-Euclideans, tore it to shreds. And we ourselves, slowly and painfully but surely, are showing that it is as false in government as it was in physics and logic. In spite of ourselves, and oftentimes very much against the grain of ancient habits, we are becoming non-Aristotelians.

An entire book is needed to show why and in what way this is true, but for the purpose here one out of the many facts which such a book would show will suffice: *Aristotelianism does not work*. The governments of peoples are not plants and animals, and no so-called logical classification of them in the terms of kinds, families, genera, and species can possibly be true. *They cannot be classified;* and the behavior of any given people proves this to be true, because no people ever knows exactly *what it is,* according to the Aristotelian classification.

Their inability to do so is thrown into gigantic relief whenever they are in a war and must confront their foes, and court their allies. This has been true of ourselves. Before our Spanish-American War we presented to Latin-American republics the face of a dictatorship, the President, using the Department of State as his weapon, being the dictator. During that war we turned to Cubans and Filipinos the face of a democracy, and while doing it represented ourselves to Europe as a republic. In World War II Great Britain was a democracy while appealing to us, a monarchy while appealing to Greece and Italy, an aristocracy at Munich, the home of the Labor Party when appealing to Russia, an empire when governing India, and at home it was a United Kingdom. Germany had an extreme dictatorship, but called it nationalist and yet at the same time called it socialist. And so it went, from country to country. The notion that there are in nature or necessity a certain fixed number of classes or kinds of "political systems" was reduced to absurdity in that War, not because the peoples concerned were stupid or hypocritical but because Aristotelianism is so wholly false, and Aristotelian nomenclature is so wholly meaningless. We ourselves have a "political system" consisting of a teeter-totter of two political parties, each one organized and authorized by law, and it ought therefore to be called everywhere bipartisanism, but instead we call ourselves either democrats or republicans. Could an Englishman stand in court under oath and declare what he is? how could he, when he is imperialist, aristocrat, monarchist, republican, democrat, and a socialist together!

The world of man is divided not into areas of land or into so-called "political units," but into *peoples.* There is in each people a general and almost uniform way in which they organize and manage their homes, do their work, carry on their sports, and amusements, dress, speak, eat, and by which they conduct their community affairs. This is not a fixed and inalterable entity, it is difficult to describe and even more difficult to name, but

## Civil Government—Politics

every man knows that there is an "American way of doing things," a "Mexican way of doing things," a German way, a French way, and so on forth, therefore it may for the sake of convenience be described as a people's way of life. It is this way of life, and not political theories, or doctrines, or "principles," which determine how any given people will find, declare, and promulgate its laws and select men to hold office in its government. Since a people's way of life is its own, since it is not duplicated anywhere else in the world and could not be duplicated out of history, it is unique, their very own; and since their way of government belongs to their way of life it necessarily also is unique. Therefore instead of describing governments as democratic, or monarchic, or communistic, etc., we should think and speak of them as the American's government, the Englishman's government, the Russian's government, etc.

From about the time of Jackson's Administration until the present generation we had a way of life which we may describe with satisfactory accuracy by the word "Committee." The father of a family was not a god, king, dictator, chieftain ruling over it but was its spokesman, its representative, he acted for it. The teachers to whom his children went to school were employed by a School Board which acted as delegates from the school district. Banks, business corporations, etc., were administered by Boards of Directors. A City Council was a body of legislators chosen to represent the citizens. A State Government or the Federal Government was a body of representatives or delegates. Churches were governed by boards of stewards, trustees, etc. Almost everything, from the largest to the smallest, even a picnic, was governed or administered, or managed by representatives, or delegates, or spokesmen, acting as a committee. If we employed this committee method in government, local, state, and national, it was not because the founders of our nation chose it, or because the Constitution compelled it, but because it was of a piece of our way of life. There are evidences on every side which prove that this way of life, a century old, has broken down, or is in process of doing so, and that somewhere within our midst a new way of life is taking shape; it is doing so slowly, and almost invisibly, as a new way of life always does; we cannot see as yet what form it will take, but we can be certain beforehand that it will differ greatly from the old one—and a man would waste his time as much to attempt to cling to the old as he would to attempt to control the new, because no way of life is ever invented by one man, or one group of men, or thought out, or theorized into existence, but comes as a vast and only half-conscious act of a whole people. Once we have a new way of life (perhaps thirty years hence) we shall have a method in government which will belong to it.

If these things be true the problem of Masonry and politics, or of Masonry's own "political system," or of Masonry and political parties, is solved before we take it up. During the Eighteenth and (the now almost equally remote) Nineteenth Centuries when men everywhere were using Aristotle's system of classification ("polity") and labeling governments by his names, hundreds of attempts were made to show to which of Aristotle's classifications a Lodge belonged. After the Mother Grand Lodge had become "Modernized" a large number of its members insisted that a Lodge is a monarchy and that the Master is its monarch. After the French and American Revolutionary wars the theorists began to declare that a Lodge is a republic, and that its officers are delegates of its membership. Since about 1920 A.D. many Masonic theorists have argued that a Lodge is a democracy. Scarcely one of Aristotle's many classifications but has had its champion, and if the Fraternity had listened to them no Mason would now know what he is in the eyes of political theory—his political clothing would have as many colors as Joseph's coat, and many more patches; it would be all patches!

The Fraternity has never paid any heed to these theorists, partly because it would not and partly because it could not. It would not now be in existence if it had. It preserved its Landmarks and its rules and regulations and its own work and teachings through centuries in which England changed its ways of life and therefore of "politics" four or five times, and in America it has preserved its identity unaltered through two such changes. It is at the present at work in forty or fifty countries (even in

Japan!), each with its own way of life and ways of government. Manifestly there has never been a period in its history when it was identified with any one way of politics else it would have perished with it; it is equally certain that it could not now be identified with one, else it could not work in so many countries which have among themselves so many ways of government. In the Aristotelian sense it has no "politics," and could not have, and therefore is not monarchic, aristocratic, dictatorial, republican, democratic, socialist, or communistic, nor could it support any "political party" outside itself which could be called by any one of those names.

There has never been a time when the Fraternity has not had in it something which can be described, non-technically, as government; and this has never been altered in its principles or fundamentals, nor could it be without destroying Freemasonry itself. Lodges and Grand Lodges act as legislative bodies. Lodge and Grand Lodge officers, certain of them, act as magistrates. It has a jurisprudence, in which are Landmarks, Constitutions, statutes, edicts, decisions, courts, rules, regulations, customs, usages, parliamentary law, and much in its etiquette is backed or implemented by its jurisprudence; and Lodges and Grand Lodges have a set of installed officers, the "installed" meaning that each office has a fixed jurisdiction with a prescribed and defined number of powers, duties and prerogatives. Together the whole of it comprises a government; but it is impossible to see where it is at any point a political government if "political" is used as the newspapers use it, because Masons as Lodges do not divide up on two sides, or adopt platforms, or participate in campaigns.

It is also impossible to see how any of the accustomary political labels can be applied to it, because it fits into no class or category; it is unique. The only true description of it (if it is necessary to use the word) is the formula: "Freemasonic Politics are freemasonic politics," which is not a repetition of words but is a recognition of the fact that the Fraternity's government is exclusively and uniquely its own, and therefore not to be described or defined in any other form or way of government. Why do Masons have these particular ways of government? Because they were necessary, because the nature of their work dictated them, because they are called for by the Craft's form of fellowship, because they were called forth by experience and practice. At no time in the Fraternity's history have its members ever been converted to any political gospel, or accepted any political creed, or espoused any political theory, or used any political watchword, because such matters have always lain outside its own province; and because within itself it has always adopted such rules and regulations as were needed by it to go on with its own work.

CHAPTER XV

## *Masonry and the Law*

IN MEN INDIVIDUALLY and in men collectively are a number of everlasting needs; in the nature of the world is that which calls forth those needs; to satisfy those needs, which no individual ever escapes, men have the three institutions which are called home, school, and government. An institution differs from every other form of collective action or association by being universally necessary, so that no people anywhere can exist without it; and it has the peculiarity that though the needs it satisfies are *in* a man, and oftentimes are invisible, yet it must have buildings, equipments, and men to work in it.

In the nature of each man, of peoples, and of the world is the law; it is one of the most difficult of all things to understand, and almost impossible to describe, yet it is so actual, so real, that if a man becomes abnormal in that in himself, which has to do with the law, it will twist him into monstrous shapes of character and may drive him insane—a rock, a piece of steel, neither of these is more real than the law! When stated in the form of words the law is, "Thou shalt not destroy another." It does not matter if you destroy a man in one minute or in one year, destroy him at one stroke, as in murder, or destroy him piecemeal by destroying his money, or belongings, or his possessions, or his property, or his freedom or whatever else he must have in order to continue to be; to destroy another by any means is to act as a criminal.

There is a law, and it does not multiply itself; what we call laws in the plural are not many laws but only many declarations of the law. A government is the institution by which our many and various needs for the law are protected or satisfied; any people without government will perish. A government may in detail or in form be in one nation unlike what it is in another, depending on their way of life, but it has its own eternal Landmarks, and always, whatever its form, it will have in it the same framework everywhere. If the citizens under a government begin a practice (such as using automobiles) and if in that practice what they do may destroy others, the government brings that practice under review and "finds" the law in it. Once it has "found" the law in that practice it "declares" it, which means that it authorizes a statement which is put on official record; when this is done it "promulgates" it, which means that citizens everywhere are put under bond to the government not to act unlawfully when engaged in the practice in question—if the practice is driving automobiles, the promulgated law commands them not to drive recklessly lest they, or their passengers, or pedestrians shall be destroyed. (It is as criminal to murder a man with an automobile as to murder him with a gun.) The last step taken by the government is to set apart a number of officers, placed under oath, and sworn to act impersonally and impartially to compel citizens to act lawfully by *means of force* (without compulsion or force there can be no government). Thus, it is now clear and as said above that there is only the law; what we call "laws" are only a number of declarations of it.

It is obvious that the law is unaltered by circumstances, is never modified to suit any one of the many races, sub-races, languages, religions, countries, or climates, in the world—wherever it is, it is always the one thing, and to suppose it to be shaped by circumstances or "environments" (whatever that word may mean!) is as impossible as that time, space, gravity, light, weight, etc., can be modified by circumstances. Some peoples do not have a complete government; if so they suffer damage or deprivation from the lack. Other peoples load up the officers of the government with tasks and duties and burdens which do not belong to government, and this attempt to unload the whole of a people's collective and general activities on a government is what is meant by nationalism (what has carrying the mail to do with the law? or conducting experimental farms?); such a government will sooner or later fall apart or else will become a totalitarian despotism and the people under it will perish; no government should ever carry any duties except such as are required by its services to the law. If these things are true it is plain that no man, Mason or non-Mason, can ever raise such a question as "What is Freemasonry's relation to government?" As well ask what are its "relations" to time or to the law of gravity. It has no "relation" of its own; Masons are under the government in exactly the same way that other men are, and Lodges are under it as other bodies are. It matters nothing to the law whether a man is a Mason or not.

Apropos of this it happens that the oldest known written Masonic record which may be described as historical is a passage in the middle of the *Regius MS.* (600 years old) in which it is clearly stated that the earliest Lodges stood under the government of the time as did other bodies of men. In 926 A.D., it says, King Athelstan, or his son Prince Edwin, or the two together, called the Freemasons together in a general assembly at York. But this was not an assembly attended exclusively by Freemasons but was called by the King in order that he, assisted by "divers lords," should consult together as to how it was best for Freemasonry to be governed or, in the scribe's own words, "How they might govern it." The King either approved rules already in use by the Craft, or else devised new rules for it; in either event old Craft rules were approved by the civil government or else new ones were ordered by it, and it was because the Craft was willing to accept the "fifteen articles" and "the fifteen points" that the King granted it a Royal Charter. This meant, as clearly as anything could be meant at the time, that the authority by which Masters of Masons ruled and governed their Lodges was an authority *delegated* by the King and his Councillors. Even if this account of the York assembly in 926 A.D. could not be proved in the courts of history because it first appears in a document written nearly 500 years after the event, and therefore is tradition rather than history, it is nevertheless a true picture of the connection between Operative Freemasonry and the civil government over a period of centuries.

That connection was so close that a number of usages, customs, and practices in Operative Freemasonry, and which we have inherited and continue to use, did not grow up out of the bosom of the art of Freemasonry itself but were the effects of laws or regulations ordered in the Craft or imposed upon it by the civil law, and a certain number of the rules and customs which the Freemasons adopted for themselves, and by themselves, they adopted because of the effect of a previous civil law or regulation. It is a fact of the greatest significance to the Ritual; and those writers who interpret everything in the Ritual as mystical or symbolic, or look for its origins far afield in distant countries or cults or in ancient times, ought to give more heed to it: a number of those things in the Ritual which we now use symbolically were not symbols originally, but were civil laws, or else were a response to civil laws.

At one time or another the government of Britain enforced on the Mason Craft directly, or enforced on it indirectly through regulations and laws directed at gilds and fraternities in general, such laws and rules as these: laws regulating wages, hours of work, the number of holidays in a year, indentures for apprentices, the care of apprentices, and commandeering of members for public duties, requisitioning of Craft funds or supplies for public use (the Masons's Company of London had to contribute funds for the settlement of North Ireland), the taking of oaths, the keeping of records, certain functions of Officers, contracts between Freemasons and their employers, impressment of Craftsmen by kings, the demand for annual reports and the forbidding, of assemblies and covines—this in modern language would mean that Freemasons were not permitted to hold meetings for public agitation or go on strike (strikes were nevertheless not uncommon). Among laws holding of crafts in general were such as, at various times required Lodges to have Patron Saints, to observe their Saints' Day each year, to wear clothing of a certain kind, to live in certain quarters, to submit work to public inspection, etc., etc. Above any of those in importance was the law (never abated or abrogated in the Middle Ages) which forbade the establishment of any permanent body of men without a charter; it is easy to see that the purpose of this law was to make every such body answerable to the civil government; it also is easy to see that this one law did more to give shape to Masonic history than any other, or any ten combined, because it was in obedience to this law that the first permanent Lodges of Free-Masons used that written charter or document which was called *The Old Charges*. Any body of men in any craft, art, or profession which attempted to work without a charter was called "an adulterine gild," and if caught and tried its officers and members suffered severe penalties. (This writer has discovered no instance of an adulterine gild of Freemasons.)

There are hundreds of forms of associations and organizations of a religious kind, or political, or esthetic, or social, etc., which are desirable, and yet are not necessary; we as a people could get along without them; in the past many peoples have gotten along without them; but neither we nor any other people has ever been able to get along without the three institutions, and that is one of the great facts about them; without families, without schooling, without government no people could long continue to exist. But an institution (by definition) is never composed of intellectual abstractions or imponderable abstractions but always must make use of buildings, equipment, money, and men and women, and since it does the buildings may burn down, the money may fall short, or be stolen, the men and women employed may fail in their duties or else may be guilty of malfeasance; an institution will therefore have questions, problems, and difficulties. The peculiarity of those questions is that *they cannot be avoided!* Questions similarly arise in organizations or associations of other kinds; many of them are very difficult; but they do not have in them a life-or-death importance. If I am in the field of theological studies I may encounter the question of who was author of the Fourth Gospel; if I am willing to work at that question for some ten or twelve years I may find an answer to it, but if I am not willing I shall not starve to death; I can take Horace Bushnell's advice to "hang it on a hook." If I am a student in the field of history I may be confronted by the problem of what was the secret agreement between Talleyrand and Metternich at the Congress of Vienna; it is a question that I could find the answer to in three years of hard work, but if I choose to evade the question I am free to do so, and will continue to be safe on the streets and have a roof over my head. But if a question arises which involves the existence of one of the institutions I *cannot evade it;* I, and the people to whom I belong, must find some answer, and we must do it at any cost of time, pain, or money, because without a house or a home we will perish, without schooling we could not work and earn money, without government neither our persons nor our property would be safe for twenty-four hours—the institutions are necessary in the same sense that food, air, and water are necessary; and this truth is one of the keys to history, because always a people will drop everything else if their institutions are threatened, and will go to any extremes of action to save them, even to the extremes of insurrection, or rebellion, or war, and will do so most promptly if that institution be their government, because the results of the loss of government are felt *immediately* in the form of anarchy, crime, mobs, riots, violence, etc.

The great difficulty which people had in the Middle Ages was with government. Their great difficulty with their governments grew out of their problems of where in government lies that which we call sovereignty, by which is meant the last word in power and authority. They tried to work the theory that this sovereignty belongs to the officers of government, that is, to the king, his colleagues, and his councillors, and these men themselves tried to act upon that theory with the doctrine that they themselves were rulers, and therefore were the government. But what if these officers of government were themselves guilty of crime? What if King Henry was guilty of murder, or King Charles guilty of treason?

It is often said that we here in the United States solved that problem with our doctrine that sovereignty lies in the *people,* and it is this, so it is said, that we mean by democracy. But this is not true. We solved the problem but not by the doctrine that sovereignty lies in the people (we have no such doctrine); we solved it by discovering the fact that *sovereignty lies in the law!* Our Constitution is a written instrument by which we set up a government in accordance with *the law;* our Supreme Court means that the

## Masonry and the Law

officers of government (including legislators) are themselves, and *qua* officers of government, as much bound to the law as any other citizens. The whole purpose of our Constitutional system is to make sure that our government itself acts lawfully whenever its officers use force to make the citizens act lawfully. If a bill enacted by the National Congress is proved to have been enacted unlawfully the Supreme Court condemns it, and it ceases to be a law (in reality, it never was one).

Lodges and their members have always been loyal in their citizenship, never conspiring against government, or asking special privileges from it, or hiding from it, or attempting to stand out from under it; and the principles of the Craft's own jurisprudence are such that if an action taken by a Mason, a Lodge, or a Grand Lodge were unlawful in the eyes of the civil government it could not be Masonically lawful. Why? Because Masonry has always identified government with *the law;* and if it has always been "politically universal" in the sense that its Lodges can work among peoples with many different forms of government it is not because it is indifferent, or "believes that one form of government is as good as another," but because it knows that any given people's own form of government will be fashioned by that people's own way of life, and that in any form of it, the sole function of a government is *the law.* It is "politically universal" because the law is universal.

Early in the 1910's Brother Madison C. Peters, of New York, delivered an address to an audience of Masons which was so much enjoyed by his hearers that upon their insistence, and after enlarging it a little, he published it as a small volume entitled *Masons as Makers of America.* Brother Peters, as it turned out, had prepared his brochure in too much haste and as a result was mistaken in a number of his facts; moreover his essay was feeble in logic, and one-sided in argument, yet for all its faults it was read by hundreds of thousands of Masons because in it he had hit upon a fact which Masons had so often noted but which no one had expressed, namely, that there is a similarity between the principles in Masonic government and the principles of the government of the United States so close, so amazingly close, that it is difficult to credit it to coincidence. With our greatly increased knowledge about Freemasonry in the Revolutionary War Period it has become impossible to believe that Masons, *as Masons,* had anything to do with the "making of America" or with writing the Constitution. Why, then, is the amazing similarity there? For a reason far more amazing than the similarity, namely, because centuries before Franklin or Washington, Freemasonry had discovered that sovereignty is not in the officers of government (kings, etc.), or in the people, but is in *the law,* and had embodied that discovery in its Doctrine of the Ancient Landmarks. These are the Landmarks; the Book of Constitutions is the instrument by which they are implemented; because it is, the Grand Lodge constituted thereby, with its Grand Master, and its Officers and members, are themselves answerable to the law in Masonry, and can never rise above it.

But if we Masons were before our National Government in this understanding of the whole point and purpose of government, we are far behind the majority of our fellow Americans in seeing the fact that when it is said that each citizen is *under* the government the story is only half told; the other half of it is the fact that to the same extent that a citizen is answerable to the law a citizen has the full use of the law; he can call upon it, he can demand that it protect him, he can command a hearing in court, he can insist that government shall defend him from anyone who seeks to destroy him. We Masons have that same right; we have been reluctant to make use of it but we ought not to be reluctant; it belongs as much to good citizenship to use the government for self-protection, as it does to act obediently to the government's declaration of the law.

The leaders, editors, and public speakers who worked for the Anti-Masonic Crusade between 1826 A.D. and the Civil War publicly and repeatedly charged the Masonic Fraternity with being a secret conspiratorial society working to overthrow the national government, and a corrupt atheistical society working to destroy Christianity. The Fraternity made no attempt to defend itself, and it is possible that its leaders could find no means to do so. A number of decisions made in the State and in the

## Masonry and the Law

National Supreme Courts since that time have made it clear that Masons can have protection against such outrageous slanders and libels as often as they are made. Freemasonry is not an unembodied set of theories, or drift of feelings, or vague "movement"; it consists of individual men; each man is identified by having his name and address in the Lodge's membership list and identifies himself by wearing insignia and lodge clothing; and by appearing in public. It is easy for him to prove himself a Mason in any civil court. Any libellous, scandalous, defamatory, damaging false statement made about Freemasonry is made about each and every one of those men in particular—it is not the slander of a theory but a harmful slander of known and locally identifiable men; those men can go into court and sue, either separately or collectively (the whole Jewish race sued an American millionaire). If Anti-Masons make true statements about us we cannot hale them into court for being Anti-Masons; but if they slander or libel us we can, not because they are Anti-Masons but because they have uttered libel.

Men and women who use stolen or forged identifications, or otherwise are impostors, frauds, charlatans, or crooks who seek Masonic relief or concoct schemes to defraud Masons and Lodges otherwise, should be arrested and tried. If a group of men set up what they call a Masonic Lodge, either actually or on paper, if they call themselves a Masonic Lodge, but are not, if they have no charter and are on the list of no Grand Lodge, they are *spurious,* and they are not spurious *Masons* because they are not Masons, nor is theirs a Spurious *Masonic* Lodge because they are not a Lodge, but are spurious men and have a spurious organization. Any regular Lodge nearest to such a spurious organization ought to indict it and hale it into court because it is not only unlawful according to Masonic law but is unlawful also according to the civil law; and the Lodge ought to bring it into court because it defrauds citizens of the community, obtains money by false pretenses, and brings their character and reputation into disrepute.

CHAPTER XVI

# *Masonic Jurisprudence*

THE ROMANS WERE the first people to discover that law and justice are one and the same. They contributed other great and permanent things to the world also, but no one of them has aroused so deeply the admiration of men; and that word is here used in its sense of gender, for in contradistinction to women and children men have a lasting love of the law, because it is that in the nature of our world which is most masculine. And in the whole of our English language with its 400,000 words there is no other combination of terms which rings such strong chords of power and music in the feelings of men as that one which centers in, and has grown out of, the old Latin word *jus,* which has always had the meaning of both law and justice. Our term "justice" itself means to "let the law prevail; to let the law have its way." "To judge" is one form of the Latin *judex,* which the Romans formed by combining *jus* with the word *dico,* which meant to say, to speak, to utter. When a case is brought before a judge he does not decide what the evidence is but finds and states the law which applies to the facts given in evidence; he says, or declares, that law; and it is the law, not the judge, which judges the case. Our word "jurisprudence" also has *jus* as one of its roots; with it is combined the Latin *prudentia,* which meant to provide for, or to provide against; it in turn was derived from *pro,* which meant ahead, to foresee, the future, combined with *video,* which meant to see, to look. In itself therefore "jurisprudence" means "as far as the law can see."

In the United States we always think of the law as belonging to government, and we do not permit associations or agencies not belonging to the government to find, declare, and state the law, nor are they permitted to have officers who can use force to compel men to act lawfully; when they attempt to do so we say that "they are taking the law into their own hands" and that is itself illegal. In Medieval Britain this was not true. The administration of law was not confined to a single government which stood at the center of the nation, but was divided up and parcelled out among great lords, cities, the church, and the gilds. Our modern gilds, fraternities, labor unions, churches and societies have their own rules and their own officers but they are not permitted to usurp the legal functions of the government. In consequence it is a question whether any private society may in the true sense of the word be said to have *laws,* and therefore to have a jurisprudence. We are discussing that question in Freemasonry now and until the discussion reaches a conclusion we can use the word "law" in Masonry with quotation marks around it, shown or implied; and we can define Masonic Jurisprudence as its own system of rules and regulations.

If this be allowed to be a correct definition we can state categorically that Masonic Jurisprudence is as old as Freemasonry itself because in its Operative Period the Fraternity had a complete system of Landmarks and rules and regulations; we can state with equal certainty that this jurisprudence was transmitted in its fundamentals with remarkably few changes; and to this we can add the fact that in the Operative Period Freemasonic rules and regulations were laws in the correct sense, because, under authority delegated by the King's government at that time, the Masonic Fraternity could impose such penalties on its own members as fines, suspension from work, or expulsion from the Craft, the last-named being a very severe penalty because it banished a Craftsman from his own world and took from him his means of livelihood.

If we take it that the Fraternity began in the Twelfth Century (the date is approximate) and that Lodges did not write down their own rules and regulations until the middle of the Fourteenth Century, the question arises as to how the Fraternity had preserved its rules and regulations during the two centuries before. The answer is, that it was by means of oral transmission.

Oral transmission was a remarkable system, and until writing came into common use, was the only system used by peoples to preserve their own chronicles and records—it was a learned profession, as much as history and authorships are now; in respect of some of its uses oral transmission was less reliable than our own system of written records and documents, in other of its uses it was more reliable, because where we now have thousands of records and thousands of men to keep them, peoples using oral transmission had only one record, and the many chroniclers had to use the same record.

Possibly the most complete records now existing of any one peoples' system of oral transmission are of Ireland. Before Christianity was brought in from Europe (not from England) by the missionaries, and when Druidism was the religion of the country, the Druids kept at the court of each king or chieftain an officer called an *ollave* whose duty it was to learn by heart the laws, the history, and the songs of the tribe, and it was worth his life to forget any of them. Under Christianity this officer was retained, but he came to be called poet instead of ollave. These poets were organized as a gild: they had their titles, officers, and ranks, and took apprentices. In the early period it took a poet twelve years to master his craft and to learn the record; by the Sixteenth Century it took him twenty years. Generation after generation these ollaves and poets preserved, in a letter-perfect form, the old chronicles, laws, and songs.

The Irish System was but a more complete and perfected form of the same system that was used everywhere else. The Operative Freemasons themselves used it, and their use of it was one of the origins of the Ritual; and it explains why it was that the authors of the first copies of the *Old Charges* in the Fourteenth Century could be so confident to believe that the rules and regulations which they wrote into the document had come down from far earlier times. Our own rules and regulations are, the body of them (and after being adapted to new uses, and rewritten in modern form), substantially the same as those written into the *Old Charges*. Our own Jurisprudence is, to repeat, very old; and it is our loss that we do not love it the more and have more emotion for it *because* it is very old; for our prejudice against the past, because it *is* the past, is a piece of stupidity, and our fear lest we be gripped by "the dead hand of the past" is a piece of superstition—loving the past has nothing to do with slavery to the past!

Socrates once raised the question "whether the soul is a simple substance" (as water is) or whether it was a compound of many things of different kinds. If Socrates could be here to examine Freemasonry he would not find any need to ask that question about it; he could see at a glance that it is a compound in which are many elements or constituents, of different kinds and sorts. Among these constituents is a kind composed of rules and regulations, which belong to Freemasonry as much as the Degrees and the symbols and Lodges belong to it; jurisprudence separates out those constituents which are concerned with rules, observes them, studies them, and seeks to know and to understand them; but it is not something external to Freemasonry because its subjects belong to what Freemasonry is; therefore a knowledge of jurisprudence is a knowledge of Freemasonry itself, a way of explaining or describing one of the things which it is; our jurisprudence is not *about* our rules and regulations, it *is* our rules and regulations.

This description of our jurisprudence is also a description of our Ancient Landmarks, which are its foundations. Among the many things which constitute Freemasonry are a number of things so fundamental to it that if they, or any one of them, are destroyed Freemasonry itself is destroyed; such fundamentals are the Ancient Landmarks. How discover them? By observation, by reasoning, by experience, and analysis.

Next after them come Constitutions and constitutional laws. The Landmarks show us what Freemasonry is, in one fundamental after another; constitutional law gives us the means to organize those fundamentals, to put them into practice, to implement them. A Landmark tells us that we cannot have Freemasonry unless we have a Lodge, constitutional law gives us the power and the agencies to erect a Lodge. Another Landmark says that we must confer three Degrees; constitutional law gives us a set of Installed Officers with which to confer them. It goes on then from one Landmark to another; for each Landmark that we find, constitutional law gives us the means to put it into effect.

Next after constitutional laws comes a large body of statutes, general rules, decisions, and edicts which may be denominated General Laws because their generality is their chief characteristic, since they are general in kind and have a general application, and apply equally to Lodges and Lodge members everywhere in a Grand Jurisdiction. In the Landmarks we have the fundamentals of which Freemasonry consists, as those fundamentals are seen in the eyes of jurisprudence; in constitutional laws we have the means or implementation by which Grand Lodges and Lodges are brought into existence as the means to make Freemasonry effective; once these Lodges and Grand Lodges are in existence they begin their work, and this work takes the form of activities of many kinds; General Laws are the rules by which these activities are separately and individually regulated.

Inside this large field of General Law is a field which may be best described as Lodge Law. A Lodge is a legislative and a judicial body; it has rules of its own in its written By-laws; it conducts trials, it collects dues; it elects and installs officers; a number of the Landmarks belong to it exclusively; it has within its own jurisdiction a privacy of its own, and within its own sphere a complete sovereignty; moreover it can, within that sphere and jurisdiction, act in its own name and with *original* authority, because unlike local bodies in many other fraternities and societies it is not a mere organ or agent for some authority outside itself. There is, therefore, such a thing as Lodge Jurisprudence; it is not as large in scope as the jurisprudence of the General Masonic Laws, still less does it have the sweep of the Landmarks, which are laws for the World Fraternity; but within its own sphere it is as fundamental and as sovereign.

In the Autumn of 1946 A.D., President (and Brother) Harry S. Truman proclaimed officially to the world that the United States had annexed a vast new territory which had added 700,000 square miles to our public domain. Professor Harold F. Clark and George T. Renner, who wrote a work on this proclamation, declared it to be one of the most epoch-making events since the discovery of the Continent by Columbus in 1492 A.D. This new territory consists of ocean bed lying as a strip around the coast of the United States and of its possessions, extending so many rods from the coast-line. But where is the coast-line? The margin where land and water meet is a shifting one, always advancing and retreating, and the two historians of the proclamation predicted that in hundreds of courts, and in the heads of thousands of lawyers, and for generations to come, that question as to where is the coast-line would be rising continually.

A student of Masonic Jurisprudence has that same question thrust upon him at every point in his studies. That Jurisprudence is only a part of Freemasonry; therefore there are other parts; where is the line between them and Jurisprudence to be drawn? The best of our authorities (jurisconsults) have never found any better answer than to say that it is a changing coast-line; it would be more convenient if we could draw the line hard and fast but we cannot, and we must do the best we can with it, and they remind us that this uncertainty in the outer boundaries of our Jurisprudence is one of the explanations of that variety in law and in laws from one Grand Jurisdiction to another which has perplexed so many Masons. Nevertheless these perplexed Masons can simplify their own particular problem to at least an appreciable degree if they will note that Masonic Jurisprudence is never to be confused with Masonic Parliamentary Law, or with Masonic Etiquette, or with Masonic traditions, usages, and customs.

CHAPTER XVII

## Masonic Parliamentary Law

WHEN THE MATHEMATICIAN DE MORGAN set out to collect the paradoxes of mathematics his first plan was to publish them in a booklet or possibly in a brochure, but by the time he had finished he filled two large volumes and only wished that he had more to use. If a Masonic author were to collect the paradoxes *in* Masonic Parliamentary Law he would have a similar experience. A paradox is anything which in appearance cannot be true, and yet which is true. Our Parliamentary Law is one of the largest of Masonic subjects and is equal in importance to Lodges, Constitutions, Landmarks, and Ritual yet only a handful of books have ever been written about it; they have been small in size, meager in content, and hard to find—even Mackey's work, the one classic among them, is out of print at the time of writing (but doubtless will be republished). Why is it that on a subject so large our literature is so silent? It is a paradox.

Any Mason, and especially any Worshipful Master (who must continually use it), will take that law to be little more than a set of club rules if he glances at it superficially, yet in almost every Masonic case thus far tried in the civil courts the judges have raised the question of our Parliamentary Law first, and before going into the evidence, because few things in Masonry are more important in the eyes of Civil Courts. In Lodge and Grand Lodge Communications nothing done is official, legal, or binding unless it is done according to Parliamentary Law, yet the phrase is seldom mentioned and it is never taught in Lodges and Grand Lodges. Through one of those oversights which are found in the oldest and largest of governmental systems of every sort, they have no Office of Parliamentarian—they do not even have an expert Parliamentarian as does the National Congress.

Our Parliamentary Law is a mirror of our history. In detail that law consists of a rule here and a usage there, almost any one of them short enough to be stated in a phrase, yet each one of these details is a crystallization of a whole chapter of history; a paleontologist can construct a whole dinosaur out of a fragment of its jaw, similarly an expert in historical research could re-write the anatomy of our Craft history out of our Parliamentary rules; Parliamentary Law is thus a major theme for our historians, yet when the writer of this paragraph reviewed the tables of contents of a complete collection of Masonic histories he could not find a chapter and scarcely a page on the subject, and this is one of the greatest of the paradoxes!

Even the name of this system by which bodies of Masons must regulate their actions is an etymologic puzzle, and apparently is in contradiction with itself; for a Lodge is not a parliament, or even similar to one, and that which is called "Law" is not law but only a set of rules; nevertheless Lodges, as well as parliaments themselves, must observe parliamentary practices, and the rules, though they are nothing but rules, and are private to Freemasonry itself, are enforced by Freemasonry in obedience to the demands and commands of the civil laws of the state.

The rules themselves, as already said, are short and are simple, are in their form almost trifling, and in their use escape attention. Yet in their purpose and effect they are Freemasonry's only guarantee that in its Lodges and Grand Lodges the greatest purposes can be secured. It is they which uphold justice, establish equity, maintain peace and harmony, protect the right (and rights also) and protect against wrongs, and alone make a Lodge regular, legal, just, lawful, orderly, and civilized, so that without them no Lodge could continue to exist as long as six months. This contrast of Parliamentary Laws in their size and appearance with the work effected by them is amazing—as amazing as the lack of attention which they have received; and when any Mason finds and realizes this for himself he discovers himself in possession of an emotional paradox. He has come upon a Cinderella in the House of Masonry, and if he feels an impulse to help her hunt for her glass slipper he ought to do it; there is a Prince close at hand and his coach is not made out of a pumpkin.

Also there is the paradox that when set forth or stated in its abstract and verbal form Masonic Parliamentary Law is as dry as flour, and as colorless, yet whenever it is at issue in any practice or action it is exciting, provocative, and full of electric shocks. This is an old secret of the arts and sciences. A text on geometry or a hand-book on mechanics can be as dull, and dreary, and full of drudgery as counting the grains of sand in a sand pile, yet in its actual use geometry is full of inspiring and satisfying emotion, and few things are less dull or more filled with motion and excitement than the actual use of machines. This ancient secret has always been known to masters and experts; they are willing to put in seven dry years of drudgery because there is no other road to glory and surprise—the rock gushes water, and the bare branch bursts into bloom. So is it with our Masonic Parliamentary Law; when it stands by itself it stands unnoted, there is no man to desire it, but if a Mason will read his own Grand Lodge Proceedings, especially the Foreign Correspondence Reports in them which are forms of discussion and debate, he will find that same apparently inert Law at the center of things where issues are fought out and Lodge fires burn.

Parliamentary Law is the art of correct procedure. Lodges and Grand Lodges are governed by its rules in the form, time and manner in which many things are done, such as: when, where, to whom, and in what form to make application; how to conduct discussion and debate; how to make motions, or to amend them; the order in which the items of business may be taken up; opening and closing of Lodges; to what Officer a thing may be referred; procedure in reprimand, trials, hearings; the conduct of Committee meetings; the form of Lodge Minutes; Formal Secretarial usages; how to call on or call off; the appointment and announcement of Committees; functions of presiding officers; the use of waivers; the giving, discussion, and disposal of reports; the when and where of actions of a certain kind; the manner of balloting; the forms used in suspensions and reinstatements; forms used in demissions and affiliations; the privileges of the floor; prerogatives and precedence. These, and a hundred other instances, in any given case consist wholly, or in part, of some rule of Parliamentary Law, or some point of it may have a determining or governing function.

An adequate and self-consistent definition of Masonic Parliamentary Law may be stated in a sentence: It is a set or system of rules adopted by a Lodge, or Grand Lodge, in order that its activities may conform to the Civil Law—where by "Civil Law" is meant the laws of its State or the Nation.

A man does not become a Mason lightly or casually. His becoming a member is an act of self-commitment. It costs him money, possibly as much as he earns in two weeks or a month, and it costs him also both time and labor. Freemasonry is an ancient organization with a place of its own in the world which is both known and recognized; its name is not a meaningless label but a descriptive term, and the mere fact that a man is a Mason tells other men many things about him. When as a Petitioner he is examined by a Committee of Investigation, that Committee's first step is to ascertain whether he brings to the Fraternity a good reputation and a sound character, because the Fraternity is entrusting its own good name to his keeping; but at the same time, and by a reciprocal implication he is entrusting his own good name *to it*. If his Lodge falls into disgrace he is disgraced. If he continues to be and to work in the Lodge year after year he invests much of himself in it, as well as his time and his money; he is entitled to have that investment protected against waste or loss. His dues and his endeavors give him no title to any portion of the Lodge's property but no Lodge could have or acquire property without the dues and endeavors of its members. A man's happiness, pleasure, serenity, peace, friendship, and good will, in a Lodge as everywhere else, are of a higher worth than money or property—what can a Lodge mean to a man if they take such things away from him? He himself, inwardly and for the sake of his own spirit, has as much at stake in the order and harmony of the Lodge as the Lodge itself; it is bad if the members fail the

Lodge, it is equally bad if a Lodge fails its members. If one member acts unlawfully when in Lodge, other members ought not to be penalized. In a Lodge as much as at home, or in church, or at work, or anywhere else a man may be slandered, traduced, libeled, affronted, or mocked, and if he has the right to look to the civil law for protection against such evils elsewhere he has the same right to look to it when in Lodge. A Lodge is a private society into which only its own members may come; it convenes behind locked and guarded doors; even the officers of the law cannot enter it while it is in tiled session because their entrance automatically closes it; yet the law is operative in the Lodge, and Parliamentary rules and safeguards are designed to make sure that nothing is done unlawfully where policemen are not present.

This philosophy of the function of Parliamentary Law in the experiences of any one member can be made both luminous and vivid if we suppose an extreme case—an extreme one and yet not impossible, because it has actually occurred more than once. A group of men in a Lodge Room engage in a quarrel; during the quarrel damage is done either to some of the men or to the property; there has been a breach of the peace; and it is carried into the courts. (A docket of Masonic cases in the United States, Canada, Britain, and Europe will show that during the past two centuries cases of this sort have been heard many times.) The first question for the court to decide is a question of Parliamentary Law: Was the Lodge Open at the time or was it not? If the Lodge was Open then the Lodge as a body is the defendant, and if found guilty the Lodge as a body is penalized. But if the Lodge was not Open then the men involved were individually responsible, and they, not the Lodge, must, if guilty, suffer the penalty. It would be difficult to show more clearly how a Parliamentary rule, small and insignificant in itself, may be charged with a large and even a portentous significance; such a rule may not mean each time that a Lodge member is answerable immediately to the Civil Law; he may be answerable to his Lodge, or his Master, or the Grand Lodge, or the Grand Master; nevertheless what he is answerable for, and answerable to whom, always somewhere involves the point or the question of lawfulness, if not directly, then by implication.

This comes home to a Worshipful Master with more weight than to any other member of a Lodge. He is presiding officer, judge, administrator, executive, spokesman; his actions and decisions carry weight; they may involve his whole Lodge or they may deeply affect some one member. What if he makes a mistake? What if disaster is the consequence of his acting or failing to act? To what, and to whom, and in what capacity is he answerable? If while making the decision or taking the action he was acting strictly according to the correct procedure of Parliamentary Law then he is answerable in his capacity as a Worshipful Master, in which case his responsibility is formal, or else the Lodge through him is answerable as a body, in which case its answerableness also is formal. But if when taking the unhappy or disastrous action the Master was acting outside of Masonic Parliamentary Law then neither the office of Master, nor any members, nor the Lodge is answerable; the Master is answerable personally, as a man, in his private capacity. It is not Brother A. B., The Worshipful Master who has done it, but Mr. A. B., the man—so great and so decisive is the action of Parliamentary Law wherever it is the point at issue. Nor does the case in a Masonic Lodge exaggerate the point; if when the Senate of the United States acts on a bill it acts in contravention of its own parliamentary rules the bill is officially null and void, for the Senate, as much as any citizen, must act lawfully when it acts.

There is a secret about the secrets of Freemasonry, and every experienced Mason knows what it is: It is that the secrets are of many kinds, and the kind which a Mason encounters depends on where he is at work, on what task he has elected for himself, on what his own interest is. One of those which a student of Freemasonry comes upon, and which gives so much charm to his studies, is the secret that *almost nothing in the Craft is what it seems*—where by "seems" is meant what things appear to be at a rapid or at a casual glance. Parliamentary Law is itself a great case in point, and it is for that reason that we have so many paradoxes about it; but if anything in the whole scope of Freemasonry, and especially among the things which bulk large in it, is not what it seems, it is that portion of a Lodge Communication which is called The Regular Order of Business.

The name itself is one of great peculiarity because a Lodge does not buy or sell anything and therefore is not in business; but if we let that peculiarity pass, and continue to employ the word, we shall have to admit that where business is everywhere else carried on in offices, stores, and behind counters with each man in it employed at some specialized task, "Business" of a Lodge is *conducted on the floor,* in the open, and every man present may take a part in it. The fact throws a new light on what a "discussion" is, at least in a Masonic Lodge, for while elsewhere a discussion may be a free and informal conversation in which everybody converses on the same subject or the same question in order to pool their thoughts, ideas, and theories, "discussion" in a Lodge is something wholly otherwise; it is, in almost literal fact, a "business," not a round-table for talk, and the purpose of it is not to have debate and speeches but *to get things done.* Furthermore, and here again "discussion" in Lodge differs from discussion elsewhere, it is not free and informal but is formal and goes according to a schedule; and those who take part in it do so not as conversationalists but as members and officers. We ought to be able to say, and without misunderstanding, "by Officers," because Lodge membership is an Office, carries its own title ("Brother"), and has its own powers, prerogatives, rights and privileges. In the "discussion" these Officers (including members) make motions, amend motions, make decisions, rescind previous action, vote, make reports, receive reports, act upon reports, listen to Minutes and correspondence, introduce resolutions; in so doing they are *taking action,* and in their taking action, the Lodge is taking action, therefore it is not an exaggeration to describe discussion on the floor as a form of "business." And since this is true we come around once again to see both the role and the importance of Parliamentary Law, because the largest single body of rules in it are the rules which regulate discussion on the floor for the purpose of making sure that the

Lodge's business, its actions and decisions, shall be official and lawful.

In its own inner reality and in its principle law is everywhere and always. "Thou shall not destroy another." If that which a man is in, that which he does, or what he works in, is such that it gives him the means and incentive to destroy others, or there is in it the danger that he may destroy others, it is said that the law is "in" such a thing. When a government finds the law thus to be "in" something which its citizens are doing, it "declares" the fact, and the various declarations are called "laws." Once it has made such declarations the government has its own officers use force to make sure that citizens do not act unlawfully. There are many kinds of such declarations of the law but the many kinds have as one characteristic in common the fact that the law applies regardless of *where* a citizen acts, or *when* he acts. "The law is ubiquitous and everlasting." It cannot be shut out. Its writs run, its voice is heard, its prescriptions hold in solitude, in the privacy of the home, inside the locked office, inside the cells of the jail, in church, as much as on the streets—there is no such thing as public law, or social law, or individual law; it is always nothing more or less than the law, and it comes home to a man wherever the man is.

It comes home to a man while he is sitting inside a Lodge Room, during a Communication, behind closed doors, as much as it does anywhere. Therefore no Lodge can keep itself secret from the law, nor does any Lodge either attempt or desire to do so; on the contrary each and every Lodge is always making sure, with a never-tiring vigilance, that it permits nothing unlawful to be said or done in any of its assemblies, not only nothing Masonically unlawful but also nothing which may be in violation of the civil law. But neither the City nor the State can send its policemen or its sheriffs to police a Lodge when it is in session, therefore the Lodge polices itself, and Masonic Parliamentary Law is the principal means by which it does so.

*Part Four*
MORE ABOUT MASONRY

CHAPTER XVIII

## *Masonry and History*

WHERE DOES HISTORY COME IN? What use does a man make of it in his daily affairs? It comes in everywhere, and he must make use of it continually, and not one man, woman, or child in the world could evade it, or avoid it, or do without it, because history is the name for one of the kinds of things of which the world is made, and it is a kind to which belong uncountable things, men, events, occurrences and activities. To try to escape from it would be like trying to escape out of space or from the law of gravitation. Millions of men start work every morning on something which they began yesterday, or last week, or last month—to pick up today where you left off yesterday, that is history. When we begin to make acquaintance with a man our first inquiry always is, "who is he?" which is to say, "Tell me about his past," and we ask for this history of him because without it we could neither know nor understand him as he now is. When a boy studies any subject in school it has a *beginning;* the end of it may be ten years away, but he must keep hold of that beginning even when he approaches the end, and when he is doing calculus or is writing his thesis for a Ph.D. he still clings to the alphabet and the tables of addition and subtraction and the forming of letters in writing because each and every study in the curriculum has a history in itself. The answer to half the questions we ask contain facts about the past—he did this a year ago; or our town decided on that twenty years ago; or this is because of what they did six months ago, etc. The greater number of things which exist or live do not come into life or existence and then leave it all in a minute, but persist, endure, last, day after day, or year after year; and not many things which occur are over as soon as they begin but need time to occur in. A war may take four years to occur in, or, as was true of two European wars, thirty years or one hundred years. If something going on now has been going on for years or for generations it is impossible to understand it now without knowledge of its past. It is this going on through a period of time, this having to know the past in order to work with the present, this fact that almost all the important things last and remain active over periods of time, that we mean by the word history. If through illness or an accident a man loses possession of his own history he becomes helpless; he is, as we say, suffering from amnesia. If the men who hate history or find it too difficult to understand could have it ignored, as Henry Ford once recommended, we might as a whole people fall ill with amnesia; a woman could starve to death in her own kitchen because she did not remember her way to the refrigerator.

Among the things which thus continue to go on year after year, and which we are unable to deal with unless we know their past, there are a number which belong to us as a people; which affect us as a people, and which we must know and understand and deal with as a people; most of them are very large things, many of them are great things, a few of them are of a life-and-death importance to us. They are so important to us as a people, and they are so necessary to each man in his daily life, that we make written records of them and teach these records to our sons and daughters in school. We do not put them through these hard drills of memory and ordeals of understanding because we are obsessed by a love or romantic passion for the past, or because we believe that the past was better than the present, or for any other reasons equally futile, but for the sake of the present; we know how often they are helpless to take action today unless they understand what occurred a century ago. History has to do with the here and now; it is contemporaneous; it is not interested in the past for the past's sake, but for the sake of the present, why do we have a Monroe Doctrine? Why do we not have free trade? Why did we choose to enter World War I? Why were we forced into World War II? Why do we maintain and pay for forty-eight governments instead of only one? Why is our religion inherently denominational? Was the Constitution adopted "way back" in 1787 A.D. or is it adopted anew each day? Why have political parties? Why do we have so many strikes? Why so much crime? We and the world together are so made that many of the affairs with which we must cope are very old affairs; we may begin something today but they may still be working at it a century from today. What is history? Suppose a man does not like it? Suppose that he would endeavor to stop it? What good would it do him, and how would he do it? If a man were caught by his neighbor trying to stop the sun from rising would not that man blush? If a man says, "History is bunk" ought he not similarly to blush, and for a like reason? and ought we not blush for him?

A number of the acts, decisions, events, and ways belonging to us as a people and which in themselves are a part of the historical process, are so large, and complex, and difficult that few of us have either the time or the means to know and understand them for ourselves, nor can we find other men among our associates able to give us that knowledge orally; we have therefore set up and set aside a profession devoted to history, and we have told off and trained (at the taxpayer's expense) a certain number of men (not a large number) to practice that profession. Only a minute fraction of history comes within their profession; and any one of them can know only a much smaller fraction, and when he teaches his students in college or writes his books he can put into either one a fraction even yet smaller; but like the mysterious materials which are put into an atomic bomb, and which also come in fractional amounts, the professional historian's own fraction of history carries a tremendous potential power, and its use is always fateful to a people, and it may under some circumstances be as hugely explosive as salts of Uranium which obliterated a whole city at one stroke. Woe to a people which trifles with history! The Nazis who trifled with German history, and taught the German people such brazen great lies about that history, discovered in 1945 A.D. how deep and how agonizing that woe can be.

Men in the other professions and arts are free with their materials and have much power over them. A musician can make and unmake his compositions to suit himself. A poet has the liberty of a bird, and has the whole of the English language to move about in at will. A sculptor can carve his block into whatever shape he pleases. An architect can make his choice among many styles and select for himself any one of uncountable details of ornamentation. An orator chooses his own subject and writes his own speech. They can be as original, and as individual, and as free as they may desire to be. In comparison with them an historian is a man of vast meekness, and of almost infinite helplessness. "Not even heaven o'er the past has power." He cannot so much as lay a finger on his own materials. It does not even belong to him. He cannot touch a hair on George Washington's head. He cannot make Caesar change his date for crossing the Rubicon. He cannot tell Genghis Khan which gate of the Great Wall to attack. If Rome fell, he can do nothing about it. If an event occurred yesterday he is no more able to alter it than he is to unbuild the Pyramids. And it is the great paradox of his profession that he not only cannot alter any event in the past but he goes to the extreme length of caution to make sure that he does not even appear to have altered it. His facts are sacred to him. And if he drudges, toils, sweats, labors, groans, and reads himself blind it is also because he is determined to know what actually did occur, and to make sure that what occurred will not be misreported. If a man finds a chapter in the history of his own people hard and painful to read he is not to cast the blame on the historian; *he* did not cause those facts to occur, and if they are hard or painful in his report of them it is because he had to report what he found; and he knows that if his fellow historians catch him trying to misrepresent events, or to twist his reports of them to please some party or interest, they hold him in contempt and read him out of the Republic of Letters.

If history is a process or kind of activity which is everlastingly going on and is a part of the world, and if it is among many other processes or activities of other kinds, it follows that there may be more of history in one kind of activity (or subject) than in another. Is it possible to devise a measuring rod by which to measure the amount of history in any given subject? There have been many in use, but possibly the simplest of them (and therefore in this place the most convenient) was the one used by Plato. To mark one end of the scale take any one or more of those things or activities which have no history in them, which means that they are unaffected by time, that no change takes place within them, and that they are not affected by changes around them. Plato himself made up a long list of these historyless realities in the world, among them being such things as time, space, mathematics, and those inviolable regularities which our fathers described as "the laws of nature." The opposite end of the scale can be marked by war, which is so completely historical in its nature that every battle in it and almost every day in it is recorded, and remembered, and the reasons for doing so are so urgent that modern armies carry their own historians into battle with them.

We can now ask ourselves the question, "where does Freemasonry stand in this scale?" The answer is that in respect of the amount of history in it it stands closer to history than to abstractions. It is almost pure history; it is as if it were a body of history come to life; so true is this that if the whole content of Freemasonry were to be divided into 200 subjects—the number is not exact but neither is it wholly guesswork—not one of them could be known and understood, at least not wholly so, except by history. The Fraternity is one of the most remarkable things in the whole world; because it is, almost every fact about it is a remarkable fact; but few of them are more remarkable, and none of them is more important, than this fact that the Fraternity is living history.

To describe or explain Freemasonry, or any particular thing in it, without a full knowledge and understanding of Masonic history would be as impossible as to attempt to explain geometry without lines, angles, circles, triangles, curves; the attempt to explain it without any reference to its history, as if its meaning could be made up by a man in his own head, is folly. It does not consist of something in any man's head but originated and developed out of external events; it did not arrive where it now is from any man's head but from the past; that past occurred in the actual and external world, was never composed of anybody's private thoughts and theories, and no man by shutting his eyes and by fabricating thoughts in his own mind can unmake that past, or alter it; he can only accept it as he finds it. Freemasonry is not theoretical but is historical.

In order to crowd much into little space we can picture the Fraternity as being a ship—though such pictures are always misleading. This ship was built by a set of master shipwrights eight or nine centuries ago. It has moved, along a route chosen by itself, and at its own speed, down from one century to another, in a voyage as long as from here to the moon; it has not yet sighted its last landfall, nor is it likely to do so for generations to come, because it has proved itself worthy to sail through any storm and on any sea. Much can happen inside a ship; work, eating, sleeping, births, illnesses, deaths, talk, and many other things; much may happen to it, from the outside, and especially if it calls at many ports.

The whole of Masonic history, whether we think of it as consisting of numberless events of an historical kind, or as written records or descriptions of those events, can therefore be divided into two large fields. One of them is Freemasonry's *internal history*, the events which have occurred within it, the movements and charges and occurrences inside Lodges and Grand Lodges and behind tiled doors. The other field is Freemasonry's *external history*, in which are such events and occurrences as have acted upon it from without, have affected it or effected it. The two fields belong to a single indivisible whole, they interact and overlap, but they are nevertheless well defined, and one of them is useless without the other. The story of the Three Degrees, the erection of the Grand Lodge System, the establishment of the High Grades, these belong to its internal history, and are instances of hundreds of other particular subjects; the story of architecture in general and of the Gothic Style especially, of the gild system, of the Liberal Arts and Sciences, of public education, these are instances of its external history. A knowledge and understanding of Masonic history must include both.

In spite of its being unchanged with history, and for all of the years it had behind it, the Fraternity was very slow and very late in finding its own professional historians, partly because for a long period Grand Lodges exercised a censorship over Masonic writings, partly because there were so few documents and other written records for historians to use, partly because the Fraternity had no way to pay historians. Until the middle of the Nineteenth Century Masons had nothing to read except the "historical introduction" of the Book of Constitutions of 1723 A.D. which was not historical, William Preston's *Illustrations* and William Hutchinson's *Spirit of Masonry* neither of which had any value as history except for the period in which they were written, and the Rev. George Oliver, whose "historical" writings were a cloudland of guesses.

Masonic historical scholarship worthy to be so called began with J. O. Halliwell's publication of the *Regius MS.* in 1838 A.D.; then, in the 1870's and 1880's, almost without warning, there came suddenly on the scene a race of giants; Gould, Hughan, Crawley, Lyon, Speth, Sadler, Rylands, Begemann, Thorp, etc., and along with them came the Quatuor Coronati Lodge of Research, the *Ars Quatuor Coronatorum* which is an Encyclopedia Britannica of historical studies. These were British; in the United States we have had Mackey, Pike, Macoy, McClenachan, Fort, Stillson, Clegg, Robertson, Newton, Pound, etc., etc., and if American Grand Lodges continue to constitute Lodges of Research as they are now beginning to do our own best historical writing may lie in the not too-distant future.

CHAPTER XIX

# *High Grades I*

(Chapter Council & Commandery)

"THE HIGH GRADES" is a name which long ago was given to the Degrees conferred in the Royal Arch, in Cryptic Masonry, in Knight Templarism, and in the Scottish Rite. The name has never been universally satisfactory but neither has any one of the other names proposed to take its place, among them being The Concordant Orders, the Auxiliary Rites, The Appendant Rites, The Additional Grades. The word "high" has in it a sense of being above, being superior to, and a certain amount of encouragement was given to that sense when in one of its lectures the Fellowcraft Degree depicts the three Degrees of Apprentice, Fellowcraft, and Master Mason in the form of three steps in a stair; if this picture were carried farther it would mean that the Fourth Degree is superior to the Third, the Fifth superior to the Fourth, etc.; but this simple arithmetical scheme cannot work because, first, no Grand Body in any of the four Rites of the High Grades is superior to a Grand Lodge, and, second, because there are *two* series using the same number after the Third Degree, one through the Royal Arch, the Council and Knight Templar, the other through the Scottish Rite. The Masons who fathered the High Grades and the Masons since who have most loved them and best understood them have always used "high" in another sense, and are carrying no suggestion that the High Grades are "above" or "superior to" the Three Degrees in the Lodge; in them it has meant that Ancient Craft Freemasonry has always had a rich and a very complex content, that among the elements in it a certain number were the best or highest, or noblest, or profoundest, and that each of the High Grades is an elaboration, or exposition, or interpretation of some one of these elements;

## High Grades I

to them therefore the subject matter of all the High Grades is contained in Ancient Craft Masonry. This explanation comes closest to the facts, and it has the great advantage of enabling us to picture the whole of Freemasonry as being single and individual, and protects us from the mistake of picturing the Fraternity as a loose collection of five independent Freemasonries. This is a better definition than the arithmetical one (after all each Degree is properly known by *name*, not by number) but even so it is not wholly satisfactory. It is probable that the easiest course to follow is not to use "High Grades" (or any other name) as either a term or a name but as a label, and merely for the purpose of roughly denoting a large number of different things and facts; it also is probable that nomenclature will never find a wholly satisfactory name, and that Masonic scholars will never be able to find a rigidly correct, adequate, and self-consistent definition for any name— ("Further Degrees," has been suggested) —the subject would overflow the definition.

A Masonic historian has a wholly different way of accounting for the origin of the High Grades and of explaining their role, or place, in the general field of Masonry. In the very beginning Operative Masonry had in it so much that was active, dynamic, growing, that it could not be diked into a single organization or captured by a single definition. Operative Freemasonry itself was but one among a number of separate organizations in the general Craft of Masonry. After it had waxed large and strong the same process began inside itself; when the first permanent Lodges were constituted many Freemasons remained outside them; after a while those permanent Lodges (using the *Old Charges*) began to expand by accepting non-Operative members, with the result that by the Seventeenth Century a number of Lodges consisted exclusively of non-Operative (Accepted, or Speculative) members; among these Lodges a new development began in 1717 A.D., with the setting up of the Grand Lodge System; and afterwards, and under the Grand Lodge leadership, another new development began when Lodges conferred three Degrees instead of two. In the meantime a number of what we should now call Side Orders grew like shoots out of the parent trunk—Masonic clubs, "Masonic Orders," "Wandering Degrees," and what for a long time were called "Masonic dilettanti"; and also in the meantime were twenty or thirty City Companies in the larger towns and cities in which Freemasons had one section of the membership. Therefore when in the second half of the Eighteenth Century a number of Royal Arch, Cryptic, Templar and Scottish Rite Degrees were formed, and when at the end of that half century those Degrees were organized into local and Grand Bodies, the historian sees in them not a new departure nor an innovation, but another overflowing of Ancient Craft Freemasonry. Nor can any historian believe that this principle of growth, this tendency to proliferate has come to an end; Freemasonry has not yet become conscious of itself as a World Fraternity, but it will do so at some unguessed date in the future; when it does so that tendency to proliferate will then produce new Masonic forms which we cannot now predict.

A Masonic philosopher would have yet another way of explaining the High Grades, and of describing their place, or role, in the Craft. Some forty-odd degrees belong to the American Masonic System of five Rites; in other countries, of which France and Sweden are conspicuous examples, yet other High Grades are in official use; this adds up, the world over, to a large number of High Grades, and it makes it impossible either to list or to number them—what, to take one case only, would be meant by "The Seventh Degree"? In the world over it would be the number used by some Masonic System for any one of ten or twelve Degrees wholly unlike each other. The Masonic philosopher does not concern himself with the *number* of them, nor is he disturbed by the size of the tableau of these High Grades; he concerns himself with the principles which various groups of these Degrees have in common. From his point of view the American System (to confine ourselves to it) is less a system of Rites than it is a group of Masonic *families*. Of these there are three; the family of Ancient Craft Freemasonry, which includes the Degrees of the Lodge, of the Cryptic Rite, and of the Royal Arch; the family of Knight Templarism; the Scottish Rite family, not including that Rites' version of the Apprentice, Fellowcraft, and Master

## High Grades I

Mason Degrees. In his eyes each of these families has a central, or fundamental, characteristic, and can be explained in the term of that characteristic. The characteristic of the Ancient Craft family is *history;* of Knight Templar Degrees, it is the idea (or principle) of a Christian *order;* of the Scottish Rite Degrees, it is philosophy (they have been called "the Masonry of the Mind").

At the present time of writing the oldest written record of the words Royal Arch is dated December 27, 1743 A.D., in the account of a Masonic procession in Yonghal Lodge, in Ireland. It is referred to again in a book published by Dr. Fifield Dassigny in 1744 A.D. The oldest known record in a Lodge Minute Book is dated December 22, 1753 A.D. in the records of Fredericksburg Lodge, The George Washington Mother Lodge, in Virginia. These and a number of other records similar to them, prove that, first, the Royal Arch was in an inchoate (or incomplete, or unorganized) condition until near the end of the Eighteenth Century; and, second, that it must have been popular among Masons or it could not have spread from Ireland, across England, and over the American Colonies in only ten years of time. The same records, however, are silent on the origin of the Degree (or Degrees); but it is probable that the Ritualistic materials which later on were separately organized in the Capitular (Royal Arch) Degrees and Chapters had been a part of the Ritualistic material and in the Masters' Lodges, the first records of which begin in 1725 A.D. In the middle of the Eighteenth Century the Royal Arch was used as a Side Order attached to Ancient Craft Lodges, but by about 1785 A.D., and afterwards the Royal Arch began to organize its own local Bodies, called Chapters, and then to organize these into Grand Chapters. The first American Grand Chapter was organized in the United States in Connecticut in 1798 A.D.; the General Grand Chapter was constituted in 1799 A.D., one year later. The esteem in which Royal Arch Masonry was held here is shown by the fact that when Thomas Smith Webb published his *Freemasons Monitor* in 1797 A.D., he signed it not in his own name but as "a Royal Arch Mason."

If the earliest known Royal Arch Masons were *in* symbolic Lodges, if the Ritualistic material belonged to the Ritual of the

Masters' Lodges, if it was conferred by many Lodges for a half century as a Side Order, if it was officially recognized by the Antient Grand Lodge, and if the two Grand Lodges in England agreed at their Union in 1813 A.D., that Royal Arch Masonry is an integral part of Ancient Craft Masonry, then it can only be so, because for some two centuries Freemasons have believed it to belong to the same family as the Three Degrees of Ancient Craft Lodges.

The Degrees conferred in a Royal Arch Chapter are (as a rule) Mark Master, Past Master, Most Excellent Master, and Royal Arch Mason. A Council of Cryptic Masons confers the Degrees of Royal Master and Select Master, and (in some Councils) of Super-excellent Master. If a student dovetails these Degrees into each other and then dovetails the Apprentice, Fellowcraft, and Master Mason Degrees into them, omitting such things as are repeated from one Degree to another, he will find before him a single body of Ritual, homogeneous in its subject-matter, its roots in Masonic history, and everywhere the same in spirit and purpose. It could almost be said that the Capitular and Cryptic Rites are a commentary in the grand style on the Three Degrees, especially of the Third Degree; and also it could almost be said that the whole family of Degrees in the three Rites could be conferred as a single Degree.

When we turn from the family of Degrees in Ancient Craft Masonry to the family of Knight Templar Degrees we find ourselves in another world of Masonry. We also find ourselves with an almost complete lack of facts or records of this Templar Family. The first mention of it in print is dated 1757 A.D. It appears to have had two centers of origin and growth, one in Europe (particularly in Germany and in France), and one in northern England. At Bristol, England, there was a Baldwyn Encampment which left behind it a written record dated in 1780 A.D., and since the document refers to "the Supreme Grand and Royal Encampment" organized Masonic Templarism must have been at work some years before that. The Grand Commandery of the United States was established in 1816 A.D. These dates show that the beginnings of Masonic Templarism were in the middle

## High Grades I

of the Eighteenth Century, and were roughly contemporaneous with the beginnings of the Royal Arch, and that the Rite was established, organized, and completed by about 1800 A.D. Since, as will be shown in a later page, the Degrees of the Scottish Rite, though possibly older, a few of them, than the Templar Degrees, were established, organized, and completed in about 1800 A.D., it means that the four Rites of High Grades were in their origin contemporaneous with each other.

At a date which may be represented by the year 1750 A.D., and during the period from that date to about 1800 A.D., we thus have a remarkable series of Masonic historical facts: The Lodges adopted three Degrees in place of two; the Antient and Modern Grand Lodges drew together in fraternal amity and practiced the same Masonry; a system of the Standard Monitor was incorporated in the Ritual; Lodges and independent Grand Lodges were planted around the world; the families of the High Grades were established and officially adopted; the Craft became a World Fraternity instead of an Anglo-Saxon or European Fraternity; the combinations of facts such as these prove that in that half-century a ground-swell moved powerfully among the sources of Freemasonry, which may be most simply described as being the Craft's preparation of itself to become a permanent World Fraternity. The greatly significant fact about Masonic Templarism is that it was one of the new forms of Freemasonry which were brought into existence by that ground-swell.

1.—By a "Knight" the early Middle Ages (possibly about 1000 A.D.) meant a professional soldier. Other crafts, arts, and professions already had been professionalized and organized into gilds. Knighthood was the soldiers' gild. It took in apprentices, gave them a severe and exacting training for many years, and then, if they were proved proficient, they were made fellows of their gild—it was a ceremony called "dubbing." Their rules and regulations were called Knighthood.

2.—For generations the Catholic Church coveted Palestine for religious reasons, and European merchants were under a great pressure to extend their trading posts and routes into the Eastern Mediterranean as far south as Egypt, but nothing came of either because Europe was divided into hundreds of small kingdoms, colonies, duchies, and free cities, and while each of these had its own corps of professional soldiers no one of them could put into the field either an army or a navy of sufficient size to be effective. Pope Urban conceived the brilliant idea of forming an army under the immediate command of himself, with each of the small nations contributing a quota, and the church adopted his plan at the Council of Clermont. Each of the quotas was to be under its own command except that its commanders agreed to follow a general plan, each to wear its own uniform except that it was also to wear the Church's badge, which was a red cross. The quotas together were the crusaders; their war upon the Mohamedan people in the Near East was called a crusade. From the first crusade in 1096 A.D., and thereafter for some 200 years the crusaders fought countless battles on land and water, won many victories and suffered many defeats; and though they failed in the end neither Europe nor Asia was ever the same afterwards. One of the roots in Knight Templar Ritual goes back to those crusades.

2.—While the crusades were under way, and in a manner strikingly like modern specialized armies, the crusaders formed among themselves, either on the Pope's insistence or with his official consent and approval, a number of separate and specialized armies which were trained and equipped for special purposes, and had their own independent organizations; among these the most important were those called Knights of the Temple, Knights of the Hospital, and the Teutonic Knights. Among these the Templars became the richest and most powerful, and had great houses and vast areas of land and almost untold money in Britain and on the continent as well as in the Near East. By the beginning of the Fourteenth Century they became too powerful, and civil government began to discuss among themselves means to curb them; but they refused to tolerate restraint, and at last the Order had to be destroyed. This abolishment was begun by Philip the Fair of France when in 1314 A.D., he burned at the stake the Order's Grand Master, Jacques de Molay, and his three principal officers. Philip's methods were criminal, and the world has never forgiven him; but the Order would have been abolished in any event, and it passed completely out of existence when Pope Clement V cancelled its charters and ordered it dissolved.

3.—Attempts were made to revive it, but they failed; and even if these attempts had succeeded the revived Order would have been illegal—each of the hard-driven peoples of Europe already carried the burden of two governments, the Church and the State; they would not tolerate a third. Another form of "revival" was, however, more successful, because they were imitative societies or fraternities which had no purpose except to perpetuate what men had most admired in the Templars. Masonic Templarism has its roots as much in these later, imitative "revivals" as in the original, and historical Order.

4.—The gilds of professional soldiers ("knighthood") were the most glamorous and romantic of any men in the Middle Ages, but it was not for that reason alone that next to the Church and to architects they made the largest and deepest impression on the Middle Ages; these soldiers also were travelers, explorers, adventurers, speakers of other languages, news-bringers from distant places, and best able to explain to stay-at-home villagers the mysteries of wages, of international politics, and diplomacy; in addition to that they also were local guardians, and that meant much at a time when there were feuds between towns, wars among dukes and earls, and no regular police forces even in the largest cities. As the generations passed there collected about these soldiers a vast amount of tradition, tales, stories, histories, poems, plays, songs, music; and at the same time the soldierly form of honor, with its attendant forms of politeness, was in time everywhere adopted and became "courtesy." This courtesy and the traditions, and the soldierly rules and regulations, came at last to form a vast body of art and culture, to which we give the general name of "chivalry." It was from this chivalry far more than from historical events or military practices that modern Masonic Templarism drew the materials of its rituals and its nomenclature.

5.—But what did the ancient art of Freemasonry, which was the art of architecture, have to do with chivalry? Until after the Third Degree and the Royal Arch were adopted and completed it could have had nothing to do with it; but once those Degrees were in use it is obvious that Freemasons began to take an interest in the Order of the Temple because it was an Order of the *Temple*—that is, Solomon's Temple. That is one of the answers to the question, "why Templarism inside the Masonic Fraternity?" The other answer is even more cogent but is not as obvious—indeed it is difficult to see. Ancient Craft Freemasonry is an Order; each Master Mason sees that it is, and he often refers to it as "The Order"; but it is doubtful if many Masons realize to the full extent what it means to Masons that their Craft is an order, how compelling is the order in it, how captivating, how much alive, and how powerful; but any Mason can realize it for himself if he will consider how a Lodge exists in the form of grades and ranks, and how hard and long a member will work to win such a rank and title as Worshipful Master. Order is one of the most living things in a Lodge; therefore the Order of the Temple also made an appeal because it was an *Order,* and a Christian Church Order.

CHAPTER XX

# High Grades II

(Scottish Rite)

WHEN WE TURN to the Ancient & Accepted Scottish Rite we once again enter a new world in Masonry with its own lands and horizons, its own skies. The historical clue to it is found in the word *European;* the clue to the interpretation of its Degrees is in the word *philosophic*. The Scottish Rite in the United States divides the nation into a Northern Jurisdiction including the States east of the Mississippi River and north of the Ohio River, and a Southern Jurisdiction including all of the other states. The Sovereign Grand Commander of the latter Jurisdiction has his seat in Washington, D.C.; of the Northern, in Boston, Massachusetts. The governing Grand Body is a Supreme Council. The two Jurisdictions differ from each other only as two Grand Lodges differ. The Rite is as a whole organized in six bodies, but the first of these called the Symbolic Lodge, and containing Apprentice, Fellowcraft, and Master Mason Degrees, is not practiced in the United States or where there are regular Grand Lodges. The Lodge of Perfection includes the Degrees from 4 to 14 inclusive; the Chapter of Rose Croix, from 15 to 18 inclusive; the Council of Kadosh, from 19 to 30 inclusive; the Consistory, includes Degrees 31 and 32; the Supreme Council confers the Thirty-third Degree. The Supreme Council of the Southern Jurisdiction is also the Mother Supreme Council of the world, and has been in continuous activity since it was constituted in Charleston, S.C., in 1801 A.D., a date which is to Scottish Rite Masonry what 1717 A.D., is to Ancient Craft Masonry.

When the first Lodges in France were constituted in the decade between 1720 A.D., and 1730 A.D., they worked under warrants from the Mother Grand Lodge at London, but they did not continue to do so for long. France and Britain had been at war, in small wars and large, for centuries (one lasted 100 years) and would continue to be until 1815 A.D., and it therefore did not sit well with French Lodge members to feel that they were subordinate to London. By another decade or two they cast loose from England, and began to set up Lodges of their own, as there was no reason why they should not, provided the Ancient Landmarks were observed, since the Grand Lodge at London had no jurisdiction over France. In Britain the new Speculative Lodges were not a new kind of Freemasonry but a new use of the Ancient Masonry. They grew up in the midst of Operative Masonry, and the first Speculative Lodges either contained many Operative members, or worked alongside Operative Lodges; therefore the Speculative Lodges did constitute a break in Masonic history, but in a form suitable to themselves, they continued to practice the ancient customs and usages, so that the Landmarks of Speculative Masonry were in literal fact *ancient* Landmarks; the thousands of new men who came into the Craft after 1717 A.D., brought no understanding of Freemasonry with them and they not infrequently tried new experiments which proved unlawful, but in due course they came to understand the Craft because they had the old Craft close at hand to teach them. When the "new men" (non-Operatives) came into Lodges in France *after* French Lodges had cut their tie with the Grand Lodges in Britain they did not have close-at-hand old Lodges and ancient customs and usages to guide or to restrain them; in consequence they indulged in a large number of experiments, created new Rites (wrote new Degrees out of hand) and at one time they had as many as 150 Degrees in operation. Many of these French Degrees were carried into other European countries; and those countries in turn (as far away as Russia) created new Rites and Degrees of their own. A number of these Degrees were in accord with the Ancient Landmarks; a number of them were legitimate elaborations of elements in the Ritual of the Ancient Craft in Britain, the homeland of Speculative Freemasonry; many were not. To step off the main highway of Masonic history, to have no official relations with the regular Grand Lodges in the English-speaking world, to

## High Grades II

experiment without restraint, these were among the characteristics of early European Freemasonry.

The widest divergence between French Masonry and the original Speculative Freemasonry in Britain, one which was not to be healed until the early Twentieth Century and then in part only, arose at the point of the aristocracy, and arose in the earliest Lodges in France. The chasm between the French aristocrat and the French commoner was wider and deeper than in any other Christian land, and since the earliest Lodges, most of them, were founded and officered by aristocrats it went against the grain to practice a Freemasonry which had been founded by workingmen, and it went still more against the grain to meet commoners on the level. A body of French Masons fathered and fostered the legend that Freemasonry had been founded by the Crusaders; they created new Degrees around emperors, kings, and princes; they made their Lodges as exclusive as possible; and they did not hesitate to use their Lodges for ecclesiastical and political purposes.

Among the many Rites and Degrees in France a number, as already said, were in conformity with the Ancient Landmarks and at the same time, like the Royal Arch, were larger or more elaborate developments of that which had long been in the Craft. In 1758 A.D., a Council of Emperors of the East and the West was organized, and it selected twenty-five of the Degrees in a system called The Rite of Perfection. This Council is said to have deputized Stephen Morin to set up Councils in the Western Hemisphere, and he said they gave him a Deputation dated 1761 A.D. (He exhibited a copy; the original was never seen by any one.) Among the Inspectors appointed by him or by his appointees, were John Mitchell and Frederick Dalcho; they established a Supreme Council in Charleston, South Carolina, in 1801 A.D.; which later transferred its seat to Washington, D.C. It was in this latter city, in 1854 A.D., that Albert Pike was elected Sovereign Grand Commander, and it was under his administration and under his august leadership, which lasted until his death in 1891 A.D., that the Rite became a Masonic World Power. He reorganized the Rite, purged it of irregularities, revised or rewrote its Degrees, wrote for its use his *Morals and Dogma*, and, as was said in a eulogy which is so often quoted, "found the Rite in a log-cabin and left it in a marble palace." It was initially from this Mother Supreme Council, and then from both it and the Northern Jurisdiction (1813 A.D.), that regular Supreme Councils throughout the world were authorized. This means that the United States is the home-land of one of the five great Rites of the Craft; it also means that the name "Ancient & Accepted Scottish Rite" can be properly used only of such Bodies as are recognized by the two American Supreme Councils.

1.—The historians of Freemasonry in the United States follow a picture of Masonic origins which has become orthodox—with few exceptions the new historian repeats in his own words the picture already drawn by his predecessors: present day American Freemasonry, so this picture goes, had its origin in the Lodges and Grand Lodges of the Colonial Period; those Bodies in turn had their own origin in Lodges and Grand Lodges in Britain; therefore American Freemasonry is in its origin not only Anglo-Saxon but is British Anglo-Saxon. In its general argument this account of our origins is sound because Speculative Freemasonry was undoubtedly of British origin. But the picture omits one of the five Rites, and therefore ceases to be a true picture; for the Scottish Rite is as integral a part of our Masonic Fraternity as is a Craft Lodge or a Royal Arch Chapter, *and its origins were in Europe!* And this is not merely one of those facts which satisfied only a curious interest; it is a fact of the first importance, and if it is overlooked there can never be either a true or an adequate history or philosophy of the Fraternity. The Anglo-Saxon mind is a great mind—no greater has ever appeared in the world; but there are many other minds in the world, and among these some four or five are its equals—the Latin mind, the Norse mind, the Teutonic mind, the Slavic mind, the Chinese mind. The historic mission of those Degrees which were organized in the Scottish Rite ("Scottish" has no reference to Scotland) was to incorporate into the Fraternity the Latin, the Teutonic, and the Norse minds. If this had not been done it is doubtful if at any time since Freemasonry ever could have become a World Masonry, just as it is

## High Grades II

doubtful, and for the same reasons, that the Anglo-Saxon mind could ever become a world mind.

2.—The early French Lodges crystallized around the idea of aristocracy—an aristocracy in the form of a caste system; in the Revolutionary period this idea was enlarged and generalized to become an aristocracy of thought, learning, talents, abilities. (The central problem of democracy is how to pay men of extraordinary ability their full wages, without granting them undemocratic privileges.) When the Rite of Perfection was transplanted to America this "idea of aristocracy" was further transformed and enlarged into the idea of "the highest to which men can attain," and since this means *any man* it is a reconciliation of the idea of a kind of aristocracy with democracy. To Albert Pike the highest attainments are the things of the mind, and in his *Morals and Dogma* the mind of man, as it is in men as thinkers, is the hero throughout his pages. This is the limitation of the Pikean vision, and in a sense it is the limitation of the Scottish Rite, because manifestly there also are "highest attainments" in the fine arts, in righteousness, in religion, and in public life. The greatest man of a people is not always the greatest thinker. There is a Masonry of the Mind, and the Scottish Rite is its prophet, and is the bearer of its message; there is a Masonry of the Heart also, and of the Conscience, and of the Masonic Community. It is only a way of saying that the Scottish Rite is not the whole of Freemasonry; that saying is not iconoclastic because it is another way of saying that Freemasonry without philosophy is unthinkable. Of the Five Masonic Rites, only the Scottish Rite is not democratic in its organization and government. Its supreme governing body, The Supreme Council is, has always been self-perpetuating, and the members do not select or have any control over it.

3.—That which most strikes the mind of a Mason or Scottish Rite Mason, is what appears to be the extraordinary contrast between the Scottish Rite and the Masonry of the Lodges in Ancient Craft Masonry. That contrast, once a Mason grasps the whole meaning and history of Freemasonry, vanishes away. A Medieval Operative Mason at work on a cathedral said to himself; "We need a large understanding of the arts and sciences to know how to design and to construct such a building as this; we must work together in harmony, and to work as a body we need a Lodge and Rules and regulations; and since we will go elsewhere to work when this building is completed we must be a Fraternity." A Scottish Rite Mason, if that Operative could have made his statement to one, would have replied: "Yes, what you say is true. But why not go a step farther and ask why the men in this country wanted a cathedral in the first place?" Men in the world of work erect buildings, build ships and railways, erect churches, hospitals, schools, and colleges, work farms, construct factories; why, in the first place, do men need such things? That question also must be asked and answered in Freemasonry's philosophy of work unless that philosophy is incomplete. Men are at work in religion; why do we need religion? They are at work in government; why do we need government? They are at work in schools; why do we need education? Men are at work on farms and in stores and in factories; why do we need them? The Thirty Degrees conferred in the five Scottish Rite Bodies are in reality nothing more than dramatizations or enacted *ideas,* which are in number possibly fifty or sixty. These ideas, without exception, are in the region of these questions. Operative Masonry was an answer to the question, *How* have architecture; Scottish Rite Masonry gives an answer to the question, *Why* have architecture. The answer to such a question can be found only by means of thought, and it is because it asks this "Why" that Scottish Rite Masonry is *philosophic* Masonry. Once we see this to be true we find ourselves in possession of the answer to another question which often perplexes Masons and Scottish Rite Masons: Why does the Scottish Rite repeat in versions of its own a number of Degrees already found in Ancient Craft Masonry, Capitular, Cryptic, and Templar Masonry? It repeats them, but it does not duplicate them; *it repeats them* with a difference, and that difference brings out of those Degrees the philosophic ideas which they contain.

CHAPTER XXI

## *Divergences*

### From the Standard Work

THE EARLIEST Operative Lodges had rites and ceremonies and a regular order of business, as we know from Fabric Rolls; and unless they were an exception to the rule, they preserved by oral transmission the history and old stories of their Craft; also we know that certain portions of their rites and ceremonies were the same in every Lodge; but as a whole the rites and ceremonies were not the same from one Lodge to another. This is shown by indirect, as well as by direct evidence; after the latter half of the Fourteenth Century, each regular *permanent* Lodge worked under a copy of the *Old Charges,* and the reading or other use of these became so firmly fixed in Lodge Work that by the time the first Grand Lodge of Speculative Masons was erected a number of portions of the *Old Charges* had become symbols in the Ritual; yet the *Old Charges* themselves were not verbally uniform from Lodge to Lodge, as we know from the many existing copies, no two of which are exact reproductions of each other.

When the Grand Lodge was constituted (1717 A.D.) there were in England and Scotland not less than 200 Lodges either wholly or in part composed of a Speculative membership; since they used a secret ritual they left no copies of it behind in print but we know from an assembling of data drawn from Lodge Minutes, Lodge histories, and from references in books and newspapers, that each Lodge was left free to use a ritual of its own; and while some portions of these rituals were the same from one Lodge to another other portions differed so much that the new Grand Lodge, which could not act except with the consent of the Lodges, was not able to secure adoption of a Uniform work; furthermore the new Grand Lodge system was as yet so incomplete and its purposes were so little understood by many local Lodges that a majority of the Lodges refused to admit that the Grand Lodge had any authority over the "working"—on two occasions its attempts to exercise authority aroused a storm of protest or rebellion. The largest change ever made in the Ritual, second only to the change which resulted when Speculative Lodges began to use the old Operative Ritual for a new purpose, was the adopting of the new Third, or Master of Masons, Degree; this new Degree was not generally or officially recognized until about 1740 A.D. but for decades afterwards a number of the Lodges continued with their old two Degrees, and among the Lodges which adopted the new Degree a number of them did so on their own terms.

The first Grand Lodge was constituted in London in 1717 A.D. After eight years other Grand Lodges were set up in Britain; one in Ireland, one at York, one "South of the River Trent," one in Scotland, and in 1751 A.D. the Antient Grand Lodge was constituted in London. Each of these Grand Jurisdictions had its own version of the Ritual, though no one of them had a uniform, official version obligatory on every one of its Lodges. The result was that when in 1813 A.D. England was made a single Grand Jurisdiction, with the present United Grand Lodge of England having exclusive territorial authority, thus ruling out all other English Grand Lodges past, present, or to come, it failed in its attempt to impose a standard, uniform Work on the Lodges; to this day any Lodge in England can of its own choice use any one of a number of "Workings." There are four principal forms.

In America the attempt to find a Uniform Work was even more difficult; Lodges here were constituted under charters from two Grand Lodges in England, from Ireland, from Scotland, and from France; the Provincial Grand Lodges were small and ill-defined; they worked in Grand Jurisdictions which were uncertain and which over-lapped; and they were too far away for the British Grand Lodges to exercise much supervision over them. The Lodges themselves were small, were not large in number, were far apart from each other, there was little visiting, the Grand Communications of the Provincial Grand Lodges were not well

## Divergences

attended. To maintain among them a Ritual everywhere uniform was impossible; Provincial Grand Lodges were satisfied if their Lodges were loyal to the fundamentals.

Therefore when these Provincial Grand Lodges became independent and sovereign Grand Lodges after the Revolutionary War not only was there a large amount of variation from one State to another, but there was as much of it inside a Grand Jurisdiction among Lodges on the same List. Each Lodge was supposed to choose for itself a version of the Work and this choice might be so unstudied and arbitrarily exercised that a Lodge would use one version under one Worshipful Master, and another version under the succeeding Worshipful Master. The Standard Monitor during the first third of the Nineteenth Century was edited and published, with few exceptions, by private Masons (Webb, Cross, Barney, Mackey, etc.) and the temptation to insert a phrase or a sentence of his own into the Ritual was more than many of those editors could resist. Even so this state of affairs might have worked itself out here as it did in Britain, giving us some five or six generally approved Workings, had not Grand Lodges been forced to take charge by the rise of a critical and dangerous evil in the form of what was called "Degree peddling." A "Degree peddler" made a living by "peddling" a version of his own from Lodge to Lodge in which two or three minor details differed from others; he would persuade the Lodge to adopt his version officially, and then would charge a fee for teaching it to the officers and other Ritualists.

When this evil had become intolerable the Lodges at last became willing to surrender to the Grand Lodges what they believed to have been their ancient right to choose a version for themselves. In response, one Grand Lodge after another adopted the doctrine of a Standard and Uniform Work; but in doing so each Grand Lodge could act only for itself, with the result that no Uniform Work ever has been adopted for the whole nation. If New York could adopt a Uniform Work for New York Lodges only, and Massachusetts for its own Lodges only and Pennsylvania for its own Lodges only, and if each of these Grand Lodges acted independently of the others, it would have been a miracle if the Work adopted had been the same word for word in those Grand Jurisdictions; and when the three grew to ten, and then to twenty, and finally to forty-nine a general or national uniformity became impossible by a process of geometrical compounding. For historical reasons, therefore, Standard Uniform Work always means that the Work is uniform within any given Grand Jurisdiction only, and is not uniform (and never was) across the nation; this difference in details of the Work from one Grand Jurisdiction to another is what is meant by *Divergences;* and it explains to a Mason why it is that when he visits a Lodge in another Grand Jurisdiction it uses a Ritual not the same in every word as the one which he had learned at home.

*Divergence* is an honest and healthy term, and carries no trace of any corrupt inheritance from either slang or profanity, so that where correctly used no man can find fault with it; but as it is used in Masonic nomenclature it carries a point which is, as we shall see, a little misleading. *Vergo* was a Latin word for a direction, a path, a tendency, a line or road laid down to be followed; the prefix *di* meant away from, to depart from, a deviation; when combined they gave us "to diverge," which means that something, or somebody, at some point, draws away from the right direction, slants away from the goal, departs a little from the path, does not turn about yet turns to one side. *Divergence* thus presupposes that the right path has been drawn, but that somebody heads a little away from it; to deviate there must be something to deviate from. Translated into Masonic circumstances this means that somewhere there is the true, orthodox, standard, uniform Work, and that in consequence a *divergence* is a fault, a failure, a heresy. And it is this which makes our own usage of it somewhat incorrect, because as the rapid synopsis of the history of the Work as given above must have made clear, there is not and never has been, in any Grand Jurisdiction, a single, ancient Uniform Work, therefore the differences from one Grand Jurisdiction to another are not divergences from it. What we have now is what the Fraternity always has had, a general Work which in its frame-work and fundamentals is everywhere the same but which in details differs from one Grand Jurisdiction

## Divergences

to another. By "standard" is meant that these fundamentals are always the standards against which a Ritual is judged; by "uniform" is meant that Grand Jurisdictions are in those fundamentals everywhere the same. If this were everywhere to be accepted as true we could describe the general Ritual, from one Grand Jurisdiction to another, as "Regular"; and in place of the somewhat misleading word "divergence" we could use the word "version"; we could then sum up the matter by saying that each Grand Jurisdiction has its own officially-approved Version of the Regular Work.

What if in visiting Lodges outside his own Grand Jurisdiction a Mason encounters a rite or a ceremony which is not only different from one used by his own Lodge, but appears to him to be *too* different? It would be almost impossible for him to encounter such a problem anywhere in the United States but he would be likely to encounter it among Lodges in parts of Europe or in almost any of the Latin countries to the south of us. It is easy to understand how there can be two versions of the same ceremony; for just as the Authorized and Revised are two versions of the same Bible, so may a ceremony be the same in spite of a difference in the words used, as, for an example, in the presentation of the apron—what difference does it make if one presentation speech is used or another as long as the apron is presented? But if in one Lodge the apron is presented, and in another Lodge it is not presented, then manifestly we do not have two versions of the same thing, because the same thing is not done in both Lodges; what we then have is not a different version (or "divergence") but an *innovation*.

If the whole of Freemasonry is conferred on a Candidate in Lodge A, and if the whole of Freemasonry is conferred in Lodge B, manifestly any differences in the version of the Ritual are not fundamental, they are, to use once again the old name, nothing but "divergences"; but if the whole of Freemasonry is conferred in Lodge A, but only a part of it is conferred in Lodge B, then Lodge B is guilty of an innovation and the idea of differences in versions of the Regular Work does not apply to it.

The same fact also is the explanation of another puzzle which mystifies many Masons. The version used among about one-half of our American Grand Jurisdictions are surprisingly close, the differences consisting of only a word or a phrase here and there; among the other half the differences widen until in a few instances they become disconcerting. The version used in Pennsylvania differs much from the one used in Massachusetts; Massachusetts differs almost as much from Colorado; and Colorado from Louisiana; and one of them in turn differs yet more widely from versions used in Canada. If that be true, why is it then that American Grand Lodges have always refused to recognize so many Lodges in Mexico, in Italy, in France, in a number of other foreign countries? If we overlook divergences here at home among our own Grand Jurisdictions why not overlook them abroad? It is because what we have in these unrecognized foreign Lodges is not a question of divergence but a question of innovation.

This abyssic difference between versions of the Regular Work and innovations in it, has its largest and most striking illustration in a chapter of Eighteenth Century Masonic history. As described early in this chapter English Lodges in 1717 A.D. were conferring only two Degrees; by 1740 A.D. the majority were conferring three Degrees, and this new Tri-Gradal System was made official; that was a difference in version (or a "divergence") in the Grand style, and it was made with almost dramatic suddenness; but instead of being everywhere questioned it was everywhere welcomed, though Freemasons in that period were more conservative than now. Yet when the Grand Lodge of England discontinued the use of the Ceremonies of Installation for Officers, Lodges everywhere rebelled, and some of them afterwards went over to the new Grand Lodge of 1751 A.D. It was because the one was a divergence, the other an innovation.

The new Degree altered nothing in the nature of Freemasonry; on the contrary it was only a new version of something as old as Freemasonry itself. But the discontinuing of the Ceremony of Installation would have destroyed Freemasonry if it had been carried on and if its implications and consequences had been worked out, because the Principal Offices of the Lodge would

*Divergences*

have been robbed of their ancient and inherent authority; the Master would have become nothing more than a presiding officer, and the Grand Mastership itself would have ceased, making the Grand Master nothing but an agent or errand runner for Grand Lodge—one Landmark after another would have gone down, and ultimately the Fraternity would have gone down with them.

*Part Five*
MORE ABOUT MASONRY

"Ye shall know the Truth and
the Truth shall make you Free"

CHAPTER XXII

## *Masonry Self-Disciplined*

WHEN THE FIRST permanent Grand Lodge was constituted in 1717 A.D. by the old Lodges only four of them are known to have participated—the dining-room in the Goose and Gridiron Tavern would have held their combined membership without crowding, because no one of them had over thirty members. If there were as many as ten other old Lodges in London at the time the fourteen together could not have assembled a crowd of 500. Few of the inhabitants of the city so much as knew of the existence of the Fraternity, though London had at the time only a small fraction of its present population. In 1721 A.D., which was four long years after the erection of the Grand Lodge, John the second Duke of Montague was elected and installed as Grand Master, and remained in office for one and one-half years. His election was a quiet and an undramatic event about which there was no gossip or rumor on the streets of the town, but as ensuing events were to show it was to be a turning point in the history of Speculative Free-Masonry, because Montague was a member of the nobility. An opportunity to sit in the same rooms with a blood relative of the King, and even possibly to enjoy with him the intimacies of the table, made so powerful an appeal to the socially aspiring that Freemasonry began to multiply. New Lodges sprang into existence almost over night, and the Fraternity began to be the talk of the town; nor did that talk have an opportunity to abate as the Duke was followed in office by other Dukes, and by Earls and Marquises. In a pamphlet published under the title of *A Free Vindication,* which is one of the most important documents in Speculative history, it is stated that in 1726 A.D., the year of its writing, there were 4,000 Freemasons in London.

The Fraternity became, in the language as then used, "a power," and it became a center of controversy for that reason. There were Whig and Tory political parties even then, at least in outline, but the most menacing controversy was that which blazed between the Hanoverians, the faction which supported the Hanoverian King George, and the Jacobites, the faction which worked to restore the Stuart family to the throne, the rancor being so bitter that in Scotland it had led to war; as soon as Freemasonry became a "power" each of these factions fought to capture it in a struggle which blazed up into an open quarrel on the floor of Grand Lodge when the Duke of Warton was Grand Master in 1723 A.D.—a fact which adds a special interest to the publication of the *Book of Constitutions* in that year.

During the Operative and Transition Periods there was some Anti-Masonry—Wyclif published a diatribe against it—but it was sporadic, though, as shown by an Anti-Masonic leaflet of 1698 A.D., it was sometimes vitriolic; but in the 1720's, and consequent to the growth described above, it became chronic, and began to accumulate a literature of its own. Along with it there grew up a deal of satire directed against the Craft, in the newspapers, on the stage, and in the coffee houses, in the form of lampoons, jokes, cartoons, and ribaldries, and these in turn led to a number of species of "mock Masonry," or societies designed to make sport of Masonic solemnities, among them being the "Gormogons" and the "Guzzletonians." And amidst this hubub there were published a number of so-called exposés, by which means clandestines or cowans tried to work their way into the lodges to ridicule.

The Fraternity met these vexing problems by having Grand Lodge act upon it officially, with edict and law, rather than to leave them work themselves out by discussion or by measures taken by Lodges. The Grand Lodges employed one means after another, as rapidly as they were called for, and enforced them with uniformity and severity. Except at one or two points,

## Masonry Self-Disciplined

and as the results were later to testify, the Craft could not have acted more wisely. Public processions were prohibited in order to avoid hooliganism on the streets—even the old customs of visiting church and of escorting the Grand Master's carriage from his residence to Grand Lodge were discontinued. Modes of recognition were altered. The Paragraphs on religion and politics in the *Book of Constitutions* were literally enforced. These various means were gathered up into a single system, and made complete, and carried to their extreme, by the official adoption of Grand Lodge censorship which included meetings, speeches, and publications, it being ordained that no Mason or Lodge could print a pamphlet or book without official approbation by the Grand Master, as is always true in any system of censorship the whole pressure was negative, censors being what they are, and this long period of *verboten* explains why it was that over a number of decades only Calcott, Hutchinson, and Preston published books of any weight, and the once so powerful voice of Masonic oratory remained so long in silence. It was not until 1783 A.D. that Captain George Smith defied censorship by publishing his *Use and Abuse of Freemasonry*, and it was not until a decade afterwards that the whole system was openly and officially set aside; since then Freemasons have been free to think and to write, and they will continue ever to be free, because grown men, if they are qualified to be Masons, will not tolerate a despotism so gratuitous, and one which violates every principle of Masonic teachings; because if the principle of censorship were established in the heart of the Craft it would destroy that very responsibility for his own thought, speech, and actions which every Mason has, first as a Candidate and then as a Member; for it is the essence of censorship to forbid a man to act upon his own responsibility.

History it so happened, preordained Freemasonry in Nineteenth Century America to repeat, almost point by point, the same course of alarm, defence, and censorship as that which was described above. The Anti-Masonic Crusade which followed the disappearance of William Morgan in 1826 A.D. was vicious, nationwide, and well organized; it set up a political party of its own, it sent hundreds of stump-speakers across the land, it published hundreds of magazines, newspapers, and books, and it won the active support of many clergymen; had there been anything in Freemasonry corrupt or evil or false it would in all certainty have completely perished, because that crusade was kept up and pursued with an almost fanatical intensity for a quarter of a century; the microscopes of its foes could find nothing false in it, and it turned again and recovered its old place and went forward. But during the decades of the attack the Fraternity set up within itself not an official censorship but a tacit rule of silence, and until the Civil War American Masonry was not only secret but almost secretive; the reason was obvious, because Masons argued that the less said in public or to the public the fewer would be the targets at which Anti-Masons could aim.

After the Civil War history took another turn, one almost as unheralded as the Anti-Masonic Crusade, and by one of the most unexpected coincidences possible to history, one that also turned out as an argument for preserving silence. The American Craft became very religious; the Master's pedestal was almost turned into a pulpit; delegates went off to Grand Lodge less to transact business than to listen to long Masonic sermons by pulpit orators; and it was accepted almost as a motto that "Freemasonry is a handmaiden to the church"; the tone and temper of the Lodge was solemn and almost funereal, and the offices of the Lodge were filled with men white in hair and beard. Along with this went not the conservatism which preserves the old because it has stood every test of analysis and research, but the conservatism which obstructs analysis and research, because it is afraid of knowledge. An "old man's silence" lay over the Craft in the 1870's and the 1880's.

This censorship by tacit consent came to an end not by rebellion or revolution or reform but for the same reason that British censorship had come to an end a century before; it was found by decades of actual practice and experience that the Fraternity could not carry on its own Masonic activities without Masonic knowledge, where knowledge is needed censorship must be cast aside because its motto is: "Thou shalt learn nothing. Thou shalt have no new knowledge." The men who moved forward to Craft leadership from about 1885 A.D. to about 1915 A.D., in person or through their writings, were almost without exception scholars, teachers, writers, historians, and encyclopedists, both here and in Britain, for the new leaders here were Fort, Stillson, Greenleaf, Drummond, Mackey, Pike, Macoy, Morris, Parvin; and in Britain were Hughan, Gould, Speth, Crowe, Woodford, Crawley, Rylands, Lyons; and in Europe were Krause, Rebold, Begemann, and others of a like kind. After one and one-half centuries of experiment with and without censorship, with and without silence, with and without books, the World Fraternity decided once and for all, and regardless of what the future may bring, that the freedom of the Masonic mind is a Landmark in Freemasonry.

No man desires to be a free man in order to be free to lie, or steal, or be ignorant, or to be rebellious, or to indulge in any other wicked or mischievous or criminal action; he desires to be free in order to be free to work and to earn wages, free to use his mind when he has need to, free to say the truth when it is the thing for him to do, free to work with others and to associate with others in peace and harmony. There is no connection between freedom and anarchy, and nothing under the starry-decked canopy of heaven could be more false than the sophistry that freedom means disorder, with every man for himself, and that order cannot be had except by the rule of a dictator or a tyrant or a despot; if history shows anything to be true it is that peoples who have the least freedom are most rebellious because they become bitter or resentful, and consequently are most in disorder.

Neither can anything be more false than the sophistry that free thought means that a man can say or think whatever may chance to enter his head, and whether it is true or false, that he has the right to believe in any notion he pleases, or to adopt any "opinion" for which he has the whim. Such vagaries would not mean that a man has a free mind, but that he has no mind. Freedom to think means whatever is *necessary* to think. It is of the very nature of free thought and of free speech that a man is free to think what he *must* think, and not what he himself decides to think, for to refuse to grasp the fact or the truth is not a form of thinking, but a form of not thinking. If I ask you what time it is, it is not you but your watch which decides your answer. If I ask you what day of the week it is it is not you but the calendar which determines what you think and what you say. If I ask you what is the area of a triangle with a base of three feet and a side of four feet and you answer that it is six feet it is not you who determines its area but the triangle itself. We do not manufacture facts or create truths but *find* them, and always they are independent of ourselves. If it be the function of the mind to find out what facts are, or what is true about facts, then it would be a contradiction in the nature of the mind to suppose that a man would demand freedom of thought in order to ignore facts or evade truths—it is among peoples where men are least free to use their own minds that the greatest amount of falseness and superstition is found because they are not permitted to find out facts or truths.

Criticism is nothing other than a man's free use of his own mind over any given field or subject matter, and the concomitant freedom to report what he finds, and not to be penalized if what he finds proves (through no fault of his) to be painful or distressing or distasteful to somebody else. Masonic criticism is a Mason's freedom to use his own mind on the subjects, questions, and problems of Freemasonry, and his freedom to report any facts or truths he finds, and without being penalized by any Lodge or Grand Lodge law or officer for doing so; since we have that freedom, since Freemasons are as free to think and to speak as they are to work or pay dues, and since that freedom is a Landmark, we have Masonic criticism free, and full, and unimpaired, and no member can be penalized or persecuted by anything or anybody if he makes use of it. But it would be as false in Freemasonry as it is elsewhere to advance the sophistry that criticism is faultfinding, or is a belittlement of things, or a running down of everybody, or is a mere advertising of failures, or is nothing but a sort of lust for destructive talk. There is no conceivable connection between criticism and fault-finding—and a man's reasoning is faulty if he believes there is. When a man lets his own intelligence play freely over any subject he is not searching for the faults in it but for the facts in it and the truths about these facts; whether what he finds is good news or bad news depends on what he finds those facts and truths to be. Who is he to dictate the facts! Would he not be under the delusion that he is a god if he tried to make the facts be what he wishes them to be! He reports what he finds. If a thing is bad he says so; if a thing is good he says so.

CHAPTER XXIII

## *Anti-Masonry*

ARCHITECTURE is a fine art, but it is not a private art, nor has it ever been a quiet art. A man cannot practice it by himself in a corner of his library or by brooding over it in his music room. Carpenters and contractors and plumbers, picked up at random, can construct any simple building (even a factory); almost any intelligent man who can use a square, saw, and hammer can frame a wooden house, shingle its roof, and nail on its siding; *such* structures are not architecture and have only a remote similarity to it. For architecture is an *art;* and it is a *public* art; as such the architect is a public figure and works in the thick of things. Everybody believes himself entitled to have his say about any new church, school-house, college, courthouse, state capitol, museum, monument, and half the time he says "no" to it, and oftentimes he says it vociferously, and nobody could count the architects who have spent half their time battling wrathful committees or fighting back at sneering newspaper editors; the careers of Roebling, Sullivan, Corbett, Hood, Pope, Wright and such men in our own day was a continuous battle.

Philistines who hate culture in general, and who are at active enmity with the fine arts, feel as they do because if culture is real and is true they themselves can have no standing in it. These mediocre persons lampoon artists with jibes and cartoons, and they picture them as thin, ineffectual, loose-handed, long-haired creatures with large and mournful eyes. The cartoon is a silly one but only a close reading of the history of the arts can show a man how silly it really is; because history proves that the fine arts have always been daring, pugnacious, aggressive; and thousands of biographies of artists (which the mediocrities never read) are life-stories of men in the midst of foes, enemies, and opponents, who battled, and bled, and oftentimes were killed; and the fine arts have as long a roll of heroes and martyrs as war or religion.

The Operative Freemasons, who were the architects of the Middle Ages, were not only not an exception to this rule but had to do more battling with foes and enemies than artists in almost any other period. Perhaps it was because they had a monopoly of their art, for it was a cornerstone of the gild system within which they operated that each gild had a monopoly of the work done in its own craft, and there is always a large amount of enmity to a monopoly, whether it is a good one or a bad one, because it leaves so many men without any voice in it. Certainly the Freemasons had a monopoly of architecture! they kept everybody away with an armed guard, and they taught nothing of their methods and secrets except to their own apprentices, and so as in other gilds and craft fraternities these apprentices were bound to keep what they had learned to themselves under oath, and on the threat of severe penalties.

Sentimental Masonic writers have drawn pictures of those Medieval Freemasons as a single, mystic, devout brotherhood; the historian Hope drew a picture of them walking down a country road at dusk, their arms around each other's shoulders, singing songs of brotherhood; it may be that such idyllic scenes occurred but if so they did not occur often; the history of themselves which they wrote into their own records when added to the history about them which was written into chronicles and borough records, gives us a picture of a wholly different kind.

The Masons often went on strike; more than once they tore a building down when their employers tried to "beat" them out of their wages; when the kings tried to lower their wages they stopped work; many times their own Lodge building was burned down—in at least three known cases the mob which burned one of them was led by a priest. Among themselves the Operative Freemasons were peaceable and quiet men, and had some drastic laws to keep them so; but their craft did not have a peaceable and quiet time.

The old picture of the Middle Ages as an Age of Faith, as

a quiet and uninterrupted interval in a period of history full of troubles and wars is a myth, and historians long have known that it was; it was more like a hurly-burly, and because they did public work, and oftentimes worked for bishops and lords and kings who were not themselves very popular Operative Masons then were at the focus of the hurly-burly. Always they had plenty of enemies and foes; Anti-Masonry went along with Masonry, and one is as ancient as the other. Because this is true no Mason ought to feel a shock when he discovers that the Fraternity has enemies and foes now, nor should he feel that there is something wrong with his Lodge or his Grand Lodge when he discovers (as he will) that the Fraternity has many enemies who would like to see it abolished; there is nothing new in this state of affairs, nor accidental; there have always been Anti-Masons and there always will be.

Now and then a timid, or thin-skinned, or ultra-conservative member tries to persuade his fellow members to keep still about this fact, or even to pretend that it is not true: "let sleeping dogs lie" (how often are such dogs really asleep?) he counsels, and thinks that the less said about Anti-Masonry the better. The Fraternity itself does not agree with him, and it never has. With its usual candor and good sense it forthrightly declares that it has foes and enemies, and it provides within itself (and with equal good sense) a large number of measures to protect itself against them. There are too many of these measures for listing and describing in one paragraph but a few of the more typical ones can be given, and with these as a clue any reader can go on to recall the others. A Petitioner is thoroughly scrutinized and investigated not only to see if he possesses the qualifications but also to make sure that he will not turn out to be a Trojan horse or a Fifth Columnist to bring trouble and dissention into a Lodge—the history of European Freemasonry is full of instances of foes introduced by this ancient scheme of a Fifth Column. The Obligation is not only most carefully worked out to cover every point but is severe, and it is backed by penalties also severe; and the whole apparatus of admonition, censure, reprimand, trial, suspension, and expulsion is designed to keep trouble makers out, or to put trouble makers out, because it is the trouble maker inside who furnishes opportunities and weapons to trouble makers on the outside. The Lodge meets behind closed doors, with a guard on the inside and another on the outside of it. The business transacted in a Communication is under the rule of secrecy and may not be reported or discussed with non-members. The Esoteric Work may nowhere be reported, spoken, or written. The Lodge permits no non-Mason to pass its door when it is in session, and it matters not who he be, not even if he is Sheriff, Governor, or President. As for the Sublime Degree itself it will take on a new meaning and stand in a new light if a student of it will view it from this standpoint of Anti-Masonry. Why should a Fraternity devoted to harmony, peace, fraternalism, charity, good will have foes and enemies? The question can be best answered by another question: why should *any* religion, church, government, people, institution have foes and enemies?

The Fraternity engages in no quarrels or brawls, and does not lift up its voice in the streets; it respects itself and therefore holds its position with dignity; furthermore it respects its own enemies (most of them) and neither despises nor holds them in contempt because they are in conflict with it, because it knows that honorable men may be in conflict with each other. If a religion believes itself to be wholly and exclusively true it is logically in conflict with other religions. The constitutional laws of a government cannot tolerate interferences from the constitutional laws of another government. Any organization which stands on principles of its own inevitably opposes a competing organization with opposite principles. Men have the inherent right of free association, and will engage in armed rebellion if that right is interfered with; but the fact that association is *free* unavoidably results in hundreds of associations with conflicting aims or purposes. Freemasonry is a free association; it is founded on principles of its own and is always willing to perish rather than to abrogate or revise them; it does not expect, and has no right to expect, that it can be immune from the rule of the world, and knows that if other free associations have opposite principles they will be logically, and therefore necessarily, at enmity with it. If they actively oppose themselves to it, it must oppose itself to them, and even though it does not openly quarrel with them, or go out and do violent battle with them.

The large number of Anti-Masonic activities about which there are many chapters among the thousand chapters in the history of the Fraternity have been not vulgar quarrels but an inevitable conflict between one principle and an opposed principle, between the Masonic teaching and an opposite teaching. This is the correct definition and the true doctrine about Anti-Masonry; except for a few occasional incidents, seldom of importance, it means nothing other than that any society or association which has principles and teachings opposed to the principles and teachings of Freemasonry, is logically and necessarily Anti-Masonic. How this definition works out can be shown by some three or four typical cases:

Clement XII issued in 1738 A.D. the first of many Papal Bulls aimed at the abolition of Freemasonry. It is difficult for any man of sound mind to see by what right these Popes took such action, because neither they nor any other set of men can speak or act for the world—Freemasonry, an American would say, is none of their business; nevertheless Clement XII acted consistently with the established principles of his church because three hundred years before (in 1326 A.D.) the Council of Avignon had excommunicated all "free associations"; and centuries before that date, and in a number of General Councils, the church had condemned free associations. Freemasonry is in law and by definition, as well as by the nature of its own Landmarks, a free association, therefore a conflict as between it and the Roman Church has always been unavoidable, and always will be because it is a conflict in principles.

In 1799 A.D. the Parliament of Great Britain enacted a law which it entitled The Combinations Act. It was, as the coffeehouses described it at the time, "a most peculiar law," but the word "peculiar" was not strong enough; the Act was not a law as any jurisconsult in the world would define "law," but was nothing but a fiat arbitrarily issued and backed up with the threat of force; it was a mere Legislative Edict, which means that the Legislature itself violated the law in the very act of enacting its so-called "law." The occasion for this act of legislative lawlessness was plain to everybody; in Ireland were many secret and conspirational political societies, there were a few of them in England; and in both Islands the Orange Society was everywhere making headway. To abolish the two or three societies it considered to be dangerous the Parliament abolished all secret societies—like the man in Charles Lamb's story who burned down his house in order to roast his pig. The law was still-born, but it remained on the books for a few years, and while it did the British Government was technically Anti-Masonic because if the law had been enforced it would have abolished Freemasonry.

After the defeat of Napoleon at Waterloo the more powerful of the States involved began a long Congress at Vienna, which turned out to be not so much a Congress as a league of nations, and officially or unofficially ruled Europe for years. To implement the scheme of rule, Metternich, its architect and its leader, devised the since-famous Triple (or Holy) Alliance, consisting of Austria, Prussia, and Russia; this was afterwards replaced by the Grand Alliance. (The Monroe Doctrine was our bulwark of defense against these Alliances.) What with Metternich, Talleyrand, the Two Alliances, and the Congress taken together there was set up in Europe a political and religious system which rested on the dogma that rulers rule by divine right. Metternich himself, once the question came round for his attention, saw that the principles of the Holy Alliance were in conflict with the principles of Freemasonry, therefore he sent out word that Freemasonry must be destroyed—it is for this reason that he may be adjudged the most powerful and the most successful Anti-Mason in history; and if his system had survived (it broke down in the 1840's) not one Lodge in Europe would have survived with it. It was one more instance of an inevitable conflict; the principles of the Holy Alliance and the principles of the Fraternity were in conflict; and they came into *conflict of themselves* because few of Metternich's colleagues had any personal quarrel with it, certainly not Metternich himself who was too much the gentleman to quarrel with anybody.

The Anti-Masonic Crusade in the United States which began in 1826 A.D. as an aftermath of the disappearance of William Morgan and the accusation that the Masons in his Lodge in Batavia, N. Y., had murdered him, would have been a Comedy of Errors if its violence had not turned it into a Comedy of Terrors, for the whole of it, as Anti-Masons themselves afterwards confessed, grew up out of a mistake (or blunder) about a matter of fact. Thurlow Weed, John Quincy Adams, Millard Fillmore and the other Anti-Masonic leaders averred that Freemasonry is a secret and conspirational society which aims to destroy the National Government, and at the same time is a secret and conspirational atheistic society which aims to destroy Christianity. Any Mason who reads these sentences can judge for himself how weirdly mistaken those charges were, because Freemasonry did not alter itself an iota as a result of this Crusade. The Anti-Masons raided some thousands of Lodge properties; read hundreds of Minute Books; analyzed every word in rites, symbols, and ceremonies they could find; and combed through the private lives of hundreds of Worshipful Masters and Grand Masters. When there was nothing more left for them to find they admitted (because they had to admit it) that they had made a blunder of epic proportions in a matter of fact, and history will continue to laugh at them as long as they are remembered.

Freemasonry began in Russia within only a few years after it was first planted in Western Europe, and it had there a long history which was checkered or broken at times but not more often than other things were under the Czars. But from the beginning of the Soviet regime it has been completely obliterated. This is a great loss because Russia occupies one-sixth of the habitable surface of the earth. Soviets are very old in Russia, for they antedate even Genghis Khan; Communism is as old as the steppes themselves; the Soviet regime is therefore not peculiar in being Communistic or in using soviets, but it is the first system in Russia or in any other land where the two have been combined to the exclusion of every other social or political method; there are small soviets and large soviets, thousands of them, but their peculiarity is that they are not used *by* the government, but *are* the government, and no soviet can exist except as a department or agency of government, or as it is controlled and inspected by an officer of the government. There is no room anywhere in this network for a free association, therefore the soviet system automatically excludes Masonic Lodges. Whether it will always do so or not it is impossible to predict, but if ever Masonic Lodges are permitted again they will not function as agencies of government or submit to inspection and regulation by government agencies because if a Lodge did so it would no longer be Masonic.

When Mussolini established Fascism in Italy one of his earliest official acts was to order Masonic leaders jailed in prisons or sent to the Lipari Islands; his "toughs" then ranged the country to mob and club Masons, to destroy Lodge rooms and buildings, steal Masonic property, and the Duce himself brought the Anti-Masonic terror to a head by offering Italian Masons a choice between two alternatives, renouncing Masonry or imprisonment and possibly death. As Fascism extended itself into Spain, Germany, Belgium, Poland, Rumania, Holland, and France, and had begun to extend itself into Britain (where Moseley claimed nearly a million members), it everywhere either destroyed Freemasonry or else began a war upon it—Petain at Vichy was as Anti-Masonic as Hitler in Berlin. From the beginning of Mussolini's Anti-Masonry until the fall of Berlin, and including persecutions by Hitler's "yellow Aryan" friends, the Japanese, some 100,000 men became martyrs of Masonry. And why? Because the principles of Fascism came into head-on collision with the principles of Masonry—where a Lodge is, fascism is not; where fascism is, a Lodge is not. It was the most bloody and awesomely tragic persecution through which Freemasonry had ever passed during the storm-troubled centuries; but the Fraternity has a long memory, and there is more than one sense in which "the strong grip of the Lion's Paw" "can raise from the dead."

It is therefore clear that they are mistaken who have pictured Anti-Masonry in the terms of quarreling, or as if it were something new, and as being possibly in some sense shameful to admit. The Fraternity is not an upstart from yesterday, or even from the day before yesterday; the world long ago accorded it a large and an established place, and it needs not to apologize for its existence, and if any man should chance to wish that it did not exist he can continue to wish, and much good it will do him. It knows its own mind; it is positive and affirmative; it has its own purposes and will neither step aside nor back down if it is opposed; and as for its Landmarks, its principles, and its teachings it will compound them for no price, and prefers non-existence to compromise; and though not belligerent it is never afraid, and not even the falling of the heavens could break down its fortitude. Where there are so many men and so many minds, so many political regimes, religions, races, and cultures, it cannot hope ever to find itself not in conflict with some one of them, at least not opposed in principle in a world where there are so many movements, and crusades, and creeds, and parties. All of these which is only another way of saying that no Mason should ever let his heart be troubled by these oppositions, past or present, for Anti-Masonry is a necessary and normal feature in the Masonic scene.

CHAPTER XXIV

# *General Topics*

(Landmarks, Bible, Secrecy, Sociability)

IN HIS *Lexicon of Freemasonry* which he published in 1845 A.D., and which was American Freemasonry's first and almost its only encyclopedia, Dr. Albert G. Mackey touched upon the subjects of the Ancient Landmarks in two short paragraphs. In his two-volume *Encyclopedia of Freemasonry* (now revised, and in three volumes) which he published originally in 1874 A.D., he included an extensive discussion of the subject and gave a descriptive list of twenty-five Landmarks. This article was notable because it was the most influential single essay (or article) ever written by a Freemason; because it embodied the best of American Masonic thought between 1845 A.D. and 1874 A.D.; and because it shows how the development of Freemasonry in the United States during some thirty years (embracing the Civil War Period) had brought the subject of Landmarks to the front. Dr. Mackey did not spend months of laborious thought and research on the subject in order to see his own private theory in print; he found the Craft working to clarify its own understanding of Landmarks because they had become crucial to the setting up a system of 49 sovereign Grand Lodges each of which must continue in fraternal relation with each and every other one, and he searched the mind of the Craft and reviewed its practices in order to assist himself to that end.

At the time of writing, one-half of the American Grand Lodges print Mackey's List in their *Codes;* of those about one-half have officially adopted the list. With two or three exceptions (New York among them) the other Grand Lodges have either officially adopted or officially approved lists of only one, or two, or three, or five up to as many as fifty-six. In their private writings Masonic authors of books or treatises on the subject have disagreed even more widely among themselves, a number of them at one extreme denying that any list is possible (Theodore Sutton Parvin was one), others, at the opposite extreme (such as Grant and Oliver), setting up lists of from 75 to 100 or more.

As has so often occurred in debates of this sort the debate did not come to an end because the debaters (including Grand Lodges) found a list upon which to agree, but came to an end because the whole debate was shifted to another ground, and the question of how many Landmarks belonged to their list became meaningless. This change in the basis of the discussion was brought about by an almost sudden and very great increase in our knowledge and understanding of Masonic history. Instead of asking what Landmarks are, and what is the number of them history asks, What has been the *function* of Landmarks throughout the history of the Fraternity?

To that question history has given the answer: *It has been to maintain and to perpetuate the identity of Freemasonry.* The Fraternity consists of men—not of a set of doctrines or dogmas. Freemasonry is the name for what those men do. Since they are men of flesh and blood at work in rooms or buildings in actual town, cities, and countries, they work under circumstances which change. How far can they carry these changes? as far as they deem it wise or expedient as long as they do not change Freemasonry itself into something else. Any organism or organization may make changes of some sort; but if a change is of a kind to destroy the organism or the organization then it is unlawful and impossible. The Landmarks are those essentials in Freemasonry which cannot be destroyed without destroying Freemasonry itself.

From the beginning of the Middle Ages until the Fifteenth Century Freemasonry did not use the Bible because it had no Bible to use. The 39 books of the Old Testament and the 27 books of the New Testament could be had, where they could be had at all, only in the form of manuscripts; since it took a professional scribe more than three years to copy the Bible manuscript by hand, and since a complete text required a thousand or two of expensive "skins" of vellum or parchment, a Bible cost

## General Topics

more than a large farm; only the largest churches had even a portion of the Books, the ablest priests had only a few books, the majority of priests could not even read it because they were illiterate. Even if less expensive copies had been purchasable Freemasons could not have owned or used a Bible because the church had a closed monopoly of it, and did not permit laymen to read it for themselves. The center of the Craft's religion was not in the Lodge but in the chapel to which the Lodge went in procession on its own Saints' days.

The first step toward having a Bible on the altar came in the middle of the Fourteenth Century when the first permanent Lodges began to work under a copy of the *Old Charges*. This manuscript was kept on a small stand or pedestal in front of the Master's station, illuminated by three candles ("Lesser Lights"). It was their "Volume of the Law." In it a number of paragraphs gave an account of the great antiquity and honorableness of the art of Freemasonry, or architecture; another group of paragraphs set forth an account of how King Athelstan had granted a Royal Charter to the Fraternity in 926 A.D.; and a concluding series of paragraphs contained the Rules and Regulations. This document was read or recited to a Candidate, in whole or in part, and on its sanction he took his Obligation.

The contents of the *Old Charges* were so sacred in the eyes of Freemasons that much of them afterwards were embodied in the Ritual, and the earliest tracing-boards were a set of designs or formalized pictures representing some of the more salient portions of them. The first edition of the *Book of Constitutions*, which was published by the Mother Grand Lodge in 1723 A.D., was nothing more than a version of the *Old Charges* adopted to Grand Lodge needs.

At about the time that Columbus discovered America a number of printers in Germany, the Lowlands, and France improved the printing-press sufficiently to make the printing of books commercially feasible. In about a century the building and operation of presses and the manufacture of paper were so much further reduced in price that by the period 1600 A.D. to 1611 A.D. the cost of a Bible was brought within the reach of men of small means, and everywhere, with an enthusiasm now difficult to measure, everybody began to read it; this popularity was many times multiplied even among children, when editions were illustrated and illuminated.

Before the constitution of the Mother Grand Lodge in 1717 A.D. Lodges kept the *Old Charges* on the "altar," or Master's pedestal; after the Grand Lodge published the *Book of Constitutions* in 1723 A.D. that Book began to replace the *Old Charges*. In 1760 A.D. the Grand Lodge officially declared the Holy Bible to be one of the Great Lights and along with the Square and Compasses it was placed on the Altar. Why this shift from one book to the other? For a number of reasons, among them being: 1) the Third Degree with the Rite organized about HA.·., Master of Masons for Solomon's Temple, brought the Bible into the Ritual, and not in the Third Degree only but also in the Cryptic and Royal Arch Degrees; 2) the rise of the Protestant Denominations everywhere quickened and greatly increased a love for the Bible because they were grounded in it instead of in tradition, church, or priesthood, and this made itself felt among Masons; 3) Solomon's Temple was the natural symbol for architecture because it was the most famous building in the world, and was believed to have been architecture's masterpiece; 4) in the Middle Ages the sanction for a man's oath was his sword, his own name, his family's name, God's name, or a charter, and among Masons it was the *Old Charges,* or (later) the Book of the Constitutions; when at the Royal Court, in the Church, in Courts of law, in the army, in public office, etc., the Bible came universally into use as a sanction for oaths Masons were led by custom to take up the same practice.

But in the Lodge the Holy Bible was not used as a theological book, but as a Great Light, one of three, and each of the other two stands on a parity with it. It is called "the Volume of the Sacred Law" because it is a continuation of the old use of the *Old Charges* and of the *Book of Constitutions,* and because it is the sanction of a Mason's oath. In the latter half of the Eighteenth Century British Lodges declared that since the Bible is used as a Volume of the Sacred Law, Masons in other countries with other religions can use their own sacred Books, and regular Grand Lodges everywhere have since taken the same position (including the 49 Grand Lodges in the United States), for which reason the V.S.L. in Lodges over the world may be represented by the Holy Bible, the Old Testament, the Koran, the Zend-Avesta, the Vedas, the Analects, etc.

The gild system, which included the whole economic life of the Middle Ages, had as one of its cornerstones the rule that any given gild had within its own territory a complete monopoly of its own kind of work—without that rule there could have been no gild system, and without the gild system in an age without schools there could have been neither training nor education for any trade, art, or profession. A gild could not maintain this monopoly of its own trade without what modern manufacturers would describe as its "know how," and without confining a knowledge of that "know how" to its own members who received it under an oath not to pass it on to outsiders; these inwardly monopolized practices, processes, and technologies were called "trade secrets." The Fraternity of Freemasons had their own trade secrets as did other crafts; such secrets were historically the origin of that Masonic secrecy which after many centuries has become almost a synonym for the word Freemasonry itself.

The Freemasons lived in a Masonic Community, and since this included their families and homes they also had privacies, another early form of secrets. Their transactions of Lodge business was confidential, and had to be so to conform to civil law as well as to their own Masonic rules and regulations; for if the civil law held a Lodge responsible for what it did no Lodge could be responsible for non-members, therefore non-members "were tiled out"; this necessarily confidential nature of Lodge business was another origin of Lodge secrecy. This form of secrecy means "members only." Another of its sources, and one which for some unknown reason has passed almost unnoted, is the nature of a Candidate's Obligation; if that Obligation is minutely analyzed in the terms of Masonic history it will be found that a Candidate takes his Obligation *to* the members of the Lodge—it is to a "you," and that "you" can include no non-members. Yet another form of the "members only" type of secrecy were the Modes of Identification, which enabled a Freemason to prove himself to be one wherever he might encounter other Freemasons. Any form of technology is a mystery to the uninitiated—the non-mathematician can make nothing of the calculus, the non-chemist is lost in a laboratory; the Freemasons had much technology, involving much geometry, chemistry, and engineering, and in an age without schools or books this was a secret of secrets.

Did the early Freemasons practice secret arts or sciences? They did in the sense that they practiced a number of them at a time when they were generally forbidden, but they had no secret form of those arts and sciences peculiarly their own—their geometry, which once was their greatest secret, was nothing other than the same geometry which the Greeks and Romans had used, and which after the invention of the printing-press was published everywhere. It is said that the Romans represented the small god of love as being blind-folded not because love blinds the eyes of its victims but because it can keep its own secrets even from those who are closest to it and who have their eyes opened the widest—it is a mystery of light; there is something at the heart of Freemasonry which every Freemason knows and yet which Freemasons cannot explain, not even to each other; it is a form of secrecy which the Ancients described by the word "ineffability."

The secrecy of Freemasonry is thus in it at many places, in many forms, for many purposes, from many origins, and it may even be that that which is most published in it is most secret—the symbols are an example. Nevertheless, and countless assertions or assumptions to the contrary notwithstanding, it is not a secret society. The society of the Carbonari of Italy in its original form concealed its own existence, hid its meeting places, its officers used assumed names, and its members kept their membership to themselves; it might flourish in a town without the town knowing of its presence. Any secret society is a society of that type. Freemasonry does not conceal its existence; it builds its temples on conspicuous corners; the names of its members and officers are published; it prints its Constitutions, laws and purposes; its members walk in public processions; Lodges publish bulletins and Grand

Lodges publish Proceedings, and the Fraternity as a whole has declared itself, expounded itself, described itself and expressed itself for the past two centuries in tens of thousands of books in forty or fifty languages. It is a society with secrets; it is not a secret society.

There are historians of small arts, and minute divisions of science, and movements of only a local fame, of cities, of counties, of states, and of peoples and nations; there also are historians who have as it were, an all-seeing eye, who see the world's history and see it as a whole, who have in their minds neither a taint nor a twist of partiality for their own folk nor prejudice against any other; like Kipling's artist, "when earth's last picture is painted," they see things now as the Great Artist's eye will see them after the world has ended. There are a few such historians now, as there have been in any age, but it is always interesting to see one's own people as they see them. What image of the American people is seen in that universal mirror? If we examine that image for ourselves, as we can if we are sufficiently impartial, we shall find that one of the outstanding peculiarities of ourselves is that almost more than any other people on earth we are the least given to feasting—we are not a festal folk, and we have few festivals. For some mysterious reason, perhaps because of an inheritance from the Puritans, we got it fixed in our minds one or two centuries ago that food and drink are somehow "material," that feasting is somehow a form of indulgence, is a little questionable, and a little gross. And since we breakfast hastily on toast and coffee, lunch on sandwiches, and perhaps eat a dinner hastily put together out of cans, bottles and paste-board boxes, it may be that we lack the festal arts because we have a national and ingrained ignorance about food. Even our religion, which most everywhere else in the world is the mother of the festal spirit, is non-festival; a church supper is something to sup, it is never anything to feast on. If at any point our American Lodges have fallen away from the Ancient Landmarks, and fallen below our early Lodges, it is at this point; we have Lodge lunches, Lodge smokers, Lodge dinners, but almost never a Lodge feast.

It is written in the first paragraph of the account of the founding of the Mother Grand Lodge in 1717 A.D. as published in the Book of Constitutions that the old Lodges in London had two (and only two) purposes in constituting a Grand Lodge: one was to establish a center of union and harmony, the other was *to revive* the Quarterly Feasts! Why feasts? because then (as it had been for centuries) the feast stood close to the very heart of the Lodge, was one of the fundamental things in the Lodge. Even in the original version of the *Old Charges,* in which everything was condensed to the fewest possible words and only essentials were included, feasts were provided for among the rules and regulations as a fixed and necessary part of the Masonic life, and on a par with wages, and Lodges, and apprentices, etc., etc. Feasts "were a third sector" in the work and scope of the Lodge, and one of the Principal Officers, the Junior Warden, had as the purpose of his office to be responsible for that sector; and in early Speculative times this Landmark was not weakened but was reinforced by giving the Junior Warden the two Stewards to assist him.

A dinner is nothing but a meal; a banquet is an occasion, where a dinner is nothing but the preliminary to a program; a feast is not a dinner or a banquet but is an *occasion;* there is food and drink in overflowing abundance and of every possible variety, it is eaten for its own sake and for the enjoyment of it, those who sit down to it remain a long time at their places, and there is always much talk, laughter, and singing, but the talking and singing go on during the eating, not as a set program after it.

In the Eighteenth Century Lodges the feast bulked so large in the life of the Lodge that in many of them the members were seated at the table when the Lodges were opened and remained at it throughout the Communication, even when the Degrees were conferred. The result was that Masonic fellowship was good fellowship; in it, as in a warm and fruitful soil, acquaintanceship, friendship, and affection could flourish—there was no grim and silent sitting on a bench, staring across at a wall. Out of this festal spirit flowered the love which Masons had for their Lodge. They brought gifts to it, and only by a reading of old Inventories can any present-day Mason measure the extent of that love; there were gifts of chairs, tables, altars, pedestals, tapestries, draperies, silver, candle-sticks, oil paintings, libraries, Bibles, mementoes, curios, regalias, and portraits. The Lodge was a home, warm, comfortable, luxurious, full of memories, and tokens, and affection, and even if a member died his presence was never wholly absent; to such a Lodge no member went grudgingly, nor had to be coaxed, nor was moved by that ghastly, cold thing called "a sense of duty," but went as if drawn by a magnet, and counted the days until he could go.

It was an old puzzle to historians until a half century ago to explain how Freemasonry was able to grow, first in Britain and America and then around the world. The puzzle was solved when historical research began to discover for the first time how large had been the place of feasts in early Lodges, and what their consequences were. The average early Lodge had only 8, 10, 15, or possibly 25 members—not enough to keep a modern American Lodge in existence—yet it flourished generation after generation, and it was those small Lodges which made Freemasonry great! It was because they *loved* their Lodges! And it so happens that Freemasonry is itself such that if in a Lodge of only ten members the ten whole-heartedly *love* it then their's is *Masonically* a larger and more powerful Lodge than one of a hundred members in which they are nothing but members, and do nothing but *attend* it now and then. It is hard to love a Lodge if it meets in a half empty room, if its walls are bare, if its furniture is ugly, if its color is drab, and if its Communications consist of nothing more than a routine turning over of Lodge "business." Business indeed! what business has any Lodge to be nothing but a machine for grinding out their work! It was not called into existence in order to have the Minutes read! Even a mystic tie will snap under the strain of cheerlessness, repetition, monotony, dullness. A Lodge needs a fire lighted in it, and the only way to have that warmth is to restore the Lodge feast, because when it is restored good fellowship and brotherly love will follow, and where good fellowship is members will fill up an empty Lodge room not only with themselves but also with their gifts.

Seldom in the large Lodges in our big cities can this fraternal and festal spirit be found or developed. It is much more prevalent and more likely to be found in small Lodges in the little towns and villages and they therefore are the backbone of Freemasonry and the best guarantee of its continuous existence and its further expansion.

CHAPTER XXV

## *Qualifications for Masonry*

THE WORD "QUALIFICATION" is a curiously distorted word, and a prime example of how the English language (like any other language) will twist itself out of shape and stand on its head like a contortionist when it needs a word which it is next to impossible for it to produce. In Latin *qualis* meant "such," but after it came into English usage "such" was twisted about until it meant "suchness." Meantime there was in Anglo-Saxon a word *swlye*, meaning such; to this was added *swa*, meaning "so"; also there was the word *swa*, meaning "who," and the neuter form (when applied to an "it") of *hwact*, which later became "what."

The Latin *qualis* with its meaning of "suchness" had an affinity with these Anglo-Saxon words, and the group of them contributed to give its full meaning to "what" as we now have it. The "fi" in "qualify" is a combining form of *facio*, meaning "to do," as "to make"; the "ation" in "qualification" means "to act." The word qualification is therefore a crystallized condensation of a whole sentence; "to do the action which gives its whatness to a thing." It can also be used as: "To do some action because of what the whatness of a thing is found to be." Thus, to give one example of this latter construction, water has the quality (or whatness, or suchness) of being a liquid, therefore to be qualified to handle it a man must have the use of containers which will hold a liquid.

The Anglo-Saxons had a "who" (or *swa*) which meant that each man had his own identity, individuality, personality, characteristics by which he can be recognized. To get at what they meant by their "what" (*lwaet*) we must picture such an individual with the "I" omitted; a rock, a chair, a cloud, any object, like a

205

man, had in it these features of characteristics; *they* are its *whatness*. This flavor of meaning must be added to the meaning of "qualification"; when it is, we have not *all* the features, characteristics, whatnesses of a thing, but certain salient ones.

A man must have a set of qualifications to become and to remain a Mason. The petitioner has in him a number of attributes, qualities, characteristics, etc., and they belong to *what* he is. Among these must be certain qualities or Freemasonry will not accept him; becoming a Freemason does not give him those qualities, he must have them *before* he becomes a Freemason. If he has it in him to become a Mason, he has it in him *before* he receives the Degrees. A man may have in him a hundred qualities, or a thousand; but Freemasonry looks for only certain ones, and if he has them Freemasonry is satisfied and ignores all the others—only certain ones are salient in *its* eyes, if he has them he is a *who* of the kind it is looking for. A man may have in himself qualities for becoming superexcellent in a thousand ways; it does not matter; he must have a certain specific number of them or he can never be elected to receive the Degrees.

But it would be a misleading explanation of the whole Doctrine of Qualifications to explain them as being just those particular qualifications which a Petitioner is required to have; this would mean that the Doctrine applies to Petitioners only, whereas it applies to Masons at every point, continuously, and as long as a man continues to be a Mason. He must have required qualifications before he can be advanced from one Degree to another; before he can hold office; before he can be appointed on a Committee; he must have a continuing set of qualifications in order to continue to be a member, and he is suspended or expelled if he ceases to have them. The Doctrine of Qualifications may therefore be defined as that rule, which intelligence, wisdom, and good judgment are to apply (hence it is a "doctrine"), which specifies what qualities (or whatness, or suchness) a man must have in himself in order to become and to continue to be a member of the Masonic Fraternity.

When Operative Freemasons demanded of a twelve year old boy that he have a stipulated number of qualities, their demands were not capricious, arbitrary, accidental, or mystical; he would have a work to do which would be onerous, hazardous, and would call for knowledge as well as skill, therefore he had to be sturdy in body, have a good brain, be willing to be trained, have the patience to go through years of work without wages, and be of a spirit to coöperate with others. The qualifications required were the qualifications made necessary by the work he had to do—the work, not the workmen, dictate the needed qualities. The same principle holds in Speculative Freemasonry. A man must learn long degrees by heart; he must be active and therefore needs health; he must be able to see, walk, and hear; he must be free in the sense of being responsible for his own acts; he must have money to pay his dues and fees; he must be willing to work on Committees and to hold office; the work of a Speculative Lodge is not the same as the work of an Operative Lodge but in one as much as in the other a member must be fit to do the work which will be assigned to him.

In his *Jurisprudence of Freemasonry* Albert G. Mackey divided his Book II on "Law Relating to Candidates" into six chapters of which the first is devoted to "The Qualifications of Candidates"; this chapter is with dubious correctness divided into sections, the first being on "The Internal Qualifications"; the second on "The External Qualifications." The dubiousness here refers to his describing a Candidate's moral and mental qualities as "external"; and the same word could be more forcibly applied to Mackey's limiting the question of qualifications to Candidates whereas, as a matter of fact, the question arises at many points in a Master Mason's career not only in Lodge but also in Grand Lodge. But though his classification may be thus open to question he covers the subject otherwise with satisfactory fullness. The heads of this list of qualifications are here quoted in his own words: the interpretations are in words of our own.

1. "Free will and accord."

Mackey takes this to mean that a Candidate must not be solicited, but the idea may be extended to include the many kinds of pressure which may be brought upon a man to do what he would not do without pressure.

2. "Uninfluenced by mercenary motives."

Here again it is better to expand the idea, because it is as un-Masonic to Petition for membership or to be a member for political, or religious, or professional motives as for motives of money.

By "internal" Mackey means such qualifications "as are known to himself only" and of which a Lodge can have only such knowledge as can "be acquired from his own solemn declarations." Preston and Webb both added two other required qualifications which also must be declared: "a favorable opinion of the Institution," and a cheerful conformity "to all the ancient established usages and customs of the Fraternity." To these could also be added a willingness to obey, a readiness to "be blindly conducted" at certain times, to hold office if called upon, to carry out orders and to obey summons from the Worshipful Master.

3. "Obey the moral law."

This is also stated as "being under the tongue of good report." This qualification can be summarized under the one word "character"; does a Petitioner have character, does he first as Candidate and later as member continue to have character? If he has, he is acceptable insofar, but no Petitioner is acceptable if he did not have character beforehand and only can promise it to have it in the future; his having character must be a long-established fact, which is the meaning of "reputation." A Candidate must be "a good man and true" from the very beginning; he cannot wait to be it; furthermore Freemasonry is not a reformatory.

4. If "he rightly understands the art, he will never be a stupid atheist, nor an irreligious libertine." These words are quoted from the original version of the Book of Constitutions. If that Book were being written now the word "stupid" would be omitted; to be an atheist, whether stupid or not, disqualifies a man; and it equally disqualifies him, it ought to be noted, if he becomes an atheist *after* he has become a member. What was meant by "irreligious libertine" in England in 1723 A.D. has long been under discussion and the debate will probably never come to an end because the phrase was widely read with different meanings, but on the whole it unquestionably meant a man who

sneers at religion, or is cynical about it. The qualification is not important because even if a man is not an atheist he may sneer at doctrines believed by others but not believed by himself; this means in effect that bigotry and sectarian animosities are no more permissible than is atheism.

5. "As to sex."

This is the simplest of qualifications because it means that women cannot be Freemasons; whatever else he is, a Petitioner, a Candidate, a member must be a man.

6. "As to age."

This means whatever age is named by law as legal age, and this may differ from one country to another. A young man under legal age is in the eyes of the law an "infant," and in many of his actions his father (or guardian) is held responsible. Obviously it would be intolerable to have in membership a man not responsible for his own actions, who would have to answer to a father or guardian for what he does in Lodge, and especially if the father or the guardian were not a Mason. An attempt was made at about 1800 A.D., to institute the system of the Masonic Lewis, by which was meant the son of a Lodge member; it was held that since the father was himself a member a Lewis could be admitted while under legal age, but the scheme was abandoned because in the eyes of the civil law each member of a lodge is legally as well as morally responsible for his actions when in Lodge. The same rule as to age would apply at the other end of the scale where because of feebleness, of extreme old age or because of senile dementia a man would not be responsible for his own actions.

7. "As to bodily conformation."

The Operative Freemasons necessarily required that an Operative had to be sound in body and have the use of his limbs, because otherwise he would not be physically able to do his work; but the Operative Masons knew nothing of any Perfect Youth Doctrine, or any doctrine of any other mystical kind, because they did not require an Apprentice to be *perfect,* but only to be sufficiently sound for his work; they did not disbar a man from work if he lost a toe, or a little finger, or even one eye. If Speculative Freemasons follow the same principle their own demands would be as rigorous, and ought to be applied without fear or favor but manifestly the physical requirements for membership in a modern American Speculative Lodge cannot be the same at every point as the demands made by Operative Lodges of six to eight centuries ago—one of the widest departures in physical qualifications is that the Operatives accepted Apprentices as young as twelve years, whereas we demand that they be not younger than twenty-one; also, where in Operative Freemasonry an Apprentice had to continue to be one for seven years in our Lodges he can pass out of his apprentice-ship in two or in four weeks. If we determine to adhere to the old Operative rules of physical qualifications *because* they are ancient then we should adhere to the whole set of them and not pick and choose arbitrarily.

The question of the physical qualifications is the most difficult one in the whole set of qualifications; it is one of the most difficult in Freemasonry; it would be made more difficult still if we went on to demand that Candidates have no diseases as well as no loss of limbs—what about tuberculosis, Bright's disease, asthma, rheumatism, and a long list of chronic degenerative maladies? If a Candidate is not a "Perfect Youth" because he has only one hand, what if he has only one lung or only one lobe to his brain? The indications are, and after nearly two centuries of debate, that the 49 American Grand Lodges will at some future time agree generally that Physical Qualifications are a general rule, and must be left to the intelligence, wisdom and good judgment of each individual Lodge.

8. "Mental Qualifications."

Dr. Mackey's discussion of this head strays out into generalities and ambiguities, for which he cannot be held at fault since the *Constitutions* and the Ritual have never made a clear, forthright statement of what the mental qualifications are. We can, however, in all modesty, take a step in that direction, especially if we do so in full consciousness that we are expressing ideas of our own. Manifestly a Candidate or a member cannot be illiterate. It is equally manifest that he cannot be insane, or be an imbecile, or an idiot, or a moron, or a dipsomaniac, or be a sufferer from chronic amnesia or loss of memory. It is also clear that the Liberal Arts and Sciences stand in the Holy of Holies, therefore it is difficult to believe that a man without any culture would be attracted to Freemasonry or even feel at home in it.

There is one outstanding qualification, or rather one whole category of qualifications, which Dr. Mackey does not mention. A Petitioner to the Degrees, and later when he becomes a Candidate, must be *personally acceptable* to the members of a Lodge, and so strict is this requirement that for lack of it alone any one member (or at most, three) can vote to reject a Petitioner. If a man does not have it in him to be "charitable," or to work in harmony with others; if he cannot be fraternal, if his behavior is intolerable, if he is given to quarreling or to intrigues or to malice, then is he as much disqualified as is the Petitioner who lacks his arms or his eyes.

"The proper study of mankind is man"—*Pope*

CHAPTER XXVI

# *Anthropology*

WHAT IS MAN? The answer to that question is called anthropology, an ancient Greek word, the first half of which was *anthropos*, meaning man, and the second the suffix form of *logos*, meaning science, system of thought, organized knowledge. With such a subject-matter anthropology is almost the largest, if not the largest, of those subjects, sciences, theologies, and organized systems of thought by means of which we understand the world. Within it are many departments, branches, divisions, specialities, among which are ethnology, the study of tribes and clans, sociology the study of the three institutions of family, school, and government, primitive culture, archeology, linguistics (study of languages); and in one of its aspects anthropology itself appears as one of the branches of philosophy. It is at the same time a necessary element or a necessary presupposition in other fields, in theology, ethics, psychology, aesthetics, physiology, anatomy, and medicine, because no one of these can work without some conception of what man is.

The question whether Freemasonry has an anthropology of its own belongs to the same category as the companion questions whether it has philosophy, theology, ethics, or politics of its own, and receives the same answer. It does not have one. There is no reason why it should have one because it is not a school, college, or association of scientists; the Ritual is not a discourse about races, tribes, clans, taboos, or tribal institutions; the subject is not mentioned in its Lectures or included in its Tenets. It is content to accept whatever is known to be true about man, but has no special theory or dogma of its own; no Masonic Frazer will ever be asked to write a *Golden Bough* about the Ritual, nor will

## Anthropology

any Hutton Webster be required to write a *Primitive Secret Society* as his Master Piece. The Craft consists of men, and does not consist of a set of doctrines or theories; it concerns itself with men, *and as men,* but it includes no anthropologic doctrine among its tests for membership.

Nevertheless Freemasonry cannot act without having certain facts and truths about man always at the front; if an anthropological theory contradicts those facts and truths Freemasonry is in disagreement with it, and at that point and to that extent Freemasons would concern themselves with anthropology—and as Masonic literature shows they have more than once done so. Freemasonry, we have said, consists not of theories or of books but of men; those men are active; they are always at work; they make plans, and they carry them out; they have purposes of their own, and they fulfill them; they have teachings, and they enforce them. None of these activities include anthropology, or even refer to it, but those things which Freemasons, millions of them, do and say and teach and feel and believe have their own *anthropologic presuppositions.*

It was not until one or two decades after the beginning of the present century that thinkers began to discover how transcendently important presuppositions are, and they did it by a new and microscopic analysis of the old Masonic subject of geometry in which they find that geometry is like our Masonic law, partly written and partly unwritten; or like our Ritual, partly exoteric and partly esoteric. The written, or, as it were, visible part of geometry are the rules, theories, and figures printed in the text; the unwritten part consists of a large number of presuppositions, axioms, postulates, assumptions which lie *behind* the written part, and which a geometrician assumes to be true although he cannot either prove them to be so, or define them. The revolutions which shook mathematicians in the Nineteenth Century were based on this part of assumptions, or presuppositions; Lobachevski (1793–1856) saw that Euclid assumed space to have three dimensions, and worked out a new geometry for more than three; Riemann (1826–66) devised one for only two. Einstein, in our own century, saw that Euclid had silently assumed that space is flat (or plane);

he worked out a geometry for a curved space. When the great power of silent and undefined or unconscious or unwritten assumptions, postulates, axioms was discovered in geometry thinkers went on to show that they have a similar power in every other subject or field, and not only in exact thinking or in science but in daily life—three-fourths of any editorial in a newspaper consists of not what the editor sets down but of what he assumes to be true but does not set down. If Freemasonry has any presuppositions about the nature of man then any thinker in any field would immediately say that those presuppositions are among the most important facts in it. What are they? It is helpful to begin the answer to that question by showing what they are not.

As soon as the atomic bombs were dropped on two cities in Japan newspapers were instantly filled with the clamor of news and editorials and articles about atoms. Millions of Americans drew the conclusion from this spate of "news" that atoms were a recent discovery, and that the atomic philosophy is a recent development in science; whereas a full-fledged atomic philosophy was developed in Greece 600 B.C., and for centuries was so influential that it almost became a religion—both Epicurus and Lucretius were among its adherents. *Atom* meant "it cannot be cut"; it was supposed that they are the ultimate particles out of which everything is made, that there is an uncountable number of them, that some are larger than others, and that if by chance a sufficient number of them happen to drift together and unite they become some object, a tree, a bird, a stone, a river, a man, what not; anything is "an accidental collocation of atoms." This would mean that everything is an illusion except atoms; that nothing is what it seems except atoms; if we say "There is a horse" we are mistaken, what we see is a thick, temporary cloud of atoms, and what we call "horse" is merely the shape it chances to take. A man is equally unreal; the believers in atomic philosophy shrink from that statement, they wriggle, and evade, and saw at words, but they ought to be held to it because if their theory is true a man, any man, you, I, is not in reality a *man* but is a conglomeration of some billions of atoms—they are real, they are absolutely real, but that which we mean by "man" is not real

## Anthropology

except as the name for the form which those atoms chanced to take. This is the answer the atomists give to the question, what is man? and there could not be an answer more wholly in contradiction to Freemasonry's presuppositions, or one in which any Freemason would more completely disbelieve.

Materialism is another philosophy which is even older than atomism and has always been far more influential. According to this theory matter is the stuff out of which everything else is made. How are things made? By the activities and changes which go on in matter itself. Any piece or kind of matter, however small, is full of motions, expansions, contractions, crackings, splittings, and other changes of a like kind which are called physical; and also is full of molecules which this or that in it is changing into something else, as when one color changes into another, and other changes of a like kind which we called chemical. The fundamental theory of Materialism is that matter is the stuff out of which any tree, animal, bird, rock, river, light, etc., etc., is made, and that its own structure and function is owing to the physical and chemical processes in matter. This theory answers the question, what is man? by saying that man is matter, and that wherever there is a quantity of matter of just the right kind, and physical and chemical processes of a certain kind go on in it, a man is the result—this is not to say that a man originated in matter and then changed into something non-material, but that he continues to be matter from beginning to end. Materialism has been described as the favorite philosophy of stupid people. The history of the materialistic philosophy over the past 2500 years bears out that satirical judgment, because of the many philosophies it has always been the most stupid and the clumsiest and most riddled by self-contradictions. It is in any event impossible for any Mason to be a materialist, even the kind of man who is a materialist without knowing it, because if Materialism were true everything in Freemasonry would be false.

Idealism is a systematized philosophy in the same sense that Materialism is, and its followers reason in very much the same manner that materialists do, but whereas materialists say that everything is made out of matter, Idealists say that everything is made out of mind. Plato and Plotinus were famous Idealists in Ancient times, Kant, Hegel, Berkeley, Green, Bradley, and Royce have been famous Idealists in Modern times. Every particular thing there is, the earth included, is not what it appears to be because it is a mere phenomenon; there is but one reality, a single absolute Mind, and what appears to be a stone or a star is not really such, is not real in its own right, but is merely a form or a movement in that one mind. "There is but one," say the Brahmins, "and that one is everywhere." Idealism is a seductive, subtle theory, very difficult to escape from if a man becomes encoiled within it, and it gains an advantage from having a name so similar to the world "ideal," and for this reason it sounds as if Idealism must consist of "ideals"; but it does not, it is as destructive of "ideals" as Materialism is, because it turns them into illusions. It answers the question what is man? by saying that he is a phenomenon in the absolute mind. If you and I are nothing but thoughts, dreams, or fancies in that Mind then we are not what we believe ourselves to be; we are not men, real in our own right, but are a mere camouflage or appearance of something not ourselves—we have no selves of our own because there is only one Self, and what we call Mankind is nothing but Maya, or illusion. If any men in the world have been non-Idealists, or Anti-Idealists, it was the Operative Masons; they did not hate matter, they did not abhor material things, they never went about in a metaphysical stupor, but worked with metal tools, were sane and sound and healthy, and it could not have crossed their minds, not even as a fancy, that the building they worked on was an illusion; and so have Freemasons been ever since. In their Lodge Room the Ashlar is as sacred as the Altar, and is on a level with it, and an Ashlar is nothing other than a stone, not a delusive, or symbolical, or make-believe stone, but a literal and ponderable piece of field-stone mined out of a quarry.

What is the ultimate reality, the stuff out of which everything else is made? The three philosophies above answer variously that it is atoms, or is matter, or is mind. Another ancient and powerful philosophy has an answer of another kind; it is the theory that behind everything else, but not robbing them of their reality, is one, absolute Being, and that within this Being is the origin of man. It is itself, however, something which requires that men shall be not all of one kind but shall be of a number of kinds, or species; these species of men differ among themselves as much as horses differ from insects, and they stand in a hierarchy of worth or excellence, the most superior species at the top, the most inferior species at the bottom; when a man is born he is not born into a single mankind, so that all other men are equally his brothers because they belong to the same family, but is born into a species.

Once man is born into a species he remains in it forever, and can no more move into another species than a cricket can change itself into a horse. Therefore the whole world of mankind is divided up into eternal castes. This is the philosophy behind the old dogmas of rulership by divine right, of being nobles by right of birth, of aristocratic powers and privileges by right of an eternal caste system of society, of feudalism which gives one caste the right of ownership but denies it to other castes, so that men in the lower castes do not even own themselves; and it is the philosophy behind slavery whenever slavery is defended on the ground that slaves belong to a lower species than their owners. It is unnecessary to say that this barbarous philosophy is the foe of every anthropologic presupposition of Freemasonry.

There is also the philosophy, powerful during the past hundred years, which a group of philosophers made out of biology, although in strict and literal fact it was not out of biology in general that they made it but out of zoölogy, which is the biology of animals. Charles Darwin began by assuming that animals are in separate species—neither he nor any other biologist could define "species" but he swept that difficulty aside and assumed it anyway. How, he asked himself, does a species originate? his answer was that it originates by that process of variation, environment, struggle for existence, and survival of the fittest for which he coined the name "evolution." Darwin then went on to say that man is an animal; since he is, he is a species, one called *homo sapiens;* he then went on to argue that this species of animal called man originated as had every other species of animal, by evolution. Neither Darwin himself nor any other man who agreed with him ever dreamed of saying that in this evolution man ceased to be an animal; the very point of the theory is that he *is* an animal; the difference between him and other animals is of the same kind as the difference among other species of animals. This theory became, as a Medieval writer had once said of the Crusades, "the world's debate," and the end is not yet, though an ever-increasing number of one-time evolutionists are forsaking the cause. Evolutionism as a philosophy of man never was well thought out; it fell apart inwardly from self-contradictions and confusions; it was never open or frank or truthful, even Darwin himself was never candid about it; and it could therefore be shown by analysis that its anthropology, or answer to the question, what is man? is impossible; but the space is not available. It can, however, be suggested that the evolutionists ought, like other philosophers, to try their theory in practice—the early Christians did so, the Communists have done so, almost every group of theologians or philosophers have done so; why should not the evolutionists? Let them, a few thousand, go somewhere and form a community, and let them go in for thoroughly treating each other as animals! They could find out if it is true by discovering how well it works out in practice. We Masons would not join their experiment; if there is anything abhorrent to Freemasonry, in its Lodge, or in its Landmarks, or in its Ritual, it is any sort of crudeness, or animalism, or sensuality, or callousness in which men treat each other as if they were mere animals.

These five or six philosophies, and a hundred others as well, differ among themselves almost as much as one opposite differs from another, yet they have in common, with only a small number of exceptions, the theory that a man never is "really" what we find him to be; he may appear to be a man, they say, "but in reality" he is not, he is always something else; he is an ex-angel, come into this world as a punishment for crimes committed in heaven; he is a wandering spirit, temporarily encased in a shell of physical body; he is an animal; he is an ex-animal; he is a very active and movable piece of matter; he is a thought in an Absolute Mind; he is a machine; always he is something other than

## Anthropology

he appears to be—it is as if these men of philosophy had agreed among themselves to admit the existence of everything except themselves!

And this fact enables us to define the anthropology which Freemasonry presupposes. It would answer the question, What is man? by saying, man is man. He is not a form of something else, or an appearance of something else, or an agency or organ of something else, but is himself, original and wholly and absolutely real in his own right. And he is whatever we find him in actuality to be. We find that he thinks, speaks, feels, has children, works, moves, acts, associates himself with others, plans, makes, and constructs; we take each of those facts about him to be completely real; if we were not to do so we could not take facts about other things to be real either because we know the facts about him in the same way that we know the facts about them. We Masons believe that men are men; we have no desire for them to be anything else.

When Masons come to speak about that which is finest in their Fraternity, about that which is nearest to being what religion is elsewhere, which moves on high reaches level with the most exalted plateaus of thought, they begin to look anxiously about them to make sure that they keep their feet on the ground; they are great believers in masculinity, and hold it to be one of the best things in a man, and it belongs to masculinity to dread those flights of idealistic fancy which blow the sails away. But there is in the whole universe no better place on which to stand than on the ground, and there is nothing higher or better anywhere than sanity, good sense, and sound wisdom, and there is no better life possible in any earth or in any heaven than the life of work; but while our law is a set of rules and regulations for workmen, and our Landmarks are drawn close to the ground, we are as free as other men to believe that there are great things in Man; we bracket together the question What do you believe about man? with the question, What do you believe about God? because one is as important to us as the other. We say in our Rituals, "There is a Grand Lodge above." We know what we mean by that saying. We do not mean that after we have changed our Way of

Being and are no longer in this world that we shall find there a Grand Lodge, with a Grand Master presiding over it; we do not mean that it is our picture of "heaven"; we believe that there is nothing better in this world than to be a man, and to be in fellowship with other men, *and we do not believe that there will be anything better in any other world.*

A Mason could if he wished (though he need not) have an anthropologic creed of his own which he could recite with complete sincerity on any of those occasions when the recital of a creed is deemed the proper thing to do: "I am content to be a man. I do not believe that I am a lump of matter, mysteriously stirred, or that I am an interesting experiment in chemistry, or that I was a plant which learned to walk, or an animal which learned to talk. I am not in fear lest I shall fall through the bottom of things to become less than a man, a devil, a demon, or what not; nor do I desire to become a superman or an angel or a disembodied spirit; I am a man here and now, I expect to continue to be a man forever."